CHINESE STORIES
FOR LANGUAGE LEARNERS

INTERMEDIATE

Chinese • Pinyin • English

LingLing

www.linglingmandarin.com

enquiries@linglingmandarin.com

FIRST EDITION

Editing by Xinrong Huo
Cover design by Ling Ling

www.linglingmandarin.com

ACKNOWLEDGEMENTS

My gratitude goes to my wonderful students who study Mandarin with me – you have inspired my writing and had given me valuable feedback to complete this book. Your support is deeply appreciated!

Special thanks go to my husband Phil, who motivated my creation and assisted with the editing and proofreading of the book.

Access FREE AUDIO

Check the **"ACCESS AUDIO"** chapter for password and full instructions (see Table of Contents)

TABLE OF CONTENTS

INTRODUCTION

Whether you have completed the first collection of stories from Book 1 of the series, **Chinese Stories for Language Learners: Elementary**, or are joining now for our new journey through stories aimed at intermediate learners, welcome and congratulations for making it this far! With this book, you will read more broadly and extensively and enjoy and experience more Chinese stories of folk tales, idioms, fables, proverbs, myths, and fun contemporary stories.

With this book, you will build up essential vocabulary and phrases at an intermediate level, mastering an additional 60 Chinese sentence patterns in context, all while being inspired by the stories behind the most influential figures from ancient to modern China. This book aims to make your Chinese learning journey fun and entertaining and give you more than just language insights but also cultural insights. Chinese culture, history, and language are inextricably linked, so prepare to discover great wisdom and valuable life lessons from many of China's greatest classics while also learning powerful Chinese proverbs and witty idioms that you can use to impress your friends and teachers. Also in store for you are beautiful and powerful stories of love and friendship, tragedy, political intrigue, military strategy, classic poetry, and much more from throughout the ages that have shaped Chinese values to this day. You will become acquainted with great men and women from ancient times to the modern day, from those who shaped the fate of entire dynasties to great actors and successful businessmen. You will gain powerful Chinese cultural insights throughout this unique learning journey full of engaging stories.

As you work through the engaging stories and activities in this book, you may find yourself wanting to further enhance your language learning journey with practical modern conversations; that's where my book **Chinese Conversations for Intermediate** can be of great help! Through short, fun stories, you'll be immersed in authentic daily conversations in modern China.

How the Book Will Help

This book features 31 stories with expanded learning content, selected and written for intermediate students. Many stories are well-known Chinese classics and touch on a range of topics. Although not necessary, following the presented order of the stories can benefit your language learning, as building vocabulary and knowledge of sentence patterns from earlier stories will aid comprehension. I encourage you to read through all the stories and benefit from the accompanying learning tools, tips, and exercises. The stories have been grouped into the below chapters:

- Chinese Myths
- Chinese Fables
- Chinese Idioms
- Chinese Proverbs
- Modern Stories
- Famous Historic Figures
- The Four Beauties of China
- Romance of the Three Kingdoms
- Chinese Poetry with Love Stories

Each story is structured to guide and assist your learning whilst making your learning journey entertaining and memorable. Far from only providing the story on its own, there is plenty of additional content, including:

- **Bilingual Story** (Simplified Chinese with Pinyin and English)
- **Chinese-only** version of the story for self-assessment
- **Key Vocabulary** list to help you to learn and review
- **Sentence Patterns** with examples in context
- **Activities and Exercises** or Discussion points to help you to reflect
- **Learning Tips and Culture Corner** to enhance your understanding
- **Free Audio** recorded by native speakers

For ancient classics and historical stories, all the words and vocabulary used are purposely written in modern Chinese, as is more appropriate for language learners. This means that some terms used may be slightly different to those used in the historical context. For example, the word for "police station" was "衙门" (yá mén) in ancient Chinese, but in the book is referred as "警察局" (jǐng chá jú) to reflect the terminology used in modern times.

Free Downloadable Audio

Great news! The audio files for the book are a FREE gift for you, as a special thanks for purchasing this book. The audio is all recorded by native speakers. Make sure you check out the instructions on the **Access Audio** page toward the back of the book for how to access and download the audio. I highly encourage you to use the audio, it will particularly help with learning the correct pronunciation and committing words to memory better.

Learn Chinese with a New Vision

Chinese is one of the most varied, dynamic, and artistic languages and has developed over 3500 years. It is one of the most spoken languages in the world, and mastering it opens doors to new opportunities in life, travel, business, and personal development.

Studying Chinese is not just about learning a new language but also exploring a different way of thinking, experiencing new perspectives, understanding a rich culture developed over thousands of years, and finding peace and balance in a life-long beneficial journey.

LEARNING TIPS

BECOME AN EFFECTIVE LEARNER

In Chinese, we have a well-known idiom 事半功倍 (shì bàn gōng bèi) (get twice the result with half the effort). You can cut short a long process with an effective learning method. It may seem obvious, but the best way to learn Chinese is to use it as often as possible, especially with Chinese speaking and listening; the more you practice, the more it will become second nature, like muscle memory.

Make the most of each story in the book by paying attention to the language flow and keep **reading it aloud** until you can read it naturally and fluently – even imagining yourself being the story teller. Use the accompanying audio to help by imitating the intonation and expression of the people in the audio. I suggest you follow this process:

1. **Read** the bilingual version of each story to identify the new words and phrases in context, referring to the Key Vocabulary list and Sentence Patterns for usage.
2. **Listen** to the audio while following the text to pick up the correct pronunciation - pause and rewind if necessary.
3. **Practice** reading the text aloud until you can read the entire story fluently. Pay attention to transitional words and phrases to master the authentic language flow.
4. **Test** yourself by heading to the Chinese version of the story, and read it without the help of Pinyin and English. Mastering the Chinese on its own is the key to level up.
5. **Listen again** to the audio. Test yourself by listening to it without the help of the text. If you miss some parts, go back to check with the text. Keep practicing until you can comprehend the audio alone.

Review and practice

Repetition is the mother of learning! Make sure you go back to each story and review the vocabularies and sentence patterns frequently. The more you review and practice, the better your Mandarin will be!

Be your own creator

You become a true master through creation and application! Apply the vocabularies, phrases, and sentence patterns you learned from each dialogue to your own conversations, whether in real-life practice or imaginary scenarios. Remember – the ultimate goal of learning Mandarin is to effectively communicate and understand the language in your own experiences. You can only achieve this by applying what you have learned in practice!

Believe in yourself

Believe in yourself and have confidence! Never be afraid of making mistakes. In real life, even advanced learners and native speakers make mistakes! Plus, mistakes only make us grow quicker! So, never let mistakes put you off. Instead, be bold, embrace and learn from mistakes!

Set Goals and Stay Committed

Have a committed learning attitude and set goals from small to big will lead you to great achievements in your Chinese learning journey. So stay committed and never give up! Just like this Chinese idiom:

Nothing Is Impossible to a Willing Heart

Chinese Myths

huà

gù

事 shì

shí èr shēng xiāo

十二生肖

The Twleve Zodiac Animals

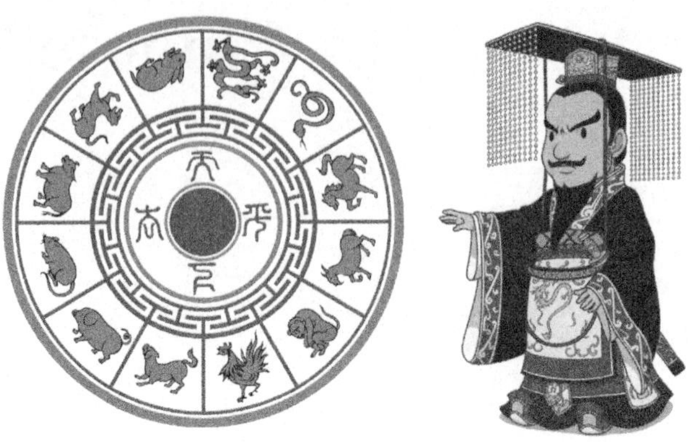

gǔ shí hòu yù dì xiǎng xuǎn shí èr zhǒng dòng wù zuò wéi shēng xiào dài biǎo

古时候，**玉帝**想选十二种动物作为生肖**代表**。

In ancient times, the **Jade Emperor** wanted to choose 12 animals as the **representatives** of zodiac.

tā pài shén xiān qù tōng zhī dòng wù men guī dìng shéi dào de zǎo jiù yǒu jī huì pái dào qián miàn

他派神仙去**通知**动物们，**规定**谁到得早就有**机会**排到前面。

He sent the immortals to **inform** the animals, and **stipulated** that whoever arrived early had a **chance** to place at the front (of the zodiac).

nà gè shí hòu māo hé lǎo shǔ shì hǎo péng yǒu dàn māo hěn xǐ huān shuì jiào jiù jiào lǎo shǔ tí xǐng tā

那个时候，猫和老鼠是**好朋友**。但猫很喜欢睡觉，就叫老鼠**提醒**它。

At that time, the cat and rat were **good friends**. But the cat liked sleeping very much, so he asked the rat to **remind** him.

kě shì lǎo shǔ wàng le lǎo shǔ zhī dào niú qǐ chuáng qǐ de zǎo jiù qù zhǎo niú dài tā qù

可是老鼠忘了。老鼠知道牛**起床起**得早，就去找牛带它去。

But the rat forgot. The rat knew that the ox **got up early**, so he went to ask the ox to help take him there.

nà shí hòu lóng hái méi yǒu jiǎo jiù qù zhǎo jī tā duì jī shuō nǐ
那时候龙还没有**角**，就去找鸡，它对鸡说："你
yǐ jīng gòu měi le bù xū yào jiǎo jiè gěi wǒ ba
已经**够**美了，不需要角，**借**给我吧。"

At that time, the dragon had no **horns**, so he went to the rooster, and said: "You are beautiful **enough**, you don't need the horns, so **lend** me your horns."

jī yī tīng dào zàn měi jiù bǎ jiǎo jiè gěi le lóng lóng mǎ shàng jué de
鸡**一**听到赞美，**就**把角借给了龙，龙马上觉得
xīn xǐ ruò kuáng
欣喜若狂。

As soon as the rooster heard the praise, he lent his horn to the dragon, and he felt **ecstatic** immediately.

bǐ sài dāng tiān lǎo shǔ zuò zài niú de bèi shàng hěn kuài jiù dào le
比赛**当天**，老鼠坐在牛的背上很快就到了。
qí tā dòng wù men yě dào le zhǐ yǒu māo hái zài shuì jiào
其他动物们也到了，**只有**猫还在睡觉。

On the day of the race, the rat sitting on the back of the ox arrived promptly. The **other** animals also arrived, **only** the cat was still sleeping.

zhè shí lǎo shǔ mǎ shàng tiào dào yù dì miàn qián yù dì shuō lǎo shǔ dào
这时，老鼠马上跳到玉帝**面前**。玉帝说老鼠到
de zuì zǎo jiù pái dì yī niú zài hòu miàn jiù pái dì èr
得**最早**，就排第一，牛在后面，就排第二。

At this time, the rat immediately jumped **in front of** the Jade Emperor. The Jade Emperor said that the rat was the **very first** to arrive, it shall rank the first, and the ox was right behind, so shall rank the second.

jiē zhe lǎo hǔ dào le pái dì sān rán hòu tù zǐ yě dào le
接着，老虎到了，排第三。然后，**兔子**也到了，
pái dì sì
排第四。

Then, came the tiger, ranking third. And, the **rabbit** also arrived, ranking fourth.

lóng lái de wǎn dàn shì gè zǐ dà hái yǒu piào liàng de jiǎo yù dì
龙来得晚，但是**个子大**，还有漂亮的角。玉帝
chāo xǐ huān tā jiù ràng tā pái dì wǔ hái shuō ràng tā ér zi pái
超喜欢它，就让他排第五，还说让它儿子排
dì liù kě shì lóng de ér zi méi lái
第六，可是龙的儿子没来。

The dragon came late, but he had a **big figure** and beautiful horns. The Jade Emperor **liked** him **so much** that he placed him fifth and also said that his son can be the sixth, but the dragon's son did not come.

zhè shí hòu miàn de shé pǎo lái shuō lóng shì wǒ gān bà ràng wǒ
这时，后面的**蛇**跑来说：“龙是我**干爸**，让我
pái dì liù ba yù dì jiù tóng yì le
排第六吧！”玉帝就**同意**了。

At this time, the **snake** behind him ran over and said, “the dragon is my **godfather**, let me rank the sixth! The Jade Emperor **agreed**.

mǎ hé yáng yě dào le tā men bù shì duì shǒu ér shì xiōng dì suǒ
马和羊也到了，他们**不是**对手，**而是**兄弟，所
yǐ bù xiǎng zhēng yù dì jué de tā men hěn yǒu lǐ mào jiù ràng tā men
以不想**争**。玉帝觉得他们很**有礼貌**，就让他们
pái dì qī hé dì bā
排第七和第八。

The horse and the sheep also arrived. They are **not** rivals, **but** brothers, so they didn’t want to **compete**. The Jade Emperor thought they were very **polite**, so he placed them the seventh and the eighth.

hóu zi běn lái zài zuì hòu miàn kě shì tā tiào de hěn kuài mǎ shàng jiù
猴子**本来**在最后面，可是他跳得很快，马上就
lái le pái le dì jiǔ
来了，排了第九。

The monkey was **originally** at the back, but he jumped so fast, so arrived immediately, hence rank the ninth.

rán hòu jī gǒu zhū yě lái le fēn bié pái dì shí dì shí
然后，鸡、狗、猪也来了，**分别**排第十，第十
yī hé dì shí èr
一和第十二。

Then, the rooster, the dog, and the pig also came, ranking tenth, eleventh, and twelfth **respectively**.

zhí dào bǐ sài hòu māo cái xǐng lái tā qì de dào chù zhuī dǎ lǎo shǔ
直到比赛后猫才醒来，它气得到处**追打**老鼠。

The cat didn’t wake up **until** after the game, and he was so angry that he **chased to beat** the mouse everywhere.

lóng yǒu le jiǎo jué de zì jǐ gèng měi le jiù bù huái gěi jī le
龙有了角觉得自己更美了，就不**还给**鸡了。
wèi le duǒ jī tā cóng cǐ zài shì jiè xiāo shī le
为了躲鸡，它从此在世界消失了。

Since the dragon had horns, he felt that he was more beautiful, so he didn’t **give it back** to the rooster. **In order to** hide from the rooster, it has since disappeared from the world.

Culture Corner

The **12 Chinese Zodiac** (十二生肖) animals are an integral part of Chinese culture and influence various aspects of daily life. The zodiac is based on a twelve-year cycle, the order of which is explained by this story of the ranking race. Each year is associated with a specific animal that represents certain personality traits and characteristics. People are believed to be influenced by the animal of the year they were born. The zodiac is used for astrological predictions and important life events, such as weddings and business ventures. It is also celebrated during the Chinese New Year and is a popular theme in art, literature, and pop culture. The Chinese Zodiac continues to play a significant role in modern Chinese culture, and is revered for its rich history and cultural significance.

老鼠违背了他对猫的承诺，没有及时提醒猫起床，**你认为他为什么会这样**？

The rat failed his promise to the cat by not reminding him to wake up in time, **why do you think he did so?**

A 它记性太差，所以忘了。
It's memory is too bad, so it forgot.

B 它的确太忙了，所以忘了。
It is indeed too busy, so forgot.

C 它没有真的把猫当朋友，不想帮它。
It didn't truly regard the cat as friend, so didn't want to help.

D 它太想赢比赛，不想多一个竞争者，就故意不提醒猫。
It wants to win the game too badly and doesn't want one more competitor, so it deliberately didn't remind the cat.

Key Vocabulary

yù dì 玉帝	*n.*	Jade Emperor	dāng tiān 当天	*n.*	on the day
dài biǎo 代表	*n.*	representative	zhǐ yǒu 只有	*conj.*	only
tōng zhī 通知	*v.*	to inform	chāo 超	*aff.*	super/very
guī dìng 规定	*v.*	to stipulate	gè zi 个子	*n.*	stature/ height
jī huì 机会	*n.*	chance/ opportunity	gān bà 干爸	*n.*	godfather
tí xǐng 提醒	*v.*	to remind	duì shǒu 对手	*n.*	rival
jiǎo 角	*n.*	horn	xiōng dì 兄弟	*n.*	mates/ brothers
gòu 够	*adj.*	enough	yǒu lǐ mào 有礼貌		polite
xīn xǐ ruò kuáng 欣喜若狂	*idiom*	ecstatic (rejoice as if one were crazy)	fēn bié 分别	*adv.*	respectively/ individually

Sentence Patterns

不是... 而是...

not ... but ...

bù shì ér shì
不是 + *A* + **而是** + *B*

tā men bù shì duì shǒu ér shì xiōng dì
他们<u>不是</u>对手，<u>而是</u>兄弟。

They are <u>not</u> rivals, <u>but</u> brothers.

为了...

in order to ..

wèi le
为了 + *purpose* + *clause*

wèi le duǒ jī tā cóng cǐ zài shì jiè xiāo shī le
<u>为了</u>躲鸡，它从此在世界消失了。

<u>In order to</u> hide from the rooster, it has since disappeared from the world.

Chinese Story

古时候，玉帝想选十二种动物作为生肖代表。

他派神仙去通知动物们，规定谁到得早就有机会排到前面。

那个时候，猫和老鼠是好朋友。但猫很喜欢睡觉，就叫老鼠提醒它。

可是老鼠忘了。老鼠知道牛起床起得早，就去找牛带它去。

那时候龙还没有角，就去找鸡，它对鸡说：“你已经够美了，不需要角，借给我吧。”

鸡一听到赞美，就把角借给了龙, 龙马上觉得欣喜若狂。

比赛当天，老鼠坐在牛的背上很快就到了。其他动物们也到了，只有猫还在睡觉 。

这时，老鼠马上跳到玉帝面前。玉帝说老鼠到得最早，就排第一，牛在后面，就排第二。

接着，老虎到了，排第三。然后，兔子也到了，排第四。

龙来得晚，但是个子大，还有漂亮的角。玉帝超喜欢它，就让他排第五,还说让它儿子排第六，可是龙的儿子没来。

这时，后面的蛇跑来说：“龙是我干爸，让我排第六吧！”玉帝就同意了。

马和羊也到了，他们不是对手，而是兄弟，所以不想争。玉帝觉得他们很有礼貌，就让他们排第七和第八。

猴子本来在最后面，可是他跳得很快，马上就来了，排了第九。

然后，鸡，狗，猪也来了，分别排第十，第十一和第十二。

直到比赛后猫才醒来，它气得到处追打老鼠。

龙有了角觉得自己更美了，就不还给鸡了。为了躲鸡，它从此在世界消失了。

chuī xiāo huì lóng nǚ

2 吹箫会龙女

Playing Flute for the Dragon Girl

yǒu yī wèi yīng jùn xiāo sǎ de xiān rén jiào hán xiāng zǐ, fēi cháng shàn cháng chuī xiāo.

有一位**英俊潇洒**的仙人叫韩湘子，非常**擅长**吹箫。

There was an very **handsome and unrestrained** immortal named Han Xiangzi, who was very **good at** playing flute.

yī cì, tā dào dōng hǎi lǚ yóu, kàn zhe lán tiān dà hǎi, táo huā fēi yáng, jiù kāi shǐ chuī xiāo.

一次，他到**东海**旅游，看着**蓝天大海**，桃花**飞扬**，就开始吹箫。

Once, he traveled to the **East China Sea**, looking at the **blue sky and the vast sea**, with peach blossoms **flying beautifully**, and he began to play flute.

tài yáng luò shān le, hǎi shàng chū xiàn le yī tiáo lóng, zài bō làng zhōng huān kuài de yóu yǒng.

太阳**落山**了，海上出现了一条**龙**，在波浪中**欢快**地游泳。

The sun was **setting**, and a **dragon** came out of the sea, swimming **merrily** in the waves.

zài xiāo shēng zhōng, lóng fēi dào hán xiāng zǐ shēn biān, wéi zhe tā tiào wǔ. hán xiāng zǐ hěn jī dòng, bèi lóng de wǔ dǎo mí zhù le.

在箫声中，龙飞到韩湘子**身边**，围着他跳舞。韩湘子很**激动**，被龙的舞蹈**迷住**了。

In the sound of the flute, the dragon came to Han Xiangzi's **side** and danced around him. Han Xiangzi was very **excited** and **fascinated** by the dragon's dance.

tū rán zhè tiáo lóng biàn chéng le yī gè nián qīng nǚ zǐ. tā shēn cái yǎo tiǎo, cháng fā piāo piāo.

突然，这条龙**变成**了一个年轻女子。她身材**窈窕**，长发飘飘。

Suddenly, the dragon **turned into** a young woman. Her body was **slim** and had long beautiful hair.

nǚ zǐ duì hán xiāng zǐ yān rán yī xiào, hán xiāng zǐ bèi tā de měi shēn shēn de jīng yà le.

女子对韩湘子**嫣然一笑**，韩湘子被她的美深深地**惊讶**了。

The woman **smiled charmingly** at Han Xiangzi, and he was deeply **astonished** by her beauty.

tā duì nǚ zǐ shuō: "yuán lái nǐ shì lóng nǚ, jīn tiān jiàn dào nǐ, zhēn shì wǒ de xìng yùn."

他对女子说："**原来**你是龙女，今天见到你，真是我的**幸运**。"

He said to her: "**It turns out** that you are a dragon girl. It is my **luck** to see you today."

lóng nǚ huí dá shuō: "wǒ yī zhí zhù zài dōng hǎi, jīn tiān dì yī cì tīng dào zhè me měi de xiāo shēng, suǒ yǐ lái kàn kan."

龙女回答说："我**一直**住在东海，今天第一次听到**这么美**的箫声，所以来看看。"

The dragon girl replied, "I have **always** lived in the East China Sea, and this is the first time I heard **such beautiful** flute sound, so I came to see it."

hán xiāng zǐ hé lóng nǚ shēn qíng de kàn zhe duì fāng, tā men yī biān sàn bù, yī biān liáo tiān, yī zhí dào shēn yè, lóng nǚ cái lí kāi.

韩湘子和龙女**深情**地看着对方，他们**一边**散步，**一边**聊天，一直到**深夜**，龙女才离开。

Han Xiangzi and the dragon girl looked at each other **affectionately**. They were walking **while** chatting, and the dragon girl didn't leave until late at night.

zài hòu lái de sān tiān, hán xiāng zǐ měi tiān dōu huì zài hǎi biān chuī xiāo, tài yáng luò shān hòu, lóng nǚ jiù huì chū lái hé tā jiàn miàn.

在后来的三天，韩湘子每天都会在**海边**吹箫，太阳落山后，龙女就会出来和他**见面**。

For the next three days, Han Xiangzi would play flute at the **seaside** every day, and after the sun set, the dragon girl would come out to **meet** him.

kě shì, dào le dì sì tiān, tài yáng luò shān le, lóng nǚ méi yǒu lái. hán xiāng zǐ bù tíng de chuī xiāo, réng rán méi yǒu děng dào lóng nǚ.

可是，到了第四天，太阳落山了，**龙女**没有来。韩湘子不停地吹箫，**仍然**没有等到龙女。

However, on the fourth day, the sun had set, yet the **dragon girl** did not come. Han Xiangzi kept playing the flute, but **still** the dragon girl never came.

hán xiāng zǐ jiù zhè yàng kōng děng le hěn duō tiān, zhí dào tā bēi tòng yù jué, zhé duàn le tā de xiāo.

韩湘子就这样**空等**了很多天，直到他**悲痛欲绝**，**折断**了他的箫。

Han Xiangzi **waited in vain** for many days, until he felt **so distraught** that he **broke** his flute.

yī tiān, yī gè lǎo tài pó tū rán chū xiàn, gào sù hán xiāng zǐ lóng nǚ shì dōng hǎi de gōng zhǔ. lóng wáng bù zhǔn tā yǔ hán xiāng zǐ jiàn miàn, jiù qiú jìn le lóng nǚ.

一天，一个**老太婆**突然出现，告诉韩湘子龙女是东海的**公主**。龙王**不准**她与韩湘子见面，就**囚禁**了龙女。

One day, an **old woman** suddenly appeared and told Han Xiangzi that the dragon girl was actually the **princess** of the East China Sea. The Dragon King had **forbidden** her to meet with Han Xiangzi, so already **imprisoned** the Dragon Girl.

rán hòu, lǎo tài pó gěi le hán xiāng zǐ yī gēn lóng nǚ sòng tā de shén zhú.

然后，老太婆给了韩湘子一根龙女送他的**神竹**。

Then, the old woman gave Han Xiangzi a **magic bamboo** gifted from the dragon girl.

hòu lái, hán xiāng zǐ bǎ shén zhú zuò chéng le xiāo, cháng cháng zài dōng hǎi biān chuī xiāo.

后来，韩湘子把神竹做成了**箫**，常常在东海边吹箫。

Later, Han Xiangzi made the magic bamboo into a **flute**, and often played flute on the east coast.

tā xiǎng, bù guǎn lóng nǚ néng bù néng lái jiàn tā, zhǐ yào tā tīng dào xiāo shēng, jiù néng gǎn dào tā de ài.

他想，**不管**龙女能不能来见他，**只要**她听到箫声，**就**能感到他的爱。

He thought that **no matter** the dragon girl could come to see him or not, **as long as** she heard the sound of the flute, she could feel his love.

Culture Corner

Han Xiangzi is a Chinese folk deity and one of the **Eight Immortals** (八仙) in Chinese mythology. He is considered a symbol of happiness, good fortune, and longevity. He is often depicted as playing a flute and is associated with music, art, and literature. Han Xiangzi is also said to be a master of alchemy, and is therefore sometimes considered a patron of scholars and students. In Chinese culture, Han Xiangzi is revered for his wisdom, his wit, and his kindness, and is often invoked for blessings and protection.

在完整的故事中，龙女是为了韩湘子偷的神笛，并因此受到重罚，再也不能与韩湘子见面。而且，要救她几乎是不可能的，也是违法的。**但如果你是韩湘子，你会怎么做？**

In the full story, the dragon girl actually stole the magical flute for Han Xiangzi and was heavily punished for it that she was never allowed to meet him again. Plus, to save her would be literally impossible and law-breaking. **But if you were Han Xiangzi, what would you do?**

A 忘记龙女，继续生活。
Forget the dragon girl and move on with life.

B 找人帮忙，一起想办法救龙女。
Find others to find ways to save the dragon girl.

C 自己去救龙女，即使死了也不怕。
Go to save the dragon girl myself, and not afraid even to die for it.

D 永远记得龙女，但是继续生活。
Remember the dragon girl forever, but move on with life.

KEY VOCABULARY

英俊潇洒 (yīng jùn xiāo sǎ)	*idiom*	handsome and unrestrained	擅长 (shàn cháng)	*v.*	good at
嫣然一笑 (yān rán yī xiào)	*idiom*	smiled charmingly	惊讶 (jīng yà)	*adj.*	astonished
蓝天大海 (lán tiān dà hǎi)	*n.*	blue sky and vast sea	幸运 (xìng yùn)	*n.* *adj.*	luck lucky
欢快 (huān kuài)	*adv.*	merrily	一直 (yī zhí)	*adv.*	always
激动 (jī dòng)	*adj.*	excited	深情 (shēn qíng)	*adj.*	affectionate
迷住 (mí zhù)	*v.*	to fascinate	深夜 (shēn yè)	*n.*	late night
悲痛欲绝 (bēi tòng yù jué)	*idiom*	extremely distraught	变成 (biàn chéng)	*v.*	to become
身材 (shēn cái)	*n.*	body figure	折断 (zhé duàn)	*v.*	to break (by hand)
窈窕 (yǎo tiǎo)	*adj.*	slim	囚禁 (qiú jìn)	*v.*	to imprison

SENTENCE PATTERNS

一边... 一边...

Indicates simultaneous actions

yī biān 一边 + *action 1* + yī biān 一边 + *action 2*

tā men yī biān sàn bù, yī biān liáo tiān
他们一边散步，一边聊天。

They were walking while chatting.

只要... 就

as long as ... then

zhǐ yào 只要 + *condition* + jiù 就 + *result*

tā xiǎng, zhǐ yào tā tīng dào xiāo shēng, jiù néng gǎn dào tā de ài
他想，只要她听到箫声，就能感到他的爱。

He thought that as long as she heard the sound of the flute, (then) she could feel his love.

Chinese Version

有一位英俊潇洒的仙人叫韩湘子，非常擅长吹箫。

一次，他到东海旅游，看着蓝天大海，桃花飞扬，就开始吹箫。

太阳落山了，海上出现了一条龙，在波浪中欢快地游泳。

在箫声中，龙飞到韩湘子身边，围着他跳舞。韩湘子很激动，被龙的舞蹈迷住了。

突然，这条龙变成了一个年轻女子。她身材窈窕，长发飘飘。

女子对韩湘子嫣然一笑，韩湘子被她的美深深惊讶了。

他对女子说："原来你是龙女，今天见到你，真是我的幸运。"

龙女回答说："我一直住在东海，今天第一次听到这么美的箫声，所以来看看。"

韩湘子和龙女深情地看着对方，他们一边散步，一边聊天，一直到深夜，龙女才离开。

在后来的三天，韩湘子每天都会在海边吹箫，太阳落山后，龙女就会出来和他见面。

可是，到了四天，太阳落山了，龙女没有来。韩湘子不停地吹箫，仍然没有等到龙女。

韩湘子就这样空等了很多天，直到他悲痛欲绝，折断了他的箫。

一天，一个老太婆突然出现，告诉韩湘子龙女是东海的公主。龙王不准她与韩湘子见面，就囚禁了龙女。

然后，老太婆给了韩湘子一根龙女送他的神竹。

后来，韩湘子把神竹做成了箫，常常在东海边吹箫。

他想，不管龙女能不能来见他，只要她听到箫声，就能感到他的爱。

Chinese Fables

yù

yán

gù

事
shì

kè zhōu qiú jiàn

刻舟求剑

Carving a Boat for a Lost Sword

chūn qiū shí qī, chǔ guó yǒu gè nián qīng de yòng jiàn gāo shǒu, xìng gé fēi cháng gǔ guài.

春秋**时期**，楚国有个年轻的**用剑高手**，性格非常**古怪**。

During the Spring and Autumn **Period**, in the state of Chu, there was a young **master swordsman**, whose personality was very **strange**.

tā chāo ài tā de jiàn, duì tā lái shuō, jiàn shì tā zuì bǎo guì de dōng xi.

他**超**爱他的剑，**对他来说**，剑是他最宝贵的东西。

He **really** loved his sword, **to** him, the sword is his most precious thing.

yǒu yī tiān, zài yī gè fēng hé rì lì de shàng wǔ, tā dài zhe jiàn zuò chuán qù guó wài lǚ xíng.

有一天，在一个**风和日丽**的上午，他带着**剑**坐船去国外**旅行**。

One day, on a **beautiful sunny** morning, he took his **sword** on a boat **travelling** to a foreign country.

dāng shí, chuán shàng chú le tā hé chuán fū, hái yǒu qí tā chéng kè.

当时，船上**除了**他和船夫，**还**有其他乘客。

At the time, **besides** him and the boatman, there were **also** other passengers on the boat.

chéng kè men yī zhí zài kāi xīn de liáo tiān, zhǐ yǒu tā méi yǒu jiā rù tā men.

乘客们一直在开心地**聊天**，只有他没有**加入**他们。

The **passengers** were **chatting** happily, only he didn't **join** them.

tā yī gè rén zuò zài chuán tóu, yī biān kàn fēng jǐng, yī biān fǔ mō tā de jiàn
他**一个人**坐在船头，**一边**看风景，**一边**抚摸他的剑。

He sat **alone** on the bow, stroking his sword **while** watching the scenery.

tū rán, lái le yī zhèn bō làng, chuán bèi zhèn le yī xià, tā de jiàn lì kè diào jìn le hé lǐ
突然，来了一阵**波浪**，船被**震**了一下，他的剑**立刻**掉进了河里。

Suddenly, came a **wave**, the boat was **shaken**, and his sword **immediately** fell into the river.

dà jiā dōu duì tā dà hǎn: wèi, nǐ de jiàn diào le, kuài xià hé qù zhǎo
大家都对他**大喊**：“喂，你的剑掉了，快下河去找。”

Everyone **yelled** to him: “Hey, your sword has fallen, go down the river to find it now.”

kě shì tā què fēi cháng dàn dìng, zhǐ huí le yī jù: bié zhāo jí, wǒ yǒu bàn fǎ
可是他却非常**淡定**，只回了一句：“别**着急**，我有办法。”

But he was very **calm**, and only replied one sentence: “Don’t **worry**, I have a way.”

tā mǎ shàng dūn xià, cóng bāo lǐ qǔ chū yī bǎ xiǎo dāo zài chuán shàng kè zì. dà jiā wèn tā wèi shén me zhè me zuò
他马上**蹲下**，从包里取出**一把小刀**在船上**刻字**。大家问他为什么这么做。

He immediately **squatted down**, took **a knife** from his bag and **engraved** on the boat. Everyone asked him why he did it.

tā méi yǒu mǎ shàng huí dá, ér shì děng kè wán le, cái shuō: zhè shì jiàn diào xià qù de jì hào
他没有马上**回答**，**而是**等刻完了，才说：“这是剑掉下去的**记号**。”

He didn’t **answer** right away, **but** waited until the engraving was over before saying, “This is the **mark** from which the sword fell.”

dà jiā dōu hěn mí huò, dàn yě méi yǒu zài wèn. jǐ gè xiǎo shí hòu, chuán dào àn biān le
大家都很**迷惑**，但也没有再问。几个小时后，船到**岸边**了。

Everyone was **confused**, but didn’t ask again. A few hours later, the boat reached the **shore**.

zhè shí hòu tā què tū rán cóng jì hào chù tiào rù le hé lǐ zài hé
这时候，他却突然从记号处**跳入**了河里，在河
lǐ yóu lái yóu qù
里**游来游去**。

At this time, he suddenly **jumped into** the river from the mark and **swam back and forth** in the river.

dà jiā kàn jiàn le dōu zhēng dà yǎn jīng jué de fēi cháng qí guài
大家看见了，都**睁大眼**睛，觉得非常**奇怪**。

When everyone saw it, they **opened** their **eyes wide** and thought it was very **strange**.

guò le yī huì ér tā shàng àn le hěn shēng qì de hǎn wèi shén
过了一会儿，他上岸了，很**生**气地喊：“为什
me wǒ zhǎo bù dào jiàn jiàn jiù shì cóng zhè gè jì hào diào xià de
么我找不到剑？剑就是从这个记号**掉下**的。”

After a while, he went ashore and shouted **angrily**: “Why can’t I find the sword? The sword **fell off** from this mark.”

dà jiā tīng dào hòu dōu hā hā dà xiào qǐ lái shuō tā shì gè shǎ dàn
大家听到后，都**哈哈大笑**起来，说他是个**傻蛋**！

After everyone heard it, they all **laughed crazily** and said he was a **dummy**.

chuán fū duì tā shuō jì hào zài chuán shàng bù dòng chuán zài hé shàng què
船夫对他说：“记号在船上不动，船在河上却
yī zhí dòng nǐ de jì hào zǎo jiù zhǎo bù dào jiàn le
一直动，你的记号早就找不到剑了！”

The **boatman** said to him: “The mark does not move on the boat, but the boat **keeps** moving on the river. Your mark is no longer the mark to locate the sword.”

Summary

This story demonstrates how remaining stuck in our ways and in **rigid thinking** (死板思维 sǐ bǎn sī wéi) can limit our ability to adapt to changing circumstances. It can also prevent us from finding creative and innovative solutions to problems. In a rapidly evolving world, the ability to be flexible, open-minded, and continuously learning is essential for success. By embracing new ideas, approaches, and methods, we increase the likelihood of achieving our goals and making progress. The lesson behind this story may be more relevant than ever.

Learning Tip

刻舟求剑 is also an idiom based on this old tale, translated literally as “carving a boat for a lost sword.” It relates to being stuck in your our ways and in rigid thinking.

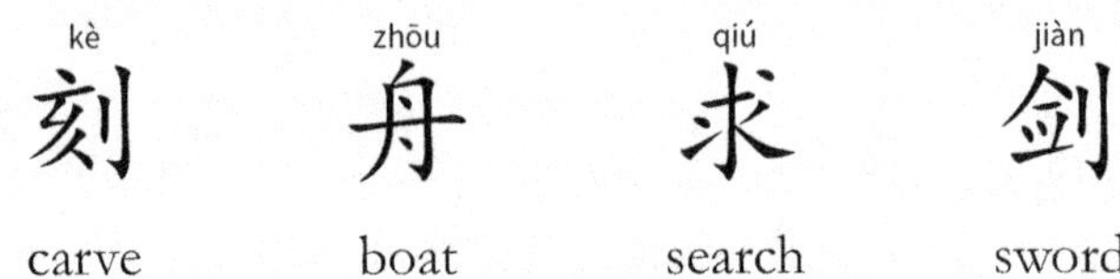

1 这种人**刻舟求剑**，肯定会一事无成。
This kind of person **stuck in his ways**, and will definitely achieve nothing.

2 要解决好这个客户问题，就不能**刻舟求剑**。
To solve this client issue well, we can’t stick with **rigid thinking**.

Write your own sentence

Key Vocabulary

shí qī 时期	*n.*	period	dàn dìng 淡定	*adj.*	calm
gāo shǒu 高手	*n.*	master/ expert	zhāo jí 着急	*adj.*	anxious/ worry
bǎo guì 宝贵	*adj.*	precious	huí dá 回答	*v.*	to answer/reply
lǚ xíng 旅行	*v.*	to travel	jì hào 记号	*n.*	mark
chéng kè 乘客	*n.*	passenger	mí huò 迷惑	*adj.*	confused
liáo tiān 聊天	*v.*	to chat	yóu lái yóu qù 游来游去	*vp.*	swim back and forth
jiā rù 加入	*v.*	to join	zhēng dà yǎn jīng 睁大眼睛	*vp.*	open eyes wide
fēng jǐng 风景	*n.*	scenery	hā hā dà xiào 哈哈大笑	*vp.*	to laugh crazily
shǎ dàn 傻蛋	*n.*	dummy	fēng hé rì lì 风和日丽	*idiom*	beautiful and sunny

Sentence patterns

对…来说

as for ... / as far as ... is concerned

duì lái shuō
对 + *someone* + **来说** + *clause*

duì tā lái shuō, jiàn shì tā zuì bǎo guì de dōng xi
对他来说，剑是他最宝贵的东西。

(as) For him, the sword is his most precious thing.

除了…还(有)…

besides ... also ...

chú le hái yǒu
除了 + *A* + **还(有)** + *B*

chuánshàng chú le tā hé chuán fū, hái yǒu qí tā chéng kè
船上除了他和船夫，还有其他乘客。

Besides him and the boatman, there were also other passengers on the boat.

CHINESE VERSION

春秋时期，楚国是有个年轻的用剑高手，性格非常古怪。

他超爱他的剑，对他来说，剑是他最宝贵的东西。

有一天，在一个风和日丽的上午，他带着剑坐船去国外旅行。

当时，船上除了他和船夫，还有其他乘客。

乘客们一直在开心地聊天，只有他没有加入他们。

他一个人坐在船头，一边看风景，一边抚摸他的剑。

突然，来了一阵波浪，船被震了一下，他的剑立刻掉进了河里。

大家都对他大喊："喂，你的剑掉了，快下河去找。"

可是他却非常淡定，只回了一句："别着急，我有办法。"

他马上蹲下，从包里取出一把小刀在船上刻字。大家问他为什么这么做。

他没有马上回答，而是等刻完了，才说："这是剑掉下去的记号。"

大家都很迷惑，但也没有再问。几个小时后，船到岸边了。

这时候，他却突然从记号处跳入了河里，在河里游来游去。

大家看见了，都睁大眼睛，觉得非常奇怪。

过了一会儿，他上岸了，很生气地喊："为什么我找不到剑？剑就是从这个记号掉下的。"

大家听到后，都哈哈大笑起来，说他是个傻蛋！

船夫对他说："记号在船上不动，船在河上却一直动，你的记号早就找不到剑了！"

shuǐ zhōng lāo yuè

水中捞月

Fishing For The Moon In Water

yī tiān wǎn shàng, yī zhī xiǎo hóu zi zài jǐng biān wán, tā wǎng jǐng lǐ kàn,
一天晚上，一只小猴子**在井边**玩，它往井里看，
jū rán fā xiàn lǐ miàn yǒu gè yuè liàng
居然发现里面有个**月亮**。

One night, a little monkey was playing **by the well**. When he looked into the well, he **suprisingly** found **the moon** in it.

xiǎo hóu zi shǒu zú wú cuò, jiù jiào: zāo gāo! yuè liàng diào jìn jǐng
lǐ le
小猴子**手足无措**，就叫："**糟糕**！月亮掉进井里了。"

The little monkey was **at a loss**, and called out, "**Oops**! The moon fell into the well.

dà hóu zi tīng jiàn hòu, pǎo guò lái kàn, yě jīng huāng le! gēn zhe jiào:
大猴子听见后，**跑过来**看，也**惊慌**了！跟着叫：
zāo gāo! yuè liàng diào jìn jǐng lǐ le
"糟糕！月亮掉进井里了。"

When the big monkey heard it, he **ran over** to see it, and **panicked**, also screamed out, "Oops! The moon fell into the well."

lǎo hóu zi tīng jiàn hòu, yě pǎo lái le, rán hòu yě yī qǐ gēn zhe jiào:
老猴子听见后，也跑来了，然后也**一起**跟着叫：
zāo gāo! yuè liàng diào jìn jǐng lǐ le, wǒ men yī dìng yào bāng máng,
"糟糕！月亮掉进井里了，我们一定要帮忙，
bǎ tā lāo qǐ lái
把它**捞起来**。"

After the old monkey heard it, he also ran over, then also screamed **together**: "Oops! The moon fell into the well, we must help to **bring it up**."

yú shì tā men zhǎo lái le qí tā hóu zi rán hòu yī qǐ pá shàng le jǐng biān de dà shù
于是，它们找来了**其他**猴子，然后一起**爬上**了井边的大树。

So they found **other** monkeys, and together they **climbed to** the big tree by the well.

lǎo hóu zi dào guà zài shù shàng lā zhù dà hóu zi de jiǎo dà hóu zi yě dào guà zhe lā zhù qí tā hóu zi de jiǎo jiù zhè yàng yī zhī jiē yī zhī
老猴子**倒挂**在树上，**拉住**大猴子的脚。大猴子也倒挂着，拉住其他猴子的脚，就这样**一只接一只**。

The old monkey **hung upside down** on the tree and **grabbed** the big monkey's feet. The big monkey also hung upside down, grabbing another monkey's feet, just like this, **one after the other**.

xiǎo hóu zi guà zài zuì xià miàn zhōng yú dào le jǐng shuǐ chù tā shēn shǒu qù lāo yuè liàng kě shì yī pèng dào shuǐ yuè liàng jiù suì le
小猴子挂在**最下面**，终于到了井水处，它**伸手**去捞月亮，可是**一**碰到水，月亮**就**碎了。

The little monkey hung **at the bottom**, and finally reached the well water. He **stretched out his hand** to fish for the moon, but **as soon as** he touched the water, the moon shattered.

xiǎo hóu zi hěn jīng yà de shuō a yuè liàng bèi wǒ zhuā suì le
小猴子很**惊讶**地说："啊！月亮被我抓**碎**了。"

The little monkey said in **shock**: "Ah! The moon was **shattered** by me."

dà jiā kāi shǐ bào yuàn xiǎo hóu zi guò le yī huì ér shuǐ miàn huī fù le píng jìng yuè liàng yòu chū xiàn le
大家开始**抱怨**小猴子。过了一会儿，水面**恢复了平静**，月亮又出现了。

Everyone started **complaining** about the little monkey. After a while, the water **calmed down** (recover peace) and the moon appeared again.

lǎo hóu zi jiù duì xiǎo hóu zi shuō nǐ hái shì zài shì yī cì ba
老猴子就对小猴子说："你**还是**再试一次**吧**。"

The old monkey said to the little monkey: You **should** just try one more time.

yú shì xiǎo hóu zi zài cì shēn shǒu qù lāo yuè liàng kě shì réng rán yī pèng dào shuǐ yuè liàng jiù suì le
于是，小猴子**再次**伸手去捞月亮。可是仍然一碰到水，月亮**就**碎了。

So the little monkey reached for the moon **again**. But **as soon as** he touched the water, the moon still shattered.

jiù zhè yàng, xiǎo hóu zi shì le jǐ cì dōu bù chéng gōng, zhí dào dà jiā dōu lèi le, zhǐ néng fàng qì。

就这样，小猴子试了几次都不**成功**，直到大家都**累**了，只能**放弃**。

Just like this, the little monkey tried several times without **success**, until everyone was **tired** and had to **give up**.

tā men wéi zhe jǐng zǒu lái zǒu qù, bù zhī dào zěn me bàn。

它们围着井**走来走去**，不知道**怎么办**。

They **walked back and forth** around the well, not knowing **what to do**.

jiù zài dà jiā hěn jǔ sàng de shí hòu, lǎo hóu zi tái tóu, kàn dào le tiān shàng yuán yuán de yuè liàng。

就在大家很**沮丧**的时候，老猴子**抬头**，看到了天上圆圆的月亮。

Just when everyone was very **depressed**, the old monkey **looked up** and saw the round moon in the sky.

tā tū rán míng bái le, sōng le kǒu qì shuō: "bié bái fèi lì qì le, yuè liàng hái zài tiān shàng, jǐng lǐ de yuè liàng zhǐ shì yǐng zi。"

它突然**明白**了，**松了口气**说："别**白费**力气了，月亮还在天上，井里的月亮只是**影子**。"

He suddenly **understood**, and said with **a sigh of relief**: "Don't **waste** your efforts, the moon is still in the sky, and the moon in the well is just a **reflection**."

hóu zi men yě zhōng yú míng bái le: yuán lái, shuǐ zhōng lāo yuè shì bù huì yǒu jié guǒ de。

猴子们也**终于**明白了：**原来**，水中捞月是不会有结果的。

The monkeys also **finally** understood: **it turns out** that fishing for the moon in the water will not yield results.

Summary

No matter how hard the monkeys try, they cannot reach the moon in the water. This tale reminds us not to waste time chasing unrealistic or unattainable goals. We must be **objective** (客观 kè guān) and **pragmatic** (务实 wù shí) when it comes to setting goals and expending effort toward achieving them, and not grasp at straws or waste effort.

Learning Tip

水中捞月 is an idiom with its origins in this fable. Literally translated as "fishing for the moon in water," it is used to describe those who wasting time and effort for unrealistic things.

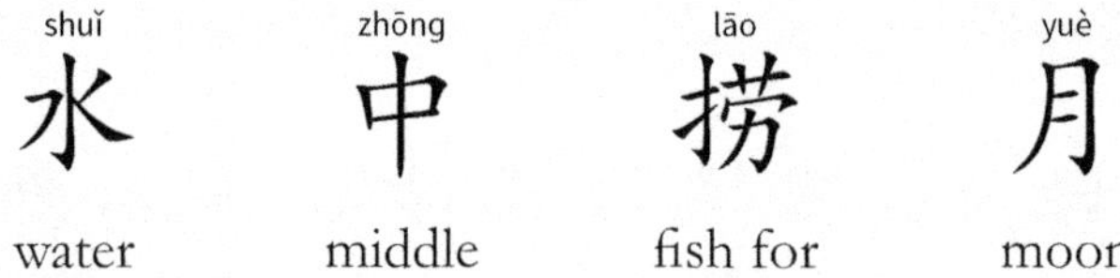

water | middle | fish for | moon

1 她想嫁给亿万富翁，真是**水中捞月。**

She wants to marry a billionaire, which is really **fishing for the moon in water.**

2 他次次尽全力去竞选总统，都失败了，最终明白是**水中捞月。**

He tried his best to run for the presidency every single time, but always failed, and finally realized that he had been **fishing for the moon in water.**

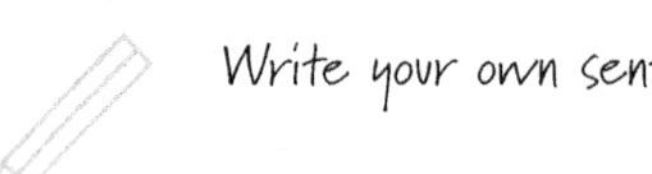

KEY VOCABULARY

Word	Part of speech	Meaning	Word	Part of speech	Meaning
shǒu zú wú cuò 手足无措	*idiom*	at a loss	huī fù 恢复	*v.*	to recover
zǒu lái zǒu qù 走来走去	*vp.*	walk back and forth	píng jìng 平静	*adj.* *n.*	peaceful peace
jīng huāng 惊慌	*adj.*	panic	chéng gōng 成功	*v.*	to succeed
yú shì 于是	*conj.*	so/ hence	fàng qì 放弃	*v.*	to give up
shēn shǒu 伸手	*v.*	stretch hand	zāo gāo 糟糕	*adj.*	oops/bad
jīng yà 惊讶	*adj.*	shocked	jǔ sàng 沮丧	*adj.*	depressed
bào yuàn 抱怨	*v.*	to complain	tái tóu 抬头	*v.*	to look up
suì 碎	*v.*	to break/ shatter	míng bái 明白	*v.*	to understand
yǐng zi 影子	*n.*	shadow/ reflection	sōng kǒu qì 松口气	*vp.*	to relieve/ relax a bit

SENTENCE PATTERNS

还是...吧

should (indicate a mild suggestion/preference)

hái shì ba
还是 + *action* + **吧**

lǎo hóu zi jiù duì xiǎo hóu zi shuō: nǐ hái shì zài shì yī cì ba
老猴子就对小猴子说：你还是再试一次吧。

The old monkey said to the little monkey: You should just try one more time.

原来...

it turns out that...

yuán lái
原来 + *clause*

yuán lái, shuǐ zhōng lāo yuè shì bù huì yǒu jié guǒ de
原来，水中捞月是不会有结果的。

It turns out that fishing for the moon in the water will not yield results.

Chinese Version

一天晚上，一只小猴子在井边玩，它往井里看，居然发现里面有个月亮。

小猴子手足无措，就叫："糟糕！月亮掉进井里了。"

大猴子听见后，跑过来看，也惊慌了！跟着叫："糟糕！月亮掉进井里了。"

老猴子听见后，也跑来了，然后也一起跟着叫："糟糕！月亮掉进井里了，我们一定要帮忙，把它捞起来。"

于是，它们找来了其他猴子，然后一起爬上了井边的大树。

老猴子倒挂在树上，拉住大猴子的脚。大猴子也倒挂着，拉住其他猴子的脚，就这样一只接一只。

小猴子挂在最下面，终于到了井水处，它伸手去捞月亮，可是一碰到水，月亮就碎了。

小猴子很惊讶地说："啊！月亮被我抓碎了。"

大家开始抱怨小猴子。过了一会儿，水面恢复了平静，月亮又出现了。

老猴子就对小猴子说："你还是再试一次吧。"

于是，小猴子再次伸手去捞月亮。可是仍然一碰到水，月亮就碎了。

就这样，小猴子试了几次都不成功，直到大家都累了，只能放弃。

它们围着井走来走去，不知道怎么办。

就在大家很沮丧的时候，老猴子抬头，看到了天上圆圆的月亮。

它突然明白了，松了口气说："别白费力气了，月亮还在天上，井里的月亮只是影子。"

猴子们也终于明白了：原来，水中捞月是不会有结果的。

Modern Stories

代 dài

故 gù

事 shì

shén mì qíng shū

神秘情书

The Secret Love Letter

dà hǎi shì dà xué lǐ yǒu míng de huā huā gōng zǐ, tā suī rán cái 21 suì, dàn yǐ jīng jiāo wǎng le 22 gè nǚ péng yǒu.

大海是大学里有名的**花花公子**，他**虽然**才21岁，**但**已经交往了22个女朋友。

Dahai is a known **playboy** (flower gentleman) in the university. **Although** he is only 21 years old, he has already dated 22 girlfriends so far.

yī xiē shì zhèng shì nǚ yǒu, jiāo wǎng shí jiān zuì cháng de shì sān gè yuè, zuì duǎn de shì liǎng gè xīng qī.

一些是**正式**女友，交往时间**最长的**是三个月，**最短的**是两个星期。

Some were **official** girlfriends, with the **longest** relationship being three months, and the **shortest** being two weeks.

hái yǒu yī xiē shì fēi zhèng shì nǚ yǒu, zhǐ shì bù dìng qī gēn tā yuē pào.

还有一些是**非正式**女友，只是**不定期**跟他**约炮**。

Others were **unofficial** girlfriends who were just **hooking up** with him **from time to time**.

dàn shì, zhè xiē duǎn zàn de nán nǚ guān xi cháng cháng ràng tā jué de hěn kōng xū.

但是，这些**短暂**的男女关系常常让他觉得很**空虚**。

But these **short-lived** relationships often left him feeling **empty**.

zài yī cì shèng dàn wǎn huì shàng, tā guān kàn le yī gè nǚ shēng xiǎo yuè de chàng gē biǎo yǎn.

在一次**圣诞晚会**上，他观看了一个女生小月的唱歌**表演**。

At a **Christmas party**, he watched a singing **performance** of a girl named Xiaoyue.

xiǎo yuè de gē shēng fēi cháng róu měi, dà hǎi bèi tā shēn shēn de mí zhù le
小月的歌声非常**柔美**，大海被她深深地**迷住**了。
Xiaoyue's singing voice was very **tender and beautiful**, and Dahai was deeply **fascinated** by her.

tā zhǔ dòng qù gēn xiǎo yuè jiāo tán, xiǎng jiā tā de wēi xìn, dàn bèi jù jué le
他**主动**去跟小月交谈，想加她的微信，但被**拒绝**了。
He **took the initiative** to talk to Xiaoyue and wanted to add her WeChat, but was **rejected**.

xiǎo yuè tiáo kǎn tā: nǐ yǒu nà me duō nǚ péng yǒu, yīng gāi hěn máng ba
小月**调侃**他："你有那么多女朋友，应该很忙吧。"
Xiaoyue **mocked** him: "You have so many girlfriends, you must be very busy."

tīng dào zhè gè, dà hǎi fēi cháng shāng gǎn. hěn kuài, tā gēn suǒ yǒu de nǚ yǒu duàn jué le guān xi
听到这个，大海非常**伤感**。很快，他**跟**所有的女友**断绝了关系**。
Hearing this, Dahai was very **sentimental**. Soon, he **cut** all his girlfriends **off**.

dàn tóng shí, tā yě fēng kuáng de ài shàng le xiǎo yuè, kāi shǐ guò zhe yī rì sān qiū de shēng huó, zhōng yú tā xiě xià le zhè fēng qíng shū:
但**同时**，他也疯狂地**爱上**了小月，开始过着**一日三秋**的生活，终于他写下了这封**情书**：
But **at the same time**, he also **fell in love** with Xiaoyue crazily, and started a life of **endless yearning** (three autumns a day), finally he wrote this **love letter**:

zài yù dào nǐ zhī qián, wǒ shì bái chī. zài yù dào nǐ zhī hòu, wǒ biàn chéng le qíng chī
在遇到你之前，我是**白痴**。在遇到你之后，我变成了**情痴**。
Before I met you, I was an **idiotic man**. After meeting you, I became a **lovesick man**.

chū mén, zhǎo bù dào lù; huí jiā, kàn bù dào mén
出门，找不到路；回家，看不到门。
When going out, I can't find the road; When returning home, I cannot see the door.

tiān qíng de shí hòu, wǒ xiǎng nǐ. xià yǔ de shí hòu, wǒ xiǎng nǐ
天晴的时候，我想你。下雨的时候，我想你。
When it's sunny, I miss you. When it's raining, I miss you.

bái tiān de shí hòu wǒ xiǎng nǐ wǎn shàng de shí hòu wǒ hái shì xiǎng nǐ
白天的时候，我想你；晚上的时候，我**还是**想你。
In daylight, I miss you. In evening, **still** I miss you.

bié rén shuō wǒ shì lù chī què bù zhī wǒ shì xīn chī
别人说我是**路痴**，却不知我是**心痴**！
Others say that I am a **road-wanderer**, but they don't know that I'm actually a **heart-wanderer**!

ài nǐ shì chī bèi nǐ ài yě shì chī
爱你是"痴"，被你爱也是"痴"。
Loving you is "lovelorn," being loved by you is also "lovelorn."

nǐ shì tiān shàng de xiǎo yuè wǒ shì dì shàng de dà hǎi
你是天上的**小月**，我是地上的**大海**。
You are the **Little Moon** (her name) in the sky, I am the **Big Sea** (his name) on the earth.

wèi shén me wǒ men zhī jiān de jù lí rú cǐ yáo yuǎn
为什么我们**之间**的距离如此**遥远**？
Why do we have such a **far** distance **between** us?

nǐ yào zěn yàng cái néng jiē shòu wǒ de chī xīn yī piàn
你要怎样才能**接受**我的**痴心一片**？
When will you **accept** my **true love** (a piece of lovelorn heart)?

xiě wán hòu tā méi yǒu shǔ míng zhǐ shì qiāo qiāo de bǎ qíng shū jì gěi le xiǎo yuè xiǎo yuè shōu dào hòu méi yǒu huí fù
写完后，他没有**署名**，只是悄悄地把**情书**寄给了小月。小月收到后没有**回复**。
After finishing writing, he did not **sign** it, but secretly sent the **love letter** to Xiaoyue. Xiaoyue did not **reply** after receiving it.

kě shì cóng nà yǐ hòu xiǎo yuè měi zhōu dōu huì shōu dào yī fēng shén mì qíng shū hé yī shù hóng méi guī
可是，**从那以后**，小月每周都会收到一封**神秘**情书和一束红玫瑰。
However, **since then**, Xiaoyue would receive a **mysterious** love letter and a bouquet of red roses every week.

bàn nián hòu xiǎo yuè zhōng yú bèi dǎ dòng le jiù zhǔ dòng lián xì le dà hǎi tā shuō wǒ zhī dào shì nǐ jì rán nǐ bù máng wǒ men míng tiān jiàn ba
半年后，小月终于被**打动**了，就主动**联系**了大海，她说："我知道是你，**既然**你不忙，我们明天见吧。"
After half a year, Xiaoyue was finally **moved**, so she took the initiative to **contact** Dahai, and she said, "I know it's you, **since** you're not busy, let's meet tomorrow."

大海欣喜若狂，因为他知道自己将会迎来一个真正的开始。

(dà hǎi xīn xǐ ruò kuáng, yīn wèi tā zhī dào zì jǐ jiāng huì yíng lái yī gè zhēn zhèng de kāi shǐ.)

Dahai felt **ecstatic** (too happy as if gone crazy), because he knew he is about to welcome a **real** beginning.

Learning Tip

痴 is a versatile character that can be used in a variety of ways to describe different forms of foolishness, silliness, or obsession, by adding it to another appropriate word. In the love letter from the story you can see several usages:

bái chī	qíng chī	lù chī	xīn chī

white obsessed	*love obsessed*	*road obsessed*	*heart obsessed*
idiot	lovesick person	road wanderer (often get lost)	heart wanderer (looking for someone to love)

Write your own sentence

你觉得小月最后选择接受大海的追求是对的吗？请给出你的理由。

Do you think it was right for Xiaoyue to finally chose to accept the pursuit of Dahai? Please give your reasons.

KEY VOCABULARY

huā huā gōng zǐ 花花公子	*idiom*	playboy	shāng gǎn 伤感	*adj.*	sentimental
zhèng shì 正式	*adj.*	formal/official	ài shàng 爱上	*v.*	fall in love with
fēi zhèng shì 非正式	*adj.*	informal/unofficial	tiáo kǎn 调侃	*v.*	to mock/tease
bù dìng qī 不定期	*adj.*	from time to time	qíng shū 情书	*n.*	love letter
duǎn zàn 短暂	*adj.*	temporary	yáo yuǎn 遥远	*adj.*	far
kōng xū 空虚	*adj.*	empty (feeling)	shǔ míng 署名	*v.*	to sign (signature)
róu měi 柔美	*adj.*	tender and beautiful	huí fù 回复	*v.*	to reply
xīn xǐ ruò kuáng 欣喜若狂	*idiom*	ecstatic	shén mì 神秘	*adj.*	secret/mysterious
yī rì sān qiū 一日三秋	*idiom*	endless yearning	jù jué 拒绝	*v.*	to reject

SENTENCE PATTERNS

虽然…但（是）

although ... but ...

suī rán dàn shì
虽然 + *clause 1* + **但（是）** + *clause 2*

tā suī rán cái suì dàn yǐ jīng jiāo wǎng le gè nǚ péng yǒu
他虽然才21岁，但已经交往了22个女朋友。

Although he is only 21 years old, he has already dated 22 girlfriends so far.

跟…断绝关系

cut ... off (relationship)

gēn duàn jué guān xi
A + **跟** + *B* + **断绝关系**

hěn kuài tā gēn suǒ yǒu de nǚ yǒu duàn jué le guān xi
很快，他跟所有的女友断绝了关系。

Soon, he cut all his girlfriends off.

Chinese Version

大海是大学里有名的花花公子，他虽然才21岁，但已经交往了22个女朋友。

一些是正式女友，交往时间最长的是三个月，最短的是两个星期。

还有一些是非正式女友，只是不定期跟他约炮。

但是，这些短暂的男女关系常常让他觉得很空虚。

在一次圣诞晚会上，他观看了一个女生小月的唱歌表演。

小月的歌声非常柔美，大海被她深深地迷住了。

他主动去跟小月交谈，想加她的微信，但被拒绝了。

小月调侃他："你有那么多女朋友，应该很忙吧。"

听到这个，大海非常伤感。很快，他跟所有的女友断绝了关系。

但同时，他也疯狂地爱上了小月，开始过着一日三秋的生活，终于他写下了这封情书：

在遇到你之前，我是白痴。在遇到你之后，我变成了情痴。

出门，找不到路；回家，看不到门。

天晴的时候，我想你。下雨的时候，我想你。

白天的时候，我想你；晚上的时候，我还是想你。

别人说我是路痴，却不知我是心痴!

爱你是"痴"，被你爱也是"痴"。

你是天上的小月，我是地上的大海。

为什么我们之间的距离如此遥远？

你要怎样才能接受我的痴心一片？

写完后，他没有署名，只是悄悄地把情书寄给了小月。小月收到后没有回复。

可是，从那以后，小月每周都会收到一封神秘情书和一束红玫瑰。

半年后，小月终于被打动了，就主动联系了大海，她说："我知道是你，既然你不忙，我们明天见吧。"

大海欣喜若狂，因为他知道自己将会迎来一个真正的开始。

mǎ yún de yǎn guāng

马云的眼光

Jack Ma's Vision

nián mǎ yún chū shēng zài zhōng guó de yī gè pǔ tōng jiā tíng tā
1964年，马云出生在中国的一个**普通**家庭。他
xiǎo de shí hòu yǒu diǎn tiáo pí cháng cháng yīn wèi gēn tóng xué dǎ jià bèi chǔ fá
小的时候有点**调皮**，常常因为跟同学打架被**处罚**。

In 1964, Jack Ma was born into an **ordinary** family in China. He was a bit **naughty** when he was young and was often **punished** for fighting with his classmates.

hòu lái mǎ yún gāo kǎo shī bài jiù qù jiǔ diàn shēn qǐng zuò fú wù yuán
后来马云高考**失败**，就去酒店**申请**做服务员，
què bèi lǎo bǎn jù jué shuō tā bù jǐn yòu shòu yòu ǎi hái zhǎng de chǒu
却被老板**拒绝**，说他不仅又瘦又矮，还长得**丑**。

Later, Jack Ma **failed** the college entrance examination, so he went to a hotel **to apply** to be a waiter, but was **rejected** by the boss, who said that he was not only thin and short, but also **ugly**.

zhī hòu zài shú rén de tuī jiàn xià mǎ yún shèn zhì zuò le yī duàn shí jiān de bān yùn gōng
之后，**在熟人的推荐下**，马云甚至做了一段时间的搬运工。

After that, **under the recommendation** of acquaintances, Ma Yun even worked as a porter for a period of time.

wèi le dà xué mèng mǎ yún jì xù cān jiā gāo kǎo dàn yòu shī bài le
为了**大学梦**，马云**继续**参加高考，但又失败了。
tā méi yǒu fàng qì dào le dì sān nián zhōng yú bèi yī suǒ dà xué lù qǔ
他没有**放弃**，到了第三年，终于被一所大学**录取**。

For the **university dream**, Jack Ma **continued** to take the college entrance examination, but failed again. He didn't **give up** and by the third year, he was finally **admitted** by a university.

zài dà xué lǐ mǎ yún zhǔ xiū yīng yǔ bì yè hòu tā zuò le yī
在大学里，马云**主修**英语。毕业后，他做了一
míng yīng yǔ lǎo shī rán hòu chéng lì le yī jiā fān yì zhōng jiè
名英语老师，然后**成立**了一家翻译**中介**。

When in university, Jack Ma **majored in** English. After graduation, he worked as an English teacher and then **established** a translation **agency**.

nián mǎ yún qù le měi guó zài jiē chù hù lián wǎng hòu
1994年，马云去了美国，在接触**互联网**后，
tā kāi shǐ fēng kuáng de xué xí diàn nǎo
他开始**疯狂**地学习电脑。

In 1994, Jack Ma went to the United States, and after coming into contact with the **internet**, he began to study computers **crazily**.

suī rán nà shí hòu hù lián wǎng zài quán shì jiè cái gāng gāng qǐ bù dàn mǎ
虽然那时候互联网在**全世界**才刚刚**起步**，但马
yún què xiāng xìn tā huì gǎi biàn shì jiè
云却**相信**它会改变世界！

Although the Internet was just **starting** in the **whole world** at that time, Jack Ma **believed** that it would change the world!

yú shì mǎ yún dǎ suàn yòng hù lián wǎng chéng lì xīn gōng sī dàn duō shù
于是，马云打算用互联网**成立**新公司，但多数
péng yǒu hé tóu zī zhě dōu fǎn duì tā
朋友和**投资者**都反对他。

So, Jack Ma planned to use the Internet to **establish** a new company, but most of his friends and **investors** were against him.

kě tā què hěn jiān dìng zài qī zi de zhī chí xià tā chéng lì le yī
可他却很**坚定**。**在**妻子**的支持下**，他成立了一
jiā wǎng luò gōng sī bù dào sān nián jiù zhuàn le wàn
家网络公司。**不到**三年，就赚了500万。

But he was very **determined**. **Under the support of** his wife, he established an Internet company. In **less than** three years, he made 5 million yuan.

nián mǎ yún yǎn guāng gèng gāo chéng lì le ā lǐ bā bā cóng
1999年，马云**眼光**更高，成立了**阿里巴巴**，**从**
shì diàn zǐ shāng wù
事电子商务。

In 1999, Jack Ma had a higher **vision** and established **Alibaba**, **engaging in** e-commerce.

jiù zhè yàng tā de shēng yì yuè lái yuè dà zhī míng dù yuè lái yuè
就这样，他的**生意**越来越大，**知名度**越来越
gāo yě xī yǐn le gèng duō de tóu zī zhě
高，也吸引了更多的**投资者**。

Through this, his **business** is getting bigger and bigger, his **popularity** is getting higher and higher, and he is attracting more **investors**.

cóng nián ā lǐ bā bā qí xià de táo bǎo jiù chéng wéi le zhōng guó

从2003年，阿里巴巴旗下的**淘宝**就成为了中国

zuì dà de líng shòu wǎng zhàn

最大的**零售网站**。

Since 2003, Alibaba's **Taobao** has become China's largest **retail site**.

mǎ yún yǐ yì rén mín bì cái fù chéng wéi le zhōng guó shǒu

2014，马云以1500亿人民币**财富**成为了中国**首**

fù nián huò dé fú bù sī zhōng shēn chéng jiù jiǎng

富，2019年获得**福布斯终身成就奖**。

In 2014, Jack Ma became the **richest man** in China with a **fortune** of 150 billion yuan, and in 2019 he won the **Forbes Lifetime Achievement Award**.

zài jìn nián de fú bù sī quán qiú yì wàn fù háo bǎng shàng tā yě yī zhí

在近年的福布斯全球**亿万富豪**榜上，他也一直

bǎng shàng yǒu míng

榜上有名。

In recent years' Forbes' World's **Billionaires** List, his **name** is always **on the list**.

bié rén zǒng shì wèn tā chéng gōng de mì mì shì shén me tā céng shuō nǐ

别人总是问他成功的**秘密**是什么，他曾说：你

de gōng sī zài nǎ lǐ bù zhòng yào zhòng yào de shì nǐ de yǎn guāng

的公司在哪里**不重要，重要的是**你的眼光。

People always ask him what is the **secret** of success. He once said: It **doesn't matter** where your company is, **what matters is** your vision.

ér zhè yě shì tā de míng zì yún de yì sī

而这，也是他的名字"云"的意思。

And this is also the meaning of his name "Yun". (Yun means vision when used for names)

你认为马云是个怎样的人？除了眼光，还有什么让他如此成功？

What kind of person do you think Jack Ma is? Besides vision, what else makes him so successful?

Key Vocabulary

tiáo pí 调皮	*adj.*	naughty	zhōng jiè 中介	*n.*	agency
chǔ fá 处罚	*v.*	to punish	hù lián wǎng 互联网	*n.*	the internet
shī bài 失败	*v.* *n.*	to fail failure	shì jiè 世界	*n.*	world
chéng gōng 成功	*v.* *n.*	to succeed success	tóu zī zhě 投资者	*n.*	investor
shēn qǐng 申请	*v.*	to apply	jiān dìng 坚定	*adj.*	determined
jù jué 拒绝	*v.*	to reject	yǎn guāng 眼光	*n.*	vision
fàng qì 放弃	*v.*	to give up	zhī míng dù 知名度	*n.*	popularity
chéng lì 成立	*v.*	to set up/ establish	cái fù 财富	*n.*	wealth/fortune
yì wàn fù háo 亿万富豪	*n.*	billionaire	shǒu fù 首富	*n.*	richest person

Sentence Patterns

在…的支持下

under/with the support of

zài 在 + *someone* + de zhī chí xià 的支持下 + *clause*

zài qī zi de zhī chí xià, tā chéng lì le yī jiā wǎng luò gōng sī
在妻子的支持下，他成立了一家网络公司。

Under the support of his wife, he established an Internet company.

…不重要，重要的是…

… doesn't matter, what matters is …

A + bù zhòng yào 不重要，zhòng yào de shì 重要的是 + *B*

nǐ de gōng sī zài nǎ lǐ bù zhòng yào, zhòng yào de shì nǐ de yǎn guāng
你的公司在哪里不重要，重要的是你的眼光。

It doesn't matter where your company is, what matters is your vision.

CHINESE VERSION

1964年，马云出生在中国的一个普通家庭。他小的时候有点调皮，常常因为跟同学打架被处罚。

后来马云高考失败，就去酒店申请做服务员，却被老板拒绝，说他不仅又瘦又矮，还长得丑。

之后，在熟人的推荐下，马云甚至做了一段时间的搬运工。

为了大学梦，马云继续参加高考，但又失败了。他没有放弃，到了第三年，终于被一所大学录取。

在大学里，马云主修英语。毕业后，他做了一名英语老师，然后成立了一家翻译中介。

1994年，马云去了美国，在接触互联网后，他开始疯狂地学习电脑。

虽然那时候互联网在全世界才刚刚起步，但马云却相信它会改变世界！

于是，马云打算用互联网成立新公司，但多数朋友和投资者都反对他。

可他却很坚定。在妻子的支持下，他成立了一家网络公司。不到三年，就赚了500万。

1999年，马云眼光更高，成立了阿里巴巴，从事电子商务。

就这样，他的生意越来越大，知名度越来越高，也吸引了更多的投资者。

从2003年，阿里巴巴旗下的淘宝就成为了中国最大的零售网站。

2014，马云以1500亿人民币财富成为了中国首富，2019年获得福布斯终身成就奖。

在近年的福布斯全球亿万富豪榜上，他也一直榜上有名。

别人总是问他成功的秘密是什么，他曾说：你的公司在哪里不重要，重要的是你的眼光。

而这，也是他的名字“云”的意思。

gōng fū chuán qí lǐ xiǎo lón

功夫传奇李小龙

Kung Fu Legend Bruce Lee

lǐ xiǎo lóng shì shì jiè zhù míng de wǔ shù jiā hé diàn yǐng yǎn yuán yě
李小龙是**世界著名**的武术家和电影**演员**，也
shì jié quán dào de chuàng shǐ rén
是“截拳道”的**创始人**。

Bruce Lee was a **world-famous** master of martial arts and movie **actor**, and the **founder** of “Jeet Kune Do”.

nián yuè rì lǐ xiǎo lóng chū shēng zài měi guó jiā zhōu jiù jīn
1940年11月27日，李小龙**出生**在美国加州**旧金**
shān tā cóng xiǎo jiù xǐ huān wǔ shù qī suì kāi shǐ liàn xí tài jí
山。他**从小**就喜欢武术，七岁开始练习“太极
quán
拳”。

Bruce Lee was **born** on November 27, 1940 in **San Francisco**, California. He had loved martial arts **since childhood**, and started practicing “Tai Chi” at the age of seven.

zài jiā rén hé péng yǒu yǎn lǐ tā jiù shì gè wǔ chī shí sì suì
在家人和朋友眼里，他就是个**武痴**。十四岁
de shí hòu tā xiàng zhù míng wǔ shù jiā yè wèn xué xí yǒng chūn quán
的时候，他**向**著名武术家叶问**学习**“咏春拳”。

In the eyes of family and friends, he is a **martial arts obsessor**. When he was fourteen, he **learned** Wing Chun **from** the famous martial arts master Ip Man.

lǐ xiǎo lóng wèi le liàn hǎo wǔ shù shí me kǔ dōu bù pà cháng cháng fèi
李小龙为了练好武术，**什么**苦**都**不怕，常常**废**
qǐn wàng shí
寝忘食。

In order to practice martial arts well, Bruce Lee was not afraid of **any** hardships and often **forgot to eat and sleep**.

zài shàng dà xué de shí hòu lǐ xiǎo lóng zài xiào yuán lǐ zǔ zhī le zhōng
在上大学的时候，李小龙在校园里**组织**了“中
guó gōng fū duì yī biān xué xí yī biān jiāo gōng fū
国功夫队”，**一边**学习，**一边**教功夫。

When he was in university, Bruce Lee **organized** a “Chinese Kung Fu Team” on campus to teach Kung Fu **while** studying.

tā bù jǐn huì hěn duō zhōng guó quán fǎ hái shēn rù xué xí xī fāng quán fǎ
他不仅会很多中国**拳法**，还**深入学习**西方拳法。
tīng shuō tā kě yǐ zài yī miǎo nèi dǎ jiǔ quán tī liù tuǐ
听说，他可以在**一秒内**打九拳，踢六腿。

He not only knew a lot of Chinese **boxing techniques**, but also **deeply studied** Western boxing techniques. **It's said that** he can hit nine punches and kick six legs **in one second**.

nián lǐ xiǎo lóng chuàng lì jié quán dào chéng wéi shì jiè wǔ
1967年，李小龙**创立**“截拳道”，成为世界武
shù dà shī tā de xué shēng lái zì shì jiè gè dì shèn zhì bāo kuò yī
术**大师**。他的学生来自**世界各地**，**甚至**包括一
xiē diàn yǐng míng xīng hé wǔ shù jiā
些电影明星和武术家。

In 1967, Bruce Lee **founded** “Jeet Kune Do” and became a **master** of martial arts in the world. His students come from **all over the world**, **even** including some movie stars and masters of martial art.

lǐ xiǎo lóng yě shì yī wèi fēi cháng yōu xiù de yǎn yuán tā shì hǎo lái wù
李小龙也是一位非常**优秀**的演员，他是好莱坞
de dì yī wèi huá rén zhǔ yǎn
的第一位华人**主演**。

Bruce Lee was also an **excellent** actor, he was the first Chinese **leading role** in Hollywood.

tōng guò diàn yǐng tā xiàng quán shì jiè jiè shào le zhōng guó gōng fū hé wén
通过电影，他**向**全世界**介绍**了中国功夫和文
huà
化。

Through films, he **introduced** Chinese Kung Fu and culture **to** the world.

tā pāi de diàn yǐng bù jǐn dǎ pò le hěn duō jì lù ér qiě chéng wéi le
他拍的电影不仅**打破**了很多**纪录**，而且成为了
shí dài de jīng diǎn
时代的经典。

The films he made not only **broke** many **records**, but also became **classics** of the era.

yí hàn de shì nián yuè rì lǐ xiǎo lóng zài xiāng gǎng pāi
遗憾的是，1973年7月20日，李小龙在香港拍
diàn yǐng sǐ wáng de yóu xì de shí hòu tū rán qù shì cái
电影《死亡的游戏》的时候，突然**去世**，才32
suì
岁。

Unfortunately, on July 20, 1973, when Bruce Lee was filming the movie “Game of Death” in Hong Kong, he **died** suddenly at the age of only 32.

lǐ xiǎo lóng shì hěn duō rén xīn zhōng de ǒu xiàng hé yīng xióng bù guǎn guò
李小龙是很多人心中的**偶像**和**英雄**。**不管**过
qù duō shǎo nián tā dōu huì yǒng yuǎn huó zài dà jiā de xīn lǐ
去多少年，他都会**永远**活在大家的心里。

Bruce Lee is an **idol** and **hero** of many people. **No matter** how many years have passed, he will **always** live in people’s hearts.

你认为李小龙是个怎样的人？你知道哪些中国或者世界武术？

What kind of person do you think Bruce Lee was? Which Chinese or world martial arts do you know of?

Key Vocabulary

zhù míng	著名	*adj.*	renowned	chuàng shǐ rén	创始人	*n.*	founder
shì jiè gè dì	世界各地	*n.*	all over the world	yōu xiù	优秀	*adj.*	excellent
wǔ shù	武术	*n.*	martial art	dǎ pò	打破	*v.*	to break
wǔ shù jiā	武术家	*n.*	martial artist	jì lù	纪录	*n.*	record
zǔ zhī	组织	*v.*	to organise	jīng diǎn	经典	*n.*	classic
gōng fū	功夫	*n.*	kung fu	yí hàn	遗憾	*n.* *adj.*	regret regretful
chuàng lì	创立	*v.*	to found/ establish	qù shì	去世	*v.*	to die/ pass away
fèi qǐn wàng shí	废寝忘食	*idiom*	forget to sleep and eat (due to hard work)	ǒu xiàng	偶像	*n.*	idol

Sentence Patterns

什么…都…

indicates an action applies to any and all things

subject + **什么** (shí me) + *noun* + **都** (dōu) + *verb*

lǐ xiǎo lóng wèi le liàn hǎo wǔ shù, shén me kǔ dōu bù pà

李小龙为了练好武术，什么苦都不怕。

In order to practice martial arts well, Bruce Lee was not afraid of any hardships.

向…介绍…

introduce … to …

A + **向** (xiàng) + *B* + **介绍** (jiè shào) + *noun*

tōng guò diàn yǐng, tā xiàng quán shì jiè jiè shào le zhōng guó gōng fū hé wén huà

通过电影，他向全世界介绍了中国功夫和文化。

Through films, he introduced Chinese Kung Fu and culture to the world.

Chinese Version

李小龙是世界著名的武术家和电影演员，也是“截拳道”的创始人。

1940年11月27日，李小龙出生在美国加州旧金山。他从小就喜欢武术，七岁开始练习“太极拳”。

在家人和朋友眼里，他就是个武痴。十四岁的时候，他向著名武术家叶问学习“咏春拳”。

李小龙为了练好武术，什么苦都不怕，常常废寝忘食。

在上大学的时候，李小龙在校园里组织了“中国功夫队”，一边学习，一边教功夫。

他不仅会很多中国拳法，还深入学习西方拳法。听说，他可以在一秒内打九拳，踢六腿。

1967年，李小龙创立“截拳道”，成为世界武术大师。他的学生来自世界各地，甚至包括一些电影明星和武术家。

李小龙也是一位非常优秀的演员。他是好莱坞的第一位华人主演。

通过电影，他向全世界介绍了中国功夫和文化。

他拍的电影不仅打破了很多记录，而且成为了时代的经典。

遗憾的是，1973年7月20日，李小龙在香港拍电影《死亡的游戏》的时候，突然去世，才32岁。

李小龙是很多人心中的偶像和英雄。不管过去多少年，他都会永远活在大家的心里。

成语故事

chéng yǔ gù shì

Chinese Idioms

8

yǎn ěr dào líng

掩耳盗铃

Cover One's Ears to Steal a Bell

chūn qiū shí qī, yī hù yǒu qián rén "fàn jiā" bèi chóu rén hài sǐ le.
春秋时期，一户**有钱**人"范家"被**仇人**害死了。
suǒ yǐ, fàn jiā de fáng zi méi yǒu rén kān guǎn.
所以，范家的房子没有人**看管**。

During the Spring and Autumn Period, a **wealthy** family, the "Fan Family," were killed by their **personal enemies**. Therefore, there was no one left **looking after** the family house.

yī gè xiǎo tōu tīng shuō fàn jiā yǒu hěn duō zhí qián de dōng xī, jiù zài
一个小偷**听说**范家有很多**值钱的东西**，就在
yī tiān yè lǐ qù fàn jiā tōu dōng xī.
一天夜里去范家**偷**东西。

A thief **heard** that the Fan's family had a lot of **valuables**, so one night he went there to **steal** things.

zài yī gè yè hēi fēng gāo de wǎn shàng, tā chuān zhe hēi yī fú, qiāo qiāo
在一个**夜黑风高**的晚上，他穿着黑衣服，**悄悄**
de lái dào fàn jiā de yuàn zi lǐ.
地来到范家的院子里。

On a **dark and windy** night, he dressed in black and **quietly** came to the Family family's yard.

tā zuǒ kàn yòu kàn, tū rán kàn dào yī kǒu dà zhōng. tā fā xiàn zhè shì
他**左看右看**，突然看到一口大钟。他发现这是
yī kǒu hěn guì de qīng tóng zhōng, yòu piào liàng yòu zhí qián.
一口很贵的**青铜钟**，又漂亮又**值钱**。

He **looked left and right**, and suddenly saw a big bell. He found that it was a very expensive **bronze bell**, beautiful and **valuable**.

xiǎo tōu gāo xìng jí le dǎ suàn bǎ zhōng tōu zǒu kě shì zhè kǒu zhōng
小偷高兴极了，**打算**把钟偷走。可是，这口钟
yòu dà yòu zhòng tā zěn me bān dōu bān bù dòng
又大又重，他**怎么**搬**都**搬不动。

The thief was very happy and **planned** to steal the bell. However, the bell was so big and heavy that **no matter how** hard he tried, he couldn't move it.

tā hěn zhāo jí xiǎng le yòu xiǎng tū rán yǒu le gè zhǔ yì bǎ zhōng
他很**着急**，想了又想，突然有了个**主意**：把钟
zá suì rán hòu yī kuài yī kuài de bān zǒu
砸碎，然后**一块一块**地搬走。

He was very **anxious**, and thought again and again, then suddenly came with an **idea**: smash the clock, and then move it away **piece by piece**.

yú shì xiǎo tōu jiù qù zhǎo le gè dà chuí zi tā bào zhe chuí zi
于是，小偷就去找了个大**锤子**。他抱着锤子，
jiā yóu de zá zhōng
加油地**砸钟**。

Hence, the thief went to find a big **hammer**. He held the hammer and thrived hard to **smash the bell**.

kě shì zhōng mǎ shàng fā shēng le jù xiǎng xià le tā yī tiào xiǎo tōu
可是，钟马上发生了巨响，**吓了**他**一跳**！小偷
hài pà jí le hěn dān xīn bié rén fā xiàn
害怕极了，很担心别人**发现**。

However, the bell immediately rang so loudly that **shocked** him **greatly**! The thief was terribly **scared** and worried that others would **find out**.

jiē zhe tā mǎ shàng zhāng kāi shuāng shǒu qù bào zhù zhōng xiǎng zhǐ zhù zhōng
接着，他马上**张开**双手去抱住钟，想**止住**钟
shēng kě zěn me dōu zhǐ bù zhù
声，可**怎么都**止不住！

So he immediately **stretched** his arms to hug the bell, trying to **stop** the sound of the bell, but **no matter how** he tried, he couldn't stop it!

tā tài hài pà le jiù yòng shǒu wǔ zhù ěr duǒ méi xiǎng dào zhè shí
他太害怕了，就用手**捂住**耳朵，**没想到**这时
hòu zhōng shēng tū rán biàn xiǎo le kuài tīng bù jiàn le
候钟声突然变小了，快听不见了！

He became so frightened that he **covered** his ears with his hands, and he **realized surprisingly** that the sound was getting smaller, almost disappearing!

yú shì xiǎo tōu mǎ shàng qù zhǎo lái liǎng kuài bù bǎ ěr duǒ wǔ zhù
于是，小偷**马上**去找来两块布，把耳朵**捂住**。
tā xiǎng xiàn zài shéi yě tīng bù dào wǒ zá zhōng le
他想：现在谁也听不到我砸钟了！

So, the thief **immediately** went to find two pieces of cloth to **cover** his ears. He believed: Now no one can hear me smashing the bell any more!

tā zài cì ná qǐ dà chuí jiā yóu de zá zhōng zhōng shēng yuè lái yuè
他**再次**拿起大锤，**加油**地砸钟。钟声越来越
dà xiǎo tōu tīng bù jiàn kě shì zhōu wéi de lín jū dōu tīng jiàn le
大，小偷听不见，可是周围的**邻居**都听见了。

He picked up the hammer **again** and **made an all-out effort** to smash the bell. The sound grew louder and louder, and the thief could not hear it, but the **neighbors** around all heard it.

hěn kuài lín jū men dōu pǎo guò lái le dà jiā kàn dào le fā shēng de
很快邻居们都**跑过来**了，大家看到了**发生**的
yī qiè jiù yī qǐ zhuō zhù le xiǎo tōu
一切，就一起**捉住**了小偷。

Very soon the neighbors **ran over**, after everyone saw what **happened**, they **caught** the thief together.

hòu lái yǎn ěr dào líng jiù yòng lái xíng róng nà xiē zì qī qī rén de
后来，“掩耳盗铃”就用来形容那些**自欺欺人**的
bèn dàn
笨蛋。

Later, the term " Cover One's Ears to Steal a Bell " became used to describe fools who **deceive themselves and others.**

Summary

This story is the original story behind the idiom 掩耳盗铃 . The image of covering one's ears to avoid hearing the ringing of a stolen bell is meant to evoke the idea of someone who is trying to deny or ignore the consequences of their actions, often to their own detriment. In modern usage, the phrase is often used to criticize someone who is being dishonest or avoiding responsibility. The idea behind the phrase is that if one tries to ignore the truth or avoid the consequences of their actions, they will ultimately be unable to hide from the truth forever and will have to face the consequences eventually.

Learning Tip

掩耳盗铃 is a Chinese idiom translated here as "cover one's ears to steal a Bell." It is similar to another idiom: **自欺欺人**, used to describe those who try to deceive themselves and others.

yǎn	ěr	dào	líng
掩	耳	盗	铃
cover	ear	steal	bell

1 他的罪行都被监控器拍到了，却还不承认，简直是在**掩耳盗铃**。

His crimes were all caught on surveillance cameras, but he didn't admit it, indeed was **deceiving himself and others**!

2 他应该大胆地去面对事实，没必要做**掩耳盗铃**的事。

He should face the facts boldly, there is no need to **do pointless things to cover up**.

Write your own sentence

Key Vocabulary

chóu rén 仇人	*n.*	personal enemies	zhǐ zhù 止住	*v.*	to stop (blood, sound)
zhí qián 值钱	*adj.*	valuable (worth money)	wǔ zhù 捂住	*v.*	to cover (by hand)
yè hēi fēng gāo 夜黑风高	*idiom*	dark and windy	zài cì 再次	*adv.*	again/ once more
dǎ suàn 打算	*v.*	plan to	jiā yóu 加油	*v.*	go all out
chuí zi 锤子	*n.*	hammer	zhōu wéi 周围	*n.*	surrounding/ around
xià le yī tiào 吓了一跳	*vp.*	heavily shocked/ scared	lín jū 邻居	*n.*	neighbour
hài pà 害怕	*adj.*	scared	fā shēng 发生	*v.*	to happen
zì qī qī rén 自欺欺人	*idiom*	deceive themselves and others	yī qiè 一切	*n.*	everything
zhuō zhù 捉住	*v.*	to catch	zhāng kāi 张开	*v.*	to stretch

Sentence Patterns

怎么都…

no matter what/how... (the result doesn't change)

zěn me 怎么 + *verb* + dōu 都 + *result*

zhè kǒu zhōng yòu dà yòu zhòng, tā zěn me bān dōu bān bù dòng.
这口钟又大又重，他怎么搬都搬不动。

The bell was so big and heavy that no matter how hard he tried, he couldn't move it.

没想到…

surprising realisation / didn't expect ...

subject + méi xiǎng dào 没想到 + *statement*

tā yòng shǒu wǔ zhù ěr duǒ, méi xiǎng dào zhè shí hòu zhōngshēng tū rán biàn xiǎo le.
他用手捂住耳朵，没想到这时候钟声突然变小了。

He covered his ears with his hands, and realized surprisingly that the sound was getting smaller.

CHINESE VERSION

春秋时期，一户有钱人“范家”被仇人害死了。所以，范家的房子没有人看管。

一个小偷听说范家有很多值钱的东西，就在一天夜里去范家偷东西。

在一个夜黑风高的晚上，他穿着黑衣服，悄悄地来到范家的院子里。

他左看右看，突然看到一口大钟。他发现这是一口很贵的青铜钟，又漂亮又值钱。

小偷高兴极了，打算把钟偷走。可是，这口钟又大又重，他怎么搬都搬不动。

他很着急，想了又想，突然有了个主意：把钟砸碎，然后一块一块地搬走。

于是，小偷就去找了个大锤子。他抱着锤子，加油地砸钟。

可是，钟马上发生了巨响，吓了他一跳！小偷害怕极了，很担心别人发现。

接着，他马上张开双手去抱住钟，想止住钟声，可怎么都止不住！

他太害怕了，就用手捂住耳朵，没想到这时候钟声突然变小了，快听不见了！

于是，小偷马上去找来两块布，把耳朵捂住。他想：现在谁也听不到我砸钟了！

他再次拿起大锤，加油地砸钟。钟声越来越大，小偷听不见，可是周围的邻居都听见了。

很快邻居们都跑过来了，大家看到了发生的一切，就一起捉住了小偷。

后来，“掩耳盗铃”就用来形容那些自欺欺人(既欺骗自己，又欺骗别人)的笨蛋。

9

zhāo sān mù sì

朝三暮四

Frequently Changing One's Mind

cóng qián yǒu gè lǎo rén hěn ài hóu zi tā rèn wéi hóu zi shì shì jiè shàng zuì cōng míng zuì kě ài de dòng wù

从前有个老人很爱猴子。他**认为**猴子是世界上**最聪明**、最可爱的动物。

Long ago, there was an old man who loved monkeys very much. He **believed** that monkeys were the **smartest** and cutest animals in the world.

tā měi tiān hé hóu zi men yī qǐ wán xiāng chǔ de hěn róng qià jiù xiàng yī jiā rén

他每天和猴子们一起玩，**相处**得很融洽，就像一家人。

He played with the monkeys every day and and **got along** very well, like a family.

lín jū men dōu jué de lǎo rén jiù xiàng hóu zi men de yé yé yú shì jiù jiào tā hóu yé

邻居们都觉得老人就像猴子们的爷爷，**于是**就叫他"猴爷"。

Neighbors thought that the old man was just like the monkey's grandfather, **so** they called him "Monkey Grandpa".

hóu yé zài yuàn zi lǐ wèi hóu zi men gài le yī jiān xiǎo wū hái zài zhōu wéi zhòng le yī xiē xiāng jiāo shù hé píng guǒ shù

猴爷在院子里为猴子们盖了一间**小屋**，还在**周围**种了一些香蕉树和苹果树。

Monkey Grandpa built a **small house** for the monkeys in the yard, and planted some banana trees and apple trees **around**.

màn màn de tā shèn zhì hé hóu zi men néng tīng dǒng bǐ cǐ de huà jiù xiàng zuì hǎo de péng yǒu

慢慢地，他**甚至**和猴子们能听懂**彼此**的话，就像最好的朋友。

Gradually, he and the monkeys could **even** understand **one another**'s words, just like best friends.

kě shì hóu yé méi shén me qián chú le yào yǎng hóu zi hái yào yǎng tā de jiā rén

可是，猴爷没什么钱，**除了**要养猴子，**还要**养他的家人。

However, Monkey Grandpa didn't have much money. **In addition to** feeding the monkeys, he **also** had to feed his family.

suí zhe hóu men zi de shù liàng yuè lái yuè duō hóu yé yuè lái yuè dān xīn wèi hóu zi de kǒu liáng bù gòu

随着猴们子的**数量**越来越多，猴爷越来越**担心**喂猴子的**口粮**不够。

As the **number** of monkeys increased, Monkey Grandpa became more and more **worried about** not having enough **food** to feed the monkeys.

yī kāi shǐ tā shěng chī jiǎn yòng nìng yuàn zì jǐ shǎo chī yě yào bǎo zhèng hóu zi men chī bǎo

一开始，他**省吃俭用**，**宁愿**自己少吃，**也要**保证猴子们吃饱。

In the beginning, he was **frugal**, and **would rather** eat less himself, **in order to** ensure that the monkeys were fully fed.

kě shì dào le dōng tiān jiā lǐ de guǒ shù méi yǒu guǒ zi hóu yé bù dé bù qù mǎi qí tā shuǐ guǒ wèi hóu zi

可是，到了冬天，家里的果树没有**果子**，猴爷**不得不**去买其他水果喂猴子。

However, in winter, the fruit trees at home had no **fruit**, and Monkey Grandpa **had to** buy other fruits to feed the monkeys.

tā méi yǒu qián mǎi hěn duō shuǐ guǒ yú shì tòng xià jué xīn zhǔn bèi jiǎn shǎo hóu zi de kǒu liáng

他没有钱买很多水果，于是**痛下决心**，准备减少猴子的口粮。

He didn't have the money to buy a lot of fruit, so **painfully made up his mind** to reduce the monkey's food.

yī tiān hóu yé duì hóu zi men shuō bǎo bèi men duì bù qǐ cóng míng tiān kāi shǐ měi zhī hóu zi měi tiān zǎo shàng zhī néng chī sān gè shuǐ guǒ wǎn shàng chī sì gè xíng ma

一天，猴爷对猴子们说："**宝贝们**，对不起，从明天开始，每只猴子每天早上只能吃三个水果，晚上吃四个，**行吗**？"

One day, Monkey Grandpa said to the monkeys: "My **babies**, I'm sorry, starting from tomorrow, each monkey can only eat three fruits in the morning and four in the evening, **okay**?"

hóu zi men hěn bù gāo xìng, dà shēng shuō: "bù xíng, tài shǎo le!
猴子们很不高兴，大声说："不行，太少了！
zhè tài bù gōng píng le!
这太**不公平**了！"

The monkeys were very unhappy and said loudly, "No, too little! This is so **un-fair**! "

yú shì, hóu yé xiǎng le yī xià, yòu shuō: "zhè yàng ba, zǎo shàng
于是，猴爷**想了一下**，又说："**这样吧**，早上
chī sì gè shuǐ guǒ, wǎn shàng chī sān gè, hǎo ma?"
吃四个水果，晚上吃三个，好吗？"

So Monkey Grandpa **thought for a while** and said, "**How about** eating four fruits in the morning and three at night, okay?"

hóu zi men tīng dào zǎo shàng shì sì gè, bǐ yǐ qián duō le yī gè, dōu
猴子们听到早上是四个，比**以前**多了一个，都
gāo xìng de hǎn: "tài hǎo le!"
高兴地**喊**："太好了！"

The monkeys heard that there were four in the morning, one more than **before**, and they all **shouted** happily: "that's great!"

hóu yé hěn kāi xīn, yīn wèi tā méi xiǎng dào zì jǐ de jì liǎng jū rán
猴爷很开心，因为他**没想到**自己的**伎俩**居然
chéng gōng le!
成功了！

Monkey Grandpa was very happy, because he **didn't expect** his **trick** to actually succeed!

hòu lái "cháo sān mù sì" jiù yòng lái xíng róng yī gè rén jīng cháng gǎi biàn zhǔ
后来"朝三暮四"就用来形容一个人经常**改变主**
yì, yòng jì liǎ piàn rén.
意，用**伎俩**骗人。

Later, "Frequently Changing One's mind (morning three, evening four)" is used to describe a person who often **changes their mind** and uses **tricks** to deceive others.

zài dāng dài zhōng guó, tè bié shì zài liàn ài guān xi zhōng, yī gè rén
在**当代**中国，特别是在**恋爱关系**中，一个人
rú guǒ tóng shí ài shàng jǐ bù tóng de rén, què bù què dìng xīn yì,
如果同时**爱上**几不同的人，却不确定心意，
jiù shì gè zhāo sān mù sì de rén.
就是个**朝三暮四**的人。

In **modern** China, especially in a **romantic relationship**, a person who **falls in love with** several different people at the same time, but is not sure of their commitment, is described as **frequently changing their mind**.

Summary

In this story behind the idiom **朝三暮四**, the old man uses a **trick** (jì liǎng 伎俩) to successfully convince his monkeys to eat less, who wrongly believed his change of mind. However, the phrase has come to symbolize inconsistency and indecision, and is used to criticize those who lack conviction and change their views frequently, indicating someone's unreliability. It may also be used when referring to people unstable in relationships.

Learning Tip

朝三暮四 is an idiom that is translated here as "frequently changing one's mind," but would be more literally be translated as "three in the morning and four in the evening." It can be used to describe those who are unstable and changeable in their behavior.

zhāo	sān	mù	sì
朝	三	暮	四
morning	three	evening	four

1 他总是随便改变大家的计划 ,真是**朝三暮四**！

He always randomly changes our plans, so **changeable**!

2 这个男的**朝三暮四**，已经有了老婆，还要去找别的女人。

This man is so **changeable** (unreliable)! Already has a wife, yet he goes to find other women.

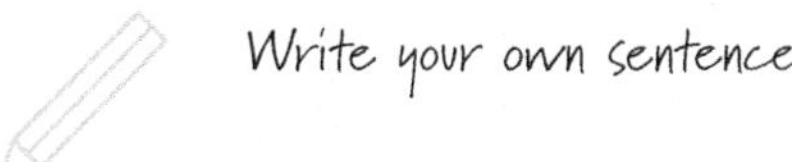

Key Vocabulary

rèn wéi 认为	*v.*	assume/ believe	wèi 喂	*v.*	to feed
cōng míng 聪明	*adj.*	smart	guǒ zi 果子	*n.*	fruit
tòng xià jué xīn 痛下决心	*idiom*	painfully decided/ made up mind	xiāng chǔ 相处	*v.*	to get along
róng qià 融洽	*adj.*	well/ harmonious	gōng píng 公平	*adj.*	fair
shen zhì 甚至	*con.*	even	hǎn 喊	*v.*	to yell/shout
bǐ cǐ 彼此	*n.*	one another	jì liǎng 伎俩	*n.*	trick
shù liàng 数量	*n.*	number/ quantity	dāng dài 当代	*n.*	modern
liàn ài guān xì 恋爱关系	*n.*	romantic relationship	kǒu liáng 口粮	*n.*	food (for animals)
shěng chī jiǎn yòng 省吃俭用	*idiom*	frugal	ài shàng 爱上	*v.*	fall in love with

Sentence Patterns

这样吧 …

how about …

zhè yàng ba
这样吧 + *suggestion*

zhè yàng ba, zǎo shàng chī sì gè shuǐ guǒ, wǎn shàng chī sān gè, hǎo ma?
这样吧，早上吃四个水果，晚上吃三个，好吗？

How about eating four fruits in the morning and three at night, okay?

宁愿 … 也

would rather … in order to …

níngyuàn yě
subject + **宁愿** + *A* + **也** + *B*

tā níng yuàn zì jǐ shǎo chī, yě yào bǎo zhèng hóu zi men chī bǎo.
他宁愿自己少吃，也要保证猴子们吃饱。

He would rather eat less himself, in order to ensure that the monkeys were fully fed.

Chinese Version

从前有个老人很爱猴子。他认为猴子是世界上最聪明、最可爱的动物。

他每天和猴子们一起玩，相处得很融洽，就像一家人。

邻居们都觉得老人就像猴子们的爷爷，于是就叫他“猴爷”。

猴爷在院子里为猴子们盖了一间小屋，还在周围种了一些香蕉树和苹果树。

慢慢地，他甚至和猴子们能听懂彼此的话，就像最好的朋友。

可是，猴爷没什么钱，除了要养猴子，还要养他的家人。

随着猴子们的数量越来越多，猴爷越来越担心喂猴子的口粮不够。

一开始，他省吃俭用，宁愿自己少吃，也要保证猴子们吃饱。

可是，到了冬天，家里的果树没有果子，猴爷不得不去买其他水果喂猴子。

他没有钱买很多水果，于是痛下决心，准备减少猴子的口粮。

一天，猴爷对猴子们说：“宝贝们，对不起，从明天开始，每只猴子每天早上只能吃三个水果，晚上吃四个，行吗？”

猴子们很不高兴，大声说：“不行，太少了！这太不公平了！”

于是，猴爷想了一下，又说:“这样吧，早上吃四个水果，晚上吃三个，好吗？”

猴子们听到早上是四个，比以前多了一个，都高兴地喊：“太好了！”

猴爷很开心，因为他没想到自己的伎俩居然成功了！

后来“朝三暮四”是用来形容一个人经常改变主意，用伎俩骗人。

在当代中国，特别是在恋爱关系中，一个人如果同时爱上几不同的人，却不确定心意，就是个朝三暮四的人。

huà lóng diǎn jīng

10 画龙点睛

Paint the Dragon, Dot the Eyes

gǔ shí hòu yǒu gè dé gāo wàng zhòng de huà jiā jiào zhāng sēng yáo, tā huà
古时候有个**德高望重**的画家叫张僧繇，他画
lóng huà de tè bié hǎo
龙画得特别好。

In ancient times, there was a **highly respected** painter named Zhang Sengyou, who was very good at drawing dragons.

yǒu yī cì, tā shòu yāo qù le yī gè sì miào huà lóng. tā huā le
有一次，他**受邀**去了一个**寺庙**画龙。他花了
jǐ tiān de shí jiān, rèn zhēn de zài sì miào de qiáng shàng huà le liǎng tiáo
几天的时间，**认真**地在寺庙的墙上画了两条
lóng
龙。

Once, he **was invited** to a **temple** to paint dragons. He spent several days **carefully** drawing two dragons on the walls of the temple.

zhè liǎng tiáo lóng kàn shàng qù huó líng huó xiàn, xī yǐn le hěn duō rén lái guān
这两条龙看上去**活灵活现**，**吸引**了很多人来观
kàn
看。

The two dragons looked **extremely vivid** and **attracted** many people to look.

dà jiā dōu zàn měi tā de huà huà jì shù. zhè shí hòu, yǒu rén què fā
大家都**赞美**他的画画技术。这时候，有人却**发**
xiàn liǎng tiáo lóng jū rán dōu méi yǒu yǎn jīng
现两条龙**居然**都没有眼睛。

Everyone **praised** his painting skills. At this time, someone **discovered** that the two dragons **surprisingly** had no eyes.

yú shì zhè rén jiào wèn zhāng sēng yáo xiān shēng nǐ wéi shén me méi
于是，这人叫问张僧繇：“先生，你**为什么**没
yǒu huà zhè liǎng tiáo lóng de yǎn jīng
有画这两条龙的眼睛？”

So, the man asked Zhang Sengyau: "Sir, **why** didn't you draw the eyes of these two dragons?"

zhāng sēng yáo huí dá bù shì wǒ bù yuàn yì huà lóng de yǎn jīng zhǐ
张僧繇**回答**：“不是我不**愿意**画龙的眼睛，只
shì wǒ dān xīn rú guǒ wǒ huà le yǎn jīng lóng jiù huì fēi zǒu
是，我担心，如果我画了眼睛，龙就会**飞走**。”

Zhang Sengyou **answered**, "It's not that I am not **willing** to draw the dragon's eyes, it's just that I'm worried that if I draw the eyes, the dragons will **fly away**."

dà jiā tīng le dōu dà xiào qǐ lái jué de tā zài chuī niú hòu
大家听了，都**大笑**起来，觉得他在**吹牛**。后
lái zhè jiàn shì jiù zài zhèn shàng chuán kāi le
来，这件事就在镇上**传开**了。

When everyone heard it, they all **laughed** and thought he was **bragging**. Later, the incident **spread** in the town.

dà jiā dōu shuō tā bù yuàn huà lóng yǎn jīng de yuán yīn bù shì zì jǐ huà huà
大家都说他不愿画龙眼睛的原因**不是**自己画画
jì shù bù gòu jiù shì tài jiāo ào gù yì zhuāng kù
技术不够，**就是**太骄傲，故意装酷。

Everyone said that the reason why he didn't want to draw dragon's eyes was **either** that he was not skilled enough in drawing, **or** that he was too proud and deliberately pretended to be cool.

zhōng yú yǒu yī tiān tā jīn bù zhù yā lì jiù qù huà lóng de yǎn jīng
终于有一天，他禁不住**压力**，就去画龙的眼睛
tā xiǎng jiù suàn lóng fēi zǒu le yě bù hòu huǐ
，他想：**就算**龙飞走了，**也**不后悔。

Finally one day, he couldn't bear the **pressure**, so he went to draw the dragon's eyes, he thought: **even if** dragons fly away, he **would** not regret it.

dāng tiān hěn duō rén dōu pǎo lái guān kàn mǎ shàng tā jiù yòng máo bǐ
当天，很多人都**跑来**观看。马上，他就用毛笔
diǎn le dì yī tiáo lóng de yǎn jīng dà jiā zàn tàn lóng gèng shēng dòng le
点了第一条龙的眼睛，大家赞叹龙更**生动**了。

On that day, many people **ran over** to look. Immediately, he used a brush to **dot** the eyes of the first dragon, and everyone praised that the dragon looked more **vivid**.

jiē zhe tā kāi shǐ diǎn dì èr tiáo lóng de yǎn jīng dàn zhè shí hòu
接着，他开始点第二条龙的眼睛，但**这时候**
tiān qì tū rán dà biàn guā qǐ le dà fēng kāi shǐ diàn shǎn léi míng
天气突然大变。刮起了大风，开始**电闪雷鸣**。

Next, he started to dot the eyes of the second dragon, but **this time** the weather changed drastically. There came a strong wind, with **lightning and thunder**.

tā gāng gāng huà wán liǎng tiáo lóng jiù tū rán dòng qǐ lái jiē zhe yī qǐ
他刚刚画**完**，两条龙就突然动起来，接着一起
xùn sù de fēi xiàng le tiān kōng
迅速地飞向了天空。

As soon as he **finished** drawing, the two dragons suddenly moved, and then flew **speedily** into the sky together.

dà jiā kàn dào zhè yī qiè dōu jīng dāi le zhè shí hòu tā men cái fā
大家看到这一切都**惊呆了**！这时候，他们才**发**
xiàn zhāng sēng yáo méi yǒu chuī niú duì tā gèng pèi fú le
现张僧繇没有**吹牛**，对他更**佩服**了！

Everyone was so **stunned** to see this! Only at this time, they **realized** that Zhang Sengyao was not **bragging**, and **admired** him even more!

hòu lái huà lóng diǎn jīng de gù shì jiù chuán kāi le yòng lái xíng róng zài
后来"画龙点睛"的故事就**传开**了。用来形容在
wán chéng yī jiàn shì de shí hòu bǎ guān jiàn de dì fāng zuò hǎo jiù néng
完成一件事的时候，把**关键**的地方做好，就能
tí shēng zhěng tǐ xiào guǒ
提升整体效果。

Later, the story of "Paint the Dragon, Dot the Eyes" **spread**. It is used to describe that upon completing a matter, doing a good job in the **key areas** can **improve** the effect of the whole.

SUMMARY

This story behind the idiom 画龙点睛 is truly one of achieving **perfection**
 wán měi
(完美) by paying attention to the delicate details. Although the great painter's dragons were already excellent, it was only by adding the finishing touches, in this case the eyes, that they came to life.

Learning Tip

画龙点睛 is a Chinese idiom translated literally as "paint the dragon, dot the eyes." It is used to describe adding the finishing touches to something to bring it to a successful conclusion.

huà 画 paint	lóng 龙 dragon	diǎn 点 dot	jīng 睛 eyes

1 他最后讲的小故事让他的整个演讲有了**画龙点睛**的效果。

The little story he told at the end gave the **finishing touch** to his entire speech.

2 挂上这幅画后，书房看上去更优雅了，真是**画龙点睛**！

After hanging this painting, the study room looks more elegant, really **adding the finishing touch**!

Write your own sentence

Key Vocabulary

dé gāo wàng zhòng 德高望重	*idiom*	well respected	jìn bù zhù 禁不住	*v.*	cannot bear/ resist
sì miào 寺庙	*n.*	temple	yā lì 压力	*n.*	pressure
rèn zhēn 认真	*adj.*	careful/ earnest	hòu huǐ 后悔	*v.*	to regret
huó líng huó xiàn 活灵活现	*idiom*	extremely vivid	shēng dòng 生动	*adj.*	vivid
xī yǐn 吸引	*v.*	to attract	diàn shǎn léi míng 电闪雷鸣	*idiom*	lightning and thunder
zàn měi 赞美	*v.*	to praise	xùn sù 迅速	*adj.*	speedy/quick
huí dá 回答	*v.*	to answer	jīng dāi 惊呆	*v.*	to stun
yuàn yì 愿意	*v.*	willing to	pèi fú 佩服	*v.*	to admire
chuī niú 吹牛	*v.*	to brag	guān jiàn 关键	*n.*	key/crucial

Sentence Patterns

不是…就是

either … or …

bù shì jiù shì
不是 + *A* + **就是** + *B*

tā bù shì zì jǐ huà huà jì shù bù gòu, jiù shì tài jiāo ào
他不是自己画画技术不够，就是太骄傲。

He was either not skilled enough in drawing, or too proud.

就算… 也

even if … would …

jiù suàn yě
就算 + *action 1* + **也** + *action 2*

tā xiǎng: jiù suàn lóng fēi zǒu le, yě bù hòu huǐ
他想：就算龙飞走了，也不后悔。

He thought: even if dragons fly away, he would not regret it.

Chinese Version

古时候有个德高望重的画家叫张僧繇，他画龙画得特别好。

有一次，他受邀去了一个寺庙画龙。他花了几天的时间，认真地在寺庙的墙上画了两条龙。

这两条龙看上去活灵活现，吸引了很多人来观看。

大家都赞美他的画画技术。这时候，有人却发现两条龙居然都没有眼睛。

于是，这人叫问张僧繇："先生，你为什么没有画这两条龙的眼睛？"

张僧繇回答："不是我不愿意画龙的眼睛，只是，我担心，如果我画了眼睛，龙就会飞走。"

大家听了，都大笑起来，觉得他在吹牛。后来，这件事就在镇上传开了。

大家都说他不愿画龙眼睛的原因不是自己画画技术不够，就是太骄傲，故意装酷。

终于有一天，他禁不住压力，就去画龙的眼睛，他想：就算龙飞走了，也不后悔。

当天，很多人都跑来观看。马上，他就用毛笔点了第一条龙的眼睛，大家赞叹龙更生动了。

接着，他开始点第二条龙的眼睛，但这时候天气突然大变。刮起了大风，开始电闪雷鸣。

他刚刚画完，两条龙就突然动起来，接着一起迅速地飞向了天空。

大家看到这一切都惊呆了！这时候，他们才发现张僧繇没有吹牛，对他更佩服了！

后来"画龙点睛"的故事就传开了。用来形容在完成一件事的时候，把关键的地方做好，就能提升整体效果。

mào sì pān ān

貌似潘安

Incredibly Handsome

pān ān shì zhōng guó gǔ dài sì dà měi nán zhī yī. tā bù jǐn chāo jí shuài, ér qiě fēi cháng yǒu cái huá, shì zhù míng de zuò jiā.

潘安是中国古代四大美男**之一**。他**不仅**超级帅，**而且**非常有才华，是著名的**作家**。

Pan An was **one of** the four most handsome men in ancient China. He was **not only** super handsome, **but also** very talented, and a famous **writer**.

pān ān chū shēng zài yī gè rú xué jiā tíng, jiā lǐ hěn fù yù, yé ye hé fù qīn dōu shì zhèng fǔ de dà guān.

潘安出生在一个**儒学**家庭，家里很**富裕**，爷爷和父亲都是**政府**的大官。

Pan An was born in a **Confucian** family, and his family was very **wealthy**. His grandfather and father were both high-ranking officals in the **government**.

tā xiǎo de shí hòu cōng míng líng lì, shí èr suì jiù néng xiě shī, bèi chēng wéi "qí tóng".

他小的时候**聪明伶俐**，十二岁就能写诗，**被称为**"奇童"。

He was **clever and witty** when he was young, and could write poems at the age of twelve, hence **was called** "the Marvelous Kid".

ér qiě yīn wèi tā zhǎng de hěn yīng jùn, bù guǎn zǒu dào nǎ lǐ dōu huì xī yǐn hěn duō rén de zhù yì.

而且因为他长得很**英俊**，不管走到哪里都会吸引很多人的**注意**。

And because he was so **handsome**, wherever he went, he attracted a lot of **attention**.

tā hěn nián qīng de shí hòu jiù zuò le guān dài rén hé shàn wèi rén mín zuò le hěn duō hǎo shì
他很年轻的时候就做了官，待人**和善**，为**人民**做了很多好事。

He became an official when he was very young, treated people **kindly**, and did a lot of good things for **the people**.

yīn wèi hěn ài táo huā tā jiù gǔ lì rén mín zài xiǎo zhèn shàng zhǒng mǎn táo huā
因为很爱**桃花**，他就**鼓励**人民在小镇上种满桃花。

Because he loved **peach blossoms** very much, he **encouraged** the people to plant peach trees in the town.

dào chūn tiān de shí hòu táo huā kāi mǎn le xiǎo zhèn xiǎo zhèn biàn de gèng měi le bèi dà jiā gǎi míng táo huā zhèn
到春天的时候，桃花开满了**小镇**。小镇变得更美了，被大家**改名**“桃花镇”。

When spring arrived, peach blossoms filled the **town**. The town became more beautiful and was **renamed** "Peach Blossom Town" by the people.

pān ān yě bèi chēng wéi huā yàng měi nán chéng wéi le hěn duō nǚ zi de mèng zhōng qíng rén
潘安也**被称为**“花样美男”，成为了很多女子的**梦中情人**。

Pan An, hence became **known as** the "Flower Beautiful Man," and became the **dream lover** of many women.

měi cì pān ān jià chē chū mén dōu huì yǐn lái hěn duō nǚ fěn sī cóng shí duō suì de xiǎo gū niang dào qī bā shí suì de lǎo tài tai dōu zhēng zhe qù kàn tā
每次潘安**驾车出门**，都会引来很多女**粉丝**。从十多岁的小姑娘到七八十岁的老太太，都**争着**去看他。

Every time Pan An **drove out**, he attracted many female **fans**. From little girls in their teens to old ladies in their seventies and eighties, they all **scrambled** to see him.

yǒu xiē nǚ fěn sī wǎng tā de chē shàng rēng xiān huā yǒu xiē nǚ fěn sī wǎng tā de chē shàng rēng shuǐ guǒ suǒ yǐ tā cháng cháng mǎn zài ér guī
有些女粉丝往他的车上**扔**鲜花，有些女粉丝往他的车上**扔**水果。所以，他常常**满载而归**。

Some fans **threw** flowers on his car, and some fans **threw** fruits on his car. He often **came home fully loaded**.

dāng shí yǒu gè nán de hěn jí dù tā, xīn xiǎng: nán dào jiù zhǐ yǒu tā nà me shòu huān yíng ma? yú shì, tā jiù gù yì mó fǎng pān ān zài jiē shàng jià chē.

当时有个男的很**嫉妒**他，心想：**难道**就只有他那么受欢迎吗？于是，他就故意**模仿**潘安在街上驾车。

At that time, there was a man very **jealous** of him, he thought: Only he can be so popular? So he deliberately **copied** Pan An to drive on the street.

jié guǒ, nà rén què yóu yú zhǎng de tài chǒu bèi hěn duō nǚ zi mà, shèn zhì hái yǒu xiē rén xiàng tā de chē zi rēng shí tóu.

结果，那人却由于长得太**丑**被很多女子骂，**甚至**还有些人向他的车子扔石头。

As a result, he was scolded by many women for being too **ugly**, some people **even** threw stones at his car.

pān ān suī rán yǒu wú shù de nǚ fěn sī, měi tiān dōu shōu dào hěn duō qíng shū hé lǐ wù, dàn tā què bù shì yī gè huā huā gōng zǐ.

潘安虽然有**无数**的女粉丝，每天都收到很多**情书**和礼物，但他却不是一个**花花公子**。

Although Pan An had **countless** female fans and received many **love letters** and gifts every day, he was not a **playboy**.

xiāng fǎn, tā duì ài qíng fēi cháng zhuān yī. zài gǔ dài, nán rén kě yǐ yǒu hěn duō qī zi, ér tā què zhǐ yǒu yī gè.

相反，他对爱情非常**专一**。在古代，男人可以有很多**妻子**，而他却只有一个。

On the contrary, he was very **committed** to love. In ancient times, a man could have many **wives**, but he had only one.

tā hé qī zi cóng xiǎo jiù dìng hūn le, jié hūn hòu gǎn qíng wěn dìng, fēi cháng xiāng ài.

他和妻子从小就**订婚**了，结婚后感情**稳定**，非常**相爱**。

He and his wife had been **engaged** since childhood, and they had a **stable** relationship after marriage and were very **in love**.

zài tā zhōng nián hòu, qī zi bìng sǐ le, tā fēi cháng shāng xīn, xiě le hěn duō shī jì niàn tā.

在他**中年**后，妻子病死了，他非常伤心，写了很多诗**纪念**她。

Reaching his **middle age**, his wife died of illness. He was very sad and wrote many poems **in memory of** her.

hòu lái, pān ān bèi juǎn rù le yī chǎng zhèng zhì dòu zhēng, bù xìng bèi
后来，潘安被**卷入**了一场政治斗争，**不幸**被
shā, cái wǔ shí sān suì
杀，才五十三岁。

Later, Pan An was **involved** in a political battle and was **unfortunately** killed at the age of only fifty-three.

pān ān shì zhōng guó lì shǐ shàng yī wèi jī hū wán měi de nán rén, bù guǎn
潘安是中国历史上一位几乎**完美**的男人，不管
shì nǎ fāng miàn, dōu shì dà jiā de bǎng yàng, mào shì pān ān yě biàn
是哪方面，都是大家的**榜样**，“貌似潘安”也变
chéng le duì yī gè nán rén wài biǎo de zuì gāo zàn měi
成了对一个男人**外表**的最高赞美。

Pan An was an almost **perfect** man in Chinese history. No matter in what aspect, he was a **role model** for many. "Looking like Pan An" has also become the highest praise of a man's **appearance**.

SUMMARY

This is a true story of one of the most handsome and beloved Chinese men in ancient China, and is the origin of the idiom 貌似潘安 (mào sì pān ān) (incredibly handsome) and 满载而归 (mǎn zài ér guī) (to come back fully loaded with good things). The reason why he was regarded as a perfect role model is not just because of his good-looking appearance, but also his **good virtues** (美德 měi dé) and **talents** (才华 cái huá) in literature. Pan An is also known as Pan Yue (潘岳 pān yuè) or by his courtesy name Anren (安仁 ān rén).

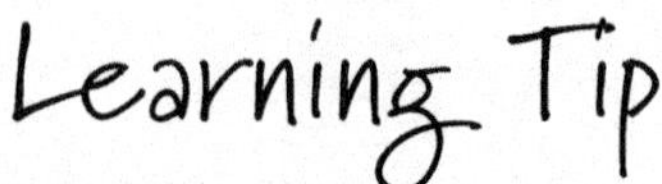

貌似潘安 is a Chinese idiom used to describe men considered particularly handsome, i.e. just like Pan An.

mào	sì	pān ān
貌	似	潘安
appearance	alike	Pan An

1 那个男明星**貌似潘安**，难怪有那么多粉丝。

That male movie star is **incredibly handsome**, no wonder has so many fans.

2 大家总是夸他**貌似潘安**，让他开心极了！

Everyone always praised him being **incredibly handsome**, making him extremely happy!

Write your own sentence

Key Vocabulary

作家	zuò jiā	*n.*	writer	粉丝	fěn sī	*n.*	fan
富裕	fù yù	*adj.*	rich/wealthy	相反	xiāng fǎn	*adj.*	contrary
满载而归	mǎn zài ér guī	*idiom*	to come back fully loaded	政府	zhèng fǔ	*n.*	government
聪明伶俐	cōng míng líng lì	*idiom*	clever and witted	模仿	mó fǎng	*v.*	to imitate/copy
英俊	yīng jùn	*adj.*	handsome	丑	chǒu	*adj.*	ugly
注意	zhù yì	*n.*	attention	无数	wú shù	*adj.*	countless
花花公子	huā huā gōng zǐ	*idiom*	playboy	和善	hé shàn	*adj.*	kind
人民	rén mín	*n.*	people (political)	专一	zhuān yī	*adj.*	committed (relationships)
鼓励	gǔ lì	*v.*	to encourage	卷入	juǎn rù	*n.*	to involve
改名	gǎi míng	*v.*	to rename	榜样	bǎng yàng	*n.*	role model
梦中情人	mèng zhōng qíng rén	*slang.*	dream lover	外表	wài biǎo	*n.*	appearance

Sentence Patterns

不仅...而且

not only ... but also

bù jǐn / ér qiě

不仅 + *A* + **而且** + *B*

tā bù jǐn chāo jí shuài, ér qiě fēi cháng yǒu cái huá

他不仅超级帅，而且非常有才华。

He was not only super handsome, but also very talented.

难道...

to form rhetorical question

nán dào

难道 + *question*

nán dào jiù zhǐ yǒu tā nà me shòu huān yíng ma

难道就只有他那么受欢迎吗？

Only he can be so popular?

Chinese Version

潘安是中国古代四大美男之一。他不仅超级帅，而且非常有才华，是著名的作家。

潘安出生在一个儒学家庭，家里很富裕，爷爷和父亲都是政府的大官。

他小的时候聪明伶俐，十二岁就能写诗，被称为“奇童”。

而且因为他长得很英俊，不管走到哪里都会吸引很多人的注意。

他很年轻的时候就做了官，待人和善，为人民做了很多好事。

因为很爱桃花，他就鼓励人民在小镇上种满桃花。

到春天的时候，桃花开满了小镇。小镇变得更美了，被大家改名“桃花镇”。

潘安也被称为“花样美男”，成为了很多女子的梦中情人。

每次潘安驾车出门，都会引来很多女粉丝。从十多岁的小姑娘到七八十岁的老太太，都争着去看他。

有些女粉丝往他的车上扔鲜花，有些女粉丝往他的车上扔水果。所以，他常常满载而归。

当时有个男的很嫉妒他，心想：难道就只有他那么受欢迎吗？于是，他就故意模仿潘安在街上驾车。

结果，那人却由于长得太丑被很多女子骂，甚至还有些人向他的车子扔石头。

潘安虽然有无数的女粉丝，每天都收到很多情书和礼物，但他却不是一个花花公子。

相反，他对爱情非常专一。在古代，男人可以有很多妻子，而他却只有一个。

他和妻子从小就订婚了，结婚后感情稳定，非常相爱。

在他中年后，妻子病死了，他非常伤心，写了很多诗纪念她。

后来，潘安被卷入了一场政治斗争，不幸被杀，才五十三岁。

潘安是中国历史上一位几乎完美的男人，不管是哪方面，都是大家的榜样，“貌似潘安”也变成了对一个男人外表的最高赞美。

诗 shī 与 yǔ 爱 ài 情 qíng

Chinese Poetry and Love Stories

que qiao xian

鹊桥仙

The Magpie Bridge

xiān yún nòng qiǎo, fēi xīng chuán hèn,
纤云弄巧，飞星传恨，
Clouds float like works of art, stars shoot with grief at heart.

yín hàn tiáo tiáo àn dù
银汉迢迢暗渡。
Across the Milky Way he meets the girl he had long waited,

jīn fēng yù lù yī xiāng féng
金风玉露一相逢，
When autumn's golden wind embraces dew of jade.

biàn shèng què rén jiān wú shù
便胜却人间无数。
All the love scenes on earth, however many, fade.

róu qíng sì shuǐ, jiā qī rú mèng
柔情似水，佳期如梦，
Their tender love flows like a stream, their happy date seems but a dream.

rěn gù què qiáo guī lù
忍顾鹊桥归路。
How could they bear to part.

liǎng qíng ruò shì jiǔ cháng shí, yòu qǐ zài zhāo zhāo mù mù
两情若是久长时，又岂在朝朝暮暮。
If their love is ever steadfast, their hearts stay together, day and night.

qín guān
秦观
1049—c. 1100 AD

Story

qín guān shì sòng cháo de zhù míng shī rén zài shì yè shàng, tā shì yī gè bǎo shǒu de zhèng zhì jiā

秦观是宋朝的**著名**诗人。在**事业**上，他是一个**保守**的政治家。

Qin Guan was a **famous** poet in the Song Dynasty. In **career**, he was a **conservative** politician.

zài gǎn qíng shàng, tā fēi cháng duō qíng, yī dàn ài shàng le, jiù bù huì fàng shǒu

在感情上，他非常**多情**，**一旦**爱上了，**就**不会放手。

In love matters, he was very **affectionate**, and **once** he fell in love, he would not let go.

qín guān nián qīng de shí hòu fēi cháng yǒu cái huá, yě shì yī wèi chéng gōng de guān yuán. dàn bù rù zhōng nián hòu, tā de shì yè shàng chū xiàn le hěn duō cuò zhé

秦观年轻的时候非常**有才华**，也是一位**成功**的官员。但**步入**中年后，他的事业上出现了很多**挫折**。

When Qin Guan was young, he was very **talented** and was a **successful** official. Buy after **entering** middle age, many **setbacks** occurred in his career.

yǒu yī nián, tā bèi huáng dì jiàng jí, bèi diào qù le hěn yuǎn de nán fāng. dào dá cháng shā de shí hòu, tā yù dào le yī wèi hěn měi de nǚ yì rén

有一年，他被皇帝**降级**，被调去了很远的南方。**到达**长沙的时候，他遇到了一位很美的女**艺人**。

One year, he was **demoted** by the emperor and transferred to the far south. When he **arrived** in Changsha, he met a very beautiful **artist**.

nǚ yì rén shàn yú tán qín, tā de qín shēng zǒng shì néng wèi qín guān fǔ píng yōu shāng. hěn kuài, tā men jiù xiāng ài le

女艺人**善于**弹琴，她的琴声总是能为秦观**抚平**忧伤。很快，他们就**相爱**了。

The artist was **good at** playing Qin (Chinese musical instrument), and her music always helped **sooth** the Qin Guan's sadness. Soon, they **fell in love**.

tā bù zài hū tā dī wēi de chū shēng, chéng nuò jiāng lái huī fù zhí wèi hòu huì lái qǔ tā

他不在乎她**低微**的出生，**承诺**将来**恢复**职位后会来娶她。

He didn't care about her **humble** origin, and **promised** to marry her after **resuming** his position in the future.

tā men fēn kāi hòu, qín guān fēi cháng xiǎng niàn tā. qī xī jié dào le,
他们**分开**后，秦观非常**想念**她。**七夕节**到了，
qín guān gěi tā xiě le zhè shǒu shī:
秦观给她写了这首诗：

After they **parted**, Qin Guan **missed** her very much. When the **Qixi Festival** (Chinese Valentine's Day) came, Qin Guan wrote her this poem:

xiān yún nòng qiǎo, fēi xīng chuán hèn,
纤云弄巧，飞星传恨，

Clouds float like works of art, stars shoot with grief at heart.

yín hàn tiáo tiáo àn dù.
银汉迢迢暗渡。

Across the Milky Way he meets the girl he had long waited,

jīn fēng yù lù yī xiāng féng,
金风玉露一相逢，

When autumn's golden wind embraces dew of jade.

biàn shèng què rén jiān wú shù.
便胜却人间无数。

All the love scenes on earth, however many, fade.

róu qíng sì shuǐ, jiā qī rú mèng,
柔情似水，佳期如梦，

Their tender love flows like a stream, their happy date seems but a dream.

rěn gù què qiáo guī lù.
忍顾鹊桥归路。

How could they bear to part.

liǎng qíng ruò shì jiǔ cháng shí, yòu qǐ zài zhāo zhāo mù mù.
两情若是久长时，又岂在朝朝暮暮。

If their love is ever steadfast, their hearts stay together, day and night.

zhè shǒu shī shì guān yú niú láng zhī nǚ de ài qíng gù shì, niú láng hé zhī
这首诗是**关于**牛郎织女的爱情故事，**牛郎和织**
nǚ fēi cháng xiāng ài.
女非常相爱。

This poem is **about** the love story of the Cowherd and the Weaver Girl. The **Cowherd** and the **Weaver Girl** were very much in love.

suī rán tā men yī nián zhǐ néng jiàn yī cì, dàn ài qíng què yǒng yuǎn jiān
虽然他们一年只能见一次，但爱情却永远**坚**
dìng
定。

Although they can only see each other once a year, their love is always **firm**.

qín guān jué de zì jǐ jiù xiàng niú láng ér tā de liàn rén jiù xiàng zhī nǚ
秦观觉得自己就像牛郎，而他的恋人就像织女
jí shǐ fēn gé hěn yuǎn tā men de xīn yě yǒng yuǎn zài yī qǐ
，即使分隔很远，他们的心也永远在一起。

Qin Guan felt that he was like the cowherd, and his **lover** was like the weaver girl. **Even though** they were far apart, their hearts were always together.

bù xìng de shì jǐ nián hòu qín guān dài zhe bù néng yǔ tā tuán yuán de
不幸的是，几年后，秦观带着不能与她团圆的
yí hàn bìng sǐ le
遗憾病死了。

Unfortunately, a few years later, Qin Guan died of illness with the **regret** of not being able to reunite with her.

ér tā de liàn rén zài tīng dào zhè gè xiāo xī hòu zǒu le zhì shǎo yī
而他的恋人，在听到这个消息后，走了至少一
bǎi gōng lǐ qù cān jiā tā de zàng lǐ
百公里去参加他的葬礼。

And his **lover**, after hearing the news, walked at least a hundred **kilometers** to attend his **funeral**.

zuì zhōng tā shāng xīn guò dù bù jiǔ yě qù shì le
最终她伤心过度，不久也去世了。

In the end, she was **too** sad and **passed away** soon after.

Culture Corner

This is one of the most renowned love poems from the Song dynasty of China, not only because it presents beautifully the love story of cowherd and weaver girl, but also relates to the true and touching story of the poet and the woman he loved. Even in modern China, the final two lines 两情若是久长时，又岂在朝朝暮暮 (if their love is ever steadfast, their hearts stay together, day and night) is used frequently in romantic talk and love letters. This poem and the story of the Cowherd and Weaver Girl that the poet references is of particular cultural relevance during **Qixi Festival** (七夕节), celebrated each year on the seventh day of the seventh lunar month, the day it is said that Cowherd and Weaver Girl are allowed to meet across the Milky Way.

Key Vocabulary

事业 (shì yè)	*n.*	career	抚平 (fǔ píng)	*v.*	to soothe
保守 (bǎo shǒu)	*adj.*	reserved/ conservative	相爱 (xiāng ài)	*v.*	to fall in love
多情 (duō qíng)	*adj.*	affectionate	低微 (dī wēi)	*adj.*	humble/inferior
放手 (fàng shǒu)	*v.*	to let go	承诺 (chéng nuò)	*v.*	to promise
挫折 (cuò zhé)	*n.*	setbacks/ difficulties	分开 (fēn kāi)	*v.*	to part
降级 (jiàng jí)	*v.*	to demote	坚定 (jiān dìng)	*adj.*	firm
到达 (dào dá)	*v.*	to arrive	恋人 (liàn rén)	*n.*	lover
艺人 (yì rén)	*n.*	artist	遗憾 (yí hàn)	*n.*	regret
善于 (shàn yú)	*v.*	be good at	至少 (zhì shǎo)	*adv.*	at least

Sentence Patterns

一旦… 就

once … (then)

一旦 (yī dàn) + *condition* + **就** (jiù) + *consequence*

他非常多情，一旦爱上了，就不会放手。
(tā fēi cháng duō qíng, yī dàn ài shàng le, jiù bù huì fàng shǒu.)

He was very affectionate, once he fell in love, he would not let go.

即使…也…

even if … (still) …

即使 (jí shǐ) + *action 1* + **也** (yě) + *action 2*

即使分隔很远，他们的心也永远在一起。
(jí shǐ fēn gé hěn yuǎn, tā men de xīn yě yǒng yuǎn zài yī qǐ.)

Even though they were far apart, their hearts were still always together.

Chinese Version

秦观是宋朝的著名诗人。在事业上，他是一个保守的政治家。

在感情上，他非常多情，一旦爱上了，就不会放手。

秦观年轻的时候非常有才华，也是一位成功的官员。但步入中年后，他的事业上出现了很多挫折。

有一年，他被皇帝降级，被调去了很远的南方。到达长沙的时候，他遇到了一位很美的女艺人。

女艺人善于弹琴，她的琴声总是能为秦观抚平忧伤。很快，他们就相爱了。

他不在乎她低微的出生，承诺将来恢复职位后会来娶她。

他们分开后，秦观非常想念她。七夕节到了，秦观给她写了这首诗：

纤云弄巧，飞星传恨，
银汉迢迢暗渡。
金风玉露一相逢，
便胜却人间无数。
柔情似水，佳期如梦，
忍顾鹊桥归路。
两情若是久长时，又岂在朝朝暮暮。

这首诗是关于牛郎织女的爱情故事，牛郎和织女非常相爱，

虽然他们一年只能见一次，但爱情却永远坚定。

秦观觉得自己就像牛郎，而他的恋人就像织女，即使分隔很远，他们的心也永远在一起。

不幸的是，几年后，秦观带着不能与她团圆的遗憾病死了。

而他的恋人，在听到这个消息后，走了至少一百公里去参加他的葬礼。

最终她伤心过度，不久也去世了。

shēng sǐ xiāng xǔ
生死相许

Till Death Do Us Part

wèn shì jiān, qíng wéi hé wù?
问世间，情为何物？
Ask the world, what is love?

zhí jiào shēng sǐ xiāng xǔ!
直教生死相许！
That even promises life and death to one another!

tiān nán dì běi shuāng fēi kè,
天南地北双飞客，
From the south sky to the north, the two geese,

lǎo chì jǐ huí hán shǔ.
老翅几回寒暑。
by their aging wings, flying from summer to winter.

huān lè qù, bié lí kǔ,
欢乐趣，别离苦，
The joy of togetherness, the sadness of parting,

jiù zhōng gèng yǒu chī ér nǚ.
就中更有痴儿女。
all melt in the yearning of two hearts.

jūn yīng yǒu yǔ, miǎo wàn lǐ céng yún,
君应有语，渺万里层云，
Should you wonder, through boundless walls of clouds,

qiān shān mù xuě, zhī yǐng xiàng shéi qù?
千山暮雪，只影向谁去？
and thousands of peaks of snow, if left alone, where would he go?

yuán hào wèn
元好问
1190—1257 AD

Story

yuán hào wèn shì zhōng guó gǔ dài zhù míng de zuò jiā, tā cóng xiǎo jiù shòu dào
元好问是中国古代著名的**作家**，他从小就受到
le hěn hǎo de jiào yù, bā suì jiù kāi shǐ xiě shī。
了很好的**教育**，八岁就开始**写诗**。

Yuan Haowen was a famous **writer** in ancient China. Since he was a child, he received a good **education**, at the age of either he began to **write poetry**.

suí zhe nián suì de zēng zhǎng, tā kāi shǐ rè ài zì rán。tā xiāng xìn huā
随着年岁的增长，他开始热爱自然。他相信花
cǎo yǒu shēng mìng, dòng wù yǒu gǎn qíng。
草有**生命**，动物有**感情**。

As he grew older, he began to love nature. He believed that flowers and plants have **life** and animals have **emotions**.

yǒu yī nián, tā qù shǒu dū cān jiā kē jǔ kǎo shì, què zài lù shàng yù
有一年，他去**首都**参加**科举考试**，却在路上遇
dào le yī gè qí guài de liè rén。
到了一个奇怪的**猎人**。

One year, he went to the **capital** take the **Imperial Examination**, yet on the way he met a strange **hunter**.

nà liè rén fēi cháng qiáng zhuàng, shǒu shàng fēn bié tí zhe liǎng zhī sǐ qù de dà
那猎人非常**强壮**，手上**分别**提着两只死去的大
yàn。yuán hǎo wèn jiù wèn tā zhè liǎng zhī dà yàn de lái yuán。
雁。元好问就问他这两只大雁的**来源**。

That hunter was very **strong**, holding two dead geese **separately** in each hand. Yuan Hao asked about the **source** of these two geese.

nà liè rén shuō tā zài dǎ liè de shí hòu, kàn dào le liǎng zhī dà yàn,
那猎人说他在打猎的时候，看到了两只**大雁**，
jiù shè xià le xiàn jǐng bǔ huò tā men。
就设下了**陷阱**捕获它们。

The hunter said that when he was hunting, he saw two **geese** and set a **trap** to catch them.

zuì hòu zhǐ bǔ dào le yī zhī。méi xiǎng dào, zài tā shā sǐ zhè zhī dà
最后只捕到了一只。**没想到**，在他杀死这只大
yàn hòu, lìng yī zhī jū rán zài shàng kōng fēi lái fēi qù。
雁后，另一只居然在上空**飞来飞去**。

Only one was caught **in the end**. **Unexpectedly**, after he killed the goose, the other goose began to **fly back and forth** above.

tā shāng xīn de jiào le yī huì ér hòu jiù yǐ zuì kuài de sù dù fēi xiàng
它伤心地**叫**了一会儿后，就以最快的速度飞向
shí bì yī tóu zhuàng sǐ le
石壁，一头**撞死**了。

After **screaming** heart-brokenly for a while, it flew to the **cliff** at full speed and **hit** his head **to death**.

liè rén shuō dāng kàn dào zhè yī qiè de shí hòu lián tā zì jǐ dōu bù gǎn
猎人说当看到这**一切**的时候，**连**他自己**都**不敢
xiāng xìn dà yàn jìng rán yǒu zhè yàng de shēn qíng
相信大雁竟然有这样的深情。

The hunter said that when looking at **all** this, **even** he himself could not believe that the wild goose had such deep affection.

yuán hào wèn tīng dào hòu fēi cháng zhèn jīng tā yǐ qián zhǐ tīng shuō guò yǒu rén
元好问听到后非常**震惊**，他以前只听说过有人
wèi le ài qíng ér xùn qíng méi xiǎng dào dòng wù yě huì zhè yàng zuò
为了爱情而**殉**情，没想到动物也会这样做。

Yuan Haowen was very **astonished** when he heard it. He had only heard of people **suicide** for love before, but didn't expect animals would do the same.

tā fēi cháng gǎn dòng yú shì tā huā qián xiàng liè rén mǎi le zhè liǎng zhī dà
他非常**感动**，于是他花钱向**猎人**买了这两只大
yàn qīn zì bǎ tā men mái le
雁，亲自把它们**埋**了。

He was very **moved**, so he bought these two geese from the **hunter** and **buried** them himself.

rán hòu tā yòu wèi tā men lì le jì niàn bēi zài jì niàn bēi shàng kè xià
然后他又为它们立了**纪念碑**，在纪念碑上**刻**下
le zhè gè gù shì
了这个故事。

Then he set a **monument** for them and **inscribed** the story on it.

tā yǐ qián yī zhí sī kǎo dào dǐ shén me shì zhēn ài xiàn zài jiàn dào
他**以前**一直思考：**到底**什么是真爱？现在见到
zhè liǎng zhī dà yàn yě zhōng yú yǒu le dá àn
这两只大雁，也**终于**有了答案。

He **used to** think all the time: what **one earth** is true love? Now that he saw these two geese, and **finally** had the answer.

tā bù zhī dào liǎng zhī dà yàn zài yī qǐ le duō shǎo nián měi nián chūn xià
他不知道两只大雁**在一起**了多少年，每年**春夏**
qiū dōng yòu yī qǐ fēi guò le duō shǎo dì fāng
秋冬，又一起飞过了多少地方。

He didn't know how many years the two geese had **been together**, or how many places they flew together every year from **spring to winter**.

dāng qí zhōng yī zhī tū rán sǐ le de shí hòu, lìng yī zhī děi rěn shòu zěn yàng de gū dú hé tòng kǔ ne

当其中一只突然死了**的时候**，另一只得忍受怎样的**孤独**和**痛苦**呢？

When one of them died suddenly, what kind of **loneliness** and **pain** did the other have to endure?

xiǎng zhe xiǎng zhe, tā jiù ná qǐ bǐ, rán hòu xiě xià le zhè shǒu shī

想着想着，他就**拿起**笔，然后写下了这首诗：

Thinking about it, he **picked up** a pen and wrote this poem:

wèn shì jiān, qíng wéi hé wù

问世间，情为何物？

Ask the world, what is love?

zhí jiào shēng sǐ xiāng xǔ

直教生死相许！

That even promises life and death to one another!

tiān nán dì běi shuāng fēi kè

天南地北双飞客，

From the south sky to the north, the two geese,

lǎo chì jǐ huí hán shǔ

老翅几回寒暑。

by their aging wings, flying from summer to winter.

huān lè qù, bié lí kǔ

欢乐趣，别离苦，

The joy of togetherness, the sadness of parting,

jiù zhōng gèng yǒu chī ér nǚ

就中更有痴儿女。

all melt in the yearning of two hearts.

jūn yīng yǒu yǔ, miǎo wàn lǐ céng yún

君应有语，渺万里层云，

Should you wonder, through boundless walls of clouds,

qiān shān mù xuě, zhī yǐng xiàng shéi qù

千山暮雪，只影向谁去？

and thousands of peaks of snow, if left alone, where would he go?

Culture Corner

This is one of the most famous love poems from ancient China that has had a profound effect on Chinese romantism. The true story behind the poem has also touched countless people's hearts and its lyrics have been used in many later poems, plays, and songs through both ancient and modern China, especially the first two lines, known by almost every Chinese person:

wèn shì jiān qíng wéi hé wù
问世间，情为何物？
zhí jiào shēng sǐ xiāng xǔ
直教生死相许

Ask the world, what is love?

That even promises life and death to one another.

Key Vocabulary

zuò jiā 作家	*n.*	writer	fēi lái fēi qù 飞来飞去	*vp.*	fly back and forth
jiào yù 教育	*n.*	education	zhèn jīng 震惊	*adj.*	astonished
shēng mìng 生命	*n.*	life	gǎn dòng 感动	*adj.*	touched/moved
gǎn qíng 感情	*n.*	emotion/feelings	jì niàn bēi 纪念碑	*n.*	monument
shǒu dū 首都	*n.*	capital	rěn shòu 忍受	*v.*	to bear
liè rén 猎人	*n.*	hunter	gū dú 孤独	*n.* *adj.*	loneliness lonely
qiáng zhuàng 强壮	*adj.*	strong (physical)	tòng kǔ 痛苦	*n.* *adj.*	pain painful
fēn bié 分别	*adv.*	separately/respectively	dà yàn 大雁	*n.*	goose
lái yuán 来源	*n.*	origin/source	xiàn jǐng 陷阱	*n.*	trap

Sentence Patterns

随着…

as …

suí zhe
随着 + *event* + *clause*

suí zhe nián sui de zēng zhǎng, tā kāi shǐ rè ài zì rán
随着年岁的增长，他开始热爱自然。

As he grew older, he began to love nature.

连…都…

even …

lián dōu
连 + *noun* + **都** + *statement*

lián tā zì jǐ dōu bù gǎn xiāng xìn dà yàn jìng rán yǒu zhè yàng de shēn qíng
连他自己都不敢相信大雁竟然有这样的深情。

Even he himself could not believe that the wild goose had such deep affection.

CHINESE VERSION

元好问是中国古代著名的作家，他从小就受到了很好的教育，八岁就开始写诗。

随着年岁的增长，他开始热爱自然。他相信花草有生命，动物有感情。

有一年，他去首都参加科举考试，却在路上遇到了一个奇怪的猎人。

那猎人非常强壮，手上分别提着两只死去的大雁。元好问就问他这两只大雁的来源。

那猎人说他在打猎的时候，看到了两只大雁，就设下了陷阱捕获它们。

最后只捕到了一只。没想到，在他杀死这只大雁后，另一只居然在上空飞来飞去。

它伤心地叫了一会儿后，就以最快的速度飞向石壁，一头撞死了。

猎人说当看到这一切的时候，连他自己都不敢相信大雁竟然有这样的深情。

元好问听到后非常震惊，他以前只听说过有人为了爱情而殉情，没想到动物也会这样做。

他非常感动，于是他花钱向猎人买了这两只大雁，亲自把它们埋了。

然后他又为它们立了纪念碑，在纪念碑上刻下了这个故事。

他以前一直思考：到底什么是真爱？现在见到这两只大雁，也终于有了答案。

他不知道两只大雁在一起了多少年，每年春夏秋冬，又一起飞过了多少地方。

当其中一只突然死了的时候，另一只得忍受怎样的孤独和痛苦呢？

想着想着，他就拿起笔，然后写下了这首诗:

问世间，情为何物?
直教生死相许!
天南地北双飞客，
老翅几回寒暑。
欢乐趣，别离苦，
就中更有痴儿女。
君应有语，
渺万里层云，
千山暮雪，
只影向谁去?

历 lì
史 shǐ
名 míng
人 rén

Famous Historical Figures

wǔ zé tiān

武则天

Wu Zetian

(First Empress of China)

wǔ zé tiān shì zhōng guó lì shǐ shàng wéi yī de nǚ huáng dì, yě shì zuì shòu
武则天是中国历史上**唯一**的女皇帝，也是最**受**
zhēng yì de nǚ zhèng zhì jiā
争议的女政治家。

Wu Zetian was the **only** empress in Chinese history and the most **controversial** female politician.

tā suī rán bù shì zuì měi de nǚ rén, què shì zuì jīng míng, zuì néng gàn
她**虽然**不是最美的女人，**却**是最精明，最能干
de nǚ rén
的女人。

Although she was not the most beautiful woman, she was certianly the most shrewd and capable woman.

wǔ zé tiān chū shēng zài yī gè guān yuán jiā tíng, cóng xiǎo jiù yǒu hěn dà
武则天**出生**在一个官员家庭，从小就有很大
de yě xīn. shí sì suì de shí hòu, tā zuò le lǎo huáng dì lǐ shì mín
的**野心**。十四岁的时候，她做了老皇帝李世民
de pín fēi
的**嫔妃**。

Wu Zetian was **born** into an official family and had great **ambitions** since she was a child. At the age of fourteen, she became the **concubine** of the old emperor Li Shimin.

lǎo huáng dì yě shì gè hěn jīng míng de rén, dāng tā fā xiàn wǔ zé tiān
老皇帝也是个很**精明**的人，当他**发现**武则天
de yě xīn hòu, xuǎn zé le yuǎn lí tā
的野心后，选择了**远离**她。

The old emperor was also a very **shrewd** man. After **discovering** Wu Zetian's ambition, he chose to **stay away** from her.

hòu lái lǎo huáng dì bìng zhòng, wǔ zé tiān gù yì qù jiē jìn tā de ér zi lǐ zhì, liǎng gè rén cháng cháng qiāo qiāo yuē huì.

后来老皇帝**病重**，武则天**故意**去接近他的儿子李治，两个人常常悄悄**约会**。

Later, when the old emperor became **severely ill**, Wu Zetian **deliberately** approached his son Li Zhi, and the two often **dated** in secret.

lǎo huáng dì sǐ hòu, lǐ zhì zuò le xīn huáng dì. kě shì, àn zhào guī dìng, wǔ zé tiān hé qí tā pín fēi dōu bèi sòng qù le sì miào zuò ní gū.

老皇帝死后，李治做了新**皇帝**。可是，**按照规定**，武则天和其他嫔妃都被送去了寺庙做**尼姑**。

After the old emperor died, Li Zhi became the new **emperor**. However, **according to** the regulations, Wu Zetian and other concubines were sent to the temple to be **nuns**.

dàn wǔ zé tiān bù fàng qì, yī zhí yǔ lǐ zhì bǎo chí lián xì, zhí dào hòu lái lǐ zhì bù gù qí tā rén de fǎn duì, jiē wǔ zé tiān huí gōng zuò pín fēi.

但武则天不放弃，一直与李治**保持联系**，直到后来李治**不顾**其他人的反对，接武则天回**宫**做嫔妃。

But Wu Zetian did not give up and **kept in touch with** Li Zhi. Until later Li Zhi **ignored** the opposition of others and took Wu Zetian back to the **palace** as a concubine.

kě shì wǔ zé tiān bìng bù mǎn zú, tā shè xiàn jǐng chú qù le lǐ zhì de huáng hòu, ràng zì jǐ dāng shàng le xīn huáng hòu, rán hòu kāi shǐ gān yù zhèng zhì.

可是武则天并不**满足**，她**设陷阱**除去了李治的**皇后**，让自己当上了新皇后，然后开始**干预**政治。

But Wu Zetian was not **satisfied**, she **set a trap** to get rid of Li Zhi's **empress consort,** and made herself the new empress consort, and then began to **interfere** in politics.

yóu yú lǐ zhì ruǎn ruò wú néng, hěn duō guó shì dōu yóu wǔ zé tiān chǔ lǐ. tā hěn yǒu zhèng zhì cái huá, lǐng dǎo néng lì yě hěn qiáng.

由于李治**软弱无能**，很多**国事**都由武则天**处理**。她很有政治才华，**领导能力**也很强。

Because Li Zhi was **weak and incompetent**, many **state affairs** were **handled** by Wu Zetian. She was politically talented and had strong **leadership skills**.

màn màn de, tā de quán lì shèn zhì chāo guò le huáng dì. huáng dì suī rán bù gāo xìng, dàn shì yě bù gǎn fǎn kàng tā.

慢慢地，她的**权力**甚至超过了皇帝。皇帝虽然不高兴，但是也不敢**反抗**她。

Gradually, her **power** even surpassed that of the emperor. Although the emperor was not happy, he did not dare to **oppose** her.

hòu lái huáng dì bìng sǐ le wǔ zé tiān chéng wéi le tài hòu tā de liǎng
后来皇帝**病死**了，武则天成为了**太后**，她的两
gè ér zi xiān hòu dāng shàng le huáng dì dàn shì dōu hěn kuài bèi tā bà miǎn
个儿子**先后**当上了皇帝，但是都很快被她**罢免**
le
了。

Later, the emperor **died of illness**, Wu Zetian became the **empress dowager**, and her two sons became emperors **one after another**, but they were both quickly **dismissed** by her.

zhōng yú zài suì de shí hòu tā zài hěn duō dà chén de zhī chí xià
终于，在67岁的时候，她在很多大臣的**支持**下
chēng dì le tā de yě xīn zhōng yú shí xiàn le chéng wéi le lì shǐ shàng
称帝了。她的野心终于实现了：**成为**了历史上
de dì yī wèi nǚ huáng dì
的第一位女皇帝。

Finally, at the age of 67, with the **support** of many ministers, she announced herself as the empress. Her ambition finally came true, **becoming** the first empress in history.

zài tā hòu lái zhí zhèng de shí wǔ nián jīng jì fā dá guó jiā qiáng dà
在她后来**执政**的十五年，**经济**发达，国家**强大**
zhèng zhì kāi míng ràng tā chéng wéi le táng cháo zuì wěi dà de huáng dì zhī
，政治**开明**，让她成为了唐朝**最伟大**的皇帝之
yī
一。

During her later fifteen years **in power**, people enjoyed a developed **economy**, a **strong** country, and political **enlightenment**, which made her one of the **greatest** emperors of Tang dynasty.

tā bā shí èr suì qù shì zhī hòu tā de ér zi chóng xīn zuò le huáng
她八十二岁**去世**，之后，她的儿子重新做了皇
dì
帝。

She **passed away** at the age of eighty-two, after which her son restored his emperor reign.

CULTURE CORNER

Wu Zetian (武则天) was a Chinese empress and ruler who lived from 624-705 AD. She was the only woman to ever rule China in her own right, and she was the first and only female emperor in the history of China. She reigned during the Tang dynasty, which was a golden age of Chinese culture, and her rule was marked by administrative and cultural reforms that helped to strengthen the empire. Wu Zetian was known for her political savvy and her ruthless pursuit of power, which earned her both respect and fear among her subjects. Having reached the highest position possible in China as a woman, against the odds, is of particular relevance; however she is a contrversial figure and for many Chinese people, she is remembered as shrewd and capable, but also manipulative and criticized for her methods of achieving and maintaing power. She has often been depicted in popular media, inclding TV dramas, films, and novels.

你认为武则天是个怎样的人。请讨论她为什么选择称帝？

What kind of person do you think Wu Zetian was? Please discuss why she chose to declare herself as empress?

A 她很爱她的国家。
She loved her country very much.

B 她的野心太大。
Her ambition was too great.

C 她太爱权力，想当统治者。
She loved power too much and wanted to be a ruler.

D 她想打破纪录，被历史记住。
She wanted to break records and be remembered by history.

Key Vocabulary

wéi yī 唯一	*adj.*	only	mǎn zú 满足	*adj.*	content/ satisfied
shòu zhēng yì 受争议	*adj.*	controversial	gān yù 干预	*n.*	to intervene
yě xīn 野心	*n.*	ambition	zhèng zhì 政治	*n.*	politics
jīng míng 精明	*adj.*	shrewd	ruǎn ruò wú néng 软弱无能	*idiom*	weak and incompetent
yuǎn lí 远离	*v.*	to stay away	quán lì 权力	*n.*	power
bìng zhòng 病重	*v.*	severely ill	bà miǎn 罢免	*v.*	to dismiss
gù yì 故意	*adj.*	deliberate	jīng jì 经济	*n.*	economy
huáng dì 皇帝	*n.*	emperor	qiáng dà 强大	*adj.*	powerful
huáng hòu 皇后	*n.*	empress consort	kāi míng 开明	*adj*	enlightened/ open-minded

Sentence Patterns

虽然... 却

although ... (but)

suī rán / què
虽然 + *clause 1* + **却** + *clause 2*

tā suī rán bù shì zuì měi de nǚ rén, què shì zuì jīng míng, zuì néng gàn de nǚ rén。
她虽然不是最美的女人，却是最精明，最能干的女人。

Although she was not the most beautiful woman, she was certianly the most shrewd and capable woman.

与... 保持联系

stay in touch/contact with ...

yǔ / bǎo chí lián xì
A + **与** + *B* + **保持联系**

dàn wǔ zé tiān bù fàng qì, yī zhí yǔ lǐ zhì bǎo chí lián xì。
但武则天不放弃，一直与李治保持联系。

But Wu Zetian did not give up and kept in touch with Li Zhi.

CHINESE VERSION

武则天是中国历史上唯一的女皇帝，也是最受争议的女政治家。

她虽然不是最美的女人，却是最精明，最能干的女人。

武则天出生在一个官员家庭，从小就有很大的野心。十四岁的时候，她做了老皇帝李世民的嫔妃。

老皇帝也是个很精明的人，当他发现武则天的野心后，选择了远离她。

后来老皇帝病重，武则天故意去接近他的儿子李治，两个人常常悄悄约会。

老皇帝死后，李治做了新皇帝。可是，按照规定，武则天和其他嫔妃都被送去了寺庙做尼姑。

但武则天不放弃，一直与李治保持联系，直到后来李治不顾其他人的反对，接武则天回宫做嫔妃。

可是武则天并不满足，她设陷阱除去了李治的皇后，让自己当上了新皇后，然后开始干预政治。

由于李治软弱无能，很多国事都由武则天处理。她很有政治才华，领导能力也很强。

慢慢地，她的权力甚至超过了皇帝。皇帝虽然不高兴，但是也不敢反抗她。

后来皇帝病死了，武则天成为了太后，她的两个儿子先后当上了皇帝，但是都很快被她罢免了。

终于，在67岁的时候，她在很多大臣的支持下称帝了。她的野心终于实现了：成为了历史上的第一位女皇帝。

在她后来执政的十五年，经济发达，国家强大，政治开明，让她成为了唐朝最伟大的皇帝之一。

她八十二岁去世，之后，她的儿子重新做了皇帝。

lán lín wán

15 兰陵王

Prince Lan Ling
(The Masked Prince)

lán líng wáng shì liù cháo shí qī zhù míng de jiāng jūn, yě shì zhōng guó sì dà měi nán zhī yī

兰陵王是六朝时期著名的**将军**，也是中国四大美男**之一**。

Prince Lanling was a famous **general** during the Six Dynasties period and was **one of** the four most handsome men in ancient China.

lán líng wáng míng jiào gāo cháng gōng, shì qí guó de wáng zǐ, cóng xiǎo jiù cōng míng líng lì、cái huá héng yì

兰陵王名叫高长恭，是齐国的**王子**，从小就**聪明伶俐**、**才华横溢**。

Prince Lanling named Gao Changgong, who was the **prince** of the state of Qi. Since he was a child, he had been **super smart** and **enormously talented**.

tā bù jǐn néng wén néng wǔ, ér qiě zhǎng xiàng yīng jùn, jì bù jiāo ào, yě bù zuò zuò, shì gè jī hū wán měi de nán zi

他不仅**能文能武**，而且长相**英俊**，**既不**骄傲，**也不**做作，是个几乎**完美**的男子。

He did not only **exceed in literature and martial arts**, but had a very **handsome** appearance, and was **neither** proud **nor** pretentious, which made him almost a **perfect** man.

tā yě yǒu hěn chū sè de jūn shì cái huá, zài hěn nián qīng de shí hòu jiù dāng shàng le jiāng jūn

他也有很**出色**的军事才华，在很年轻的时候就**当上**了将军。

He also had **excellent** military talent and **became** a general at a very young age.

kě shì yóu yú tā de liǎn tài jùn měi zài zhàn chǎng shàng bù néng wēi hè dí
可是由于他的脸太**俊美**，在战场上不能**威吓**敌
rén suǒ yǐ tā jiù qǐng rén wèi tā zuò le yī gè zhēng níng de miàn jù
人。所以，他就请人为他做了一个**狰狞**的面具。

But because his face was so **pretty** that he could not **intimidate** the enemy on the battlefield. So, he asked a **hideous** mask made for him.

hòu lái měi cì dǎ zhàng tā dōu huì dài shàng miàn jù yóu yú tā cháng cháng
后来每次**打仗**，他都会戴上面具。由于他常常
dǎ shèng zhàng qí guó de rén mín hěn chóng bài tā chēng tā wéi zhàn shén
打胜仗，齐国的人民很**崇拜**他，称他为**战神**。

Later, every time he **fought in wars**, he would wear the mask. Because he often **won battles**, the people of Qi state **admired** him very much and called him the **God of War**.

yǒu yī cì dí guó de jǐ wàn shì bīng bāo wéi le qí guó de jīn yōng chéng
有一次，敌国的几万**士兵**包围了齐国的**金墉城**
lán líng wáng què dài lǐng wǔ bǎi jīng ruì bù duì chōng jìn bāo wéi dào dá
，兰陵王却带领五百**精锐部队**冲进包围，到达
chéng mén xià
城门下。

Once, tens of thousands of **soldiers** from the enemy state surrounded **Jinyong City** in the state of Qi, yet Prince Lanling managed to lead 500 **elite troops** into the siege and reached under the city wall.

tā dāng shí dài zhe miàn jù yīn cǐ chéng shàng de shì bīng men dōu bù què dìng
他当时**戴**着面具，因此城上的士兵们都**不确定**
shì shéi yú shì jiào tā zhāi xià miàn jù
是谁，于是叫他**摘下**面具。

As he was **wearing** a mask by then, the soldiers in the city were **not sure** who it was, so they told him to **take off** the mask.

zài tā zhāi xià miàn jù de shí hòu shì bīng men rèn chū le tā lì kè
在他摘下面具的时候，士兵们**认出**了他，立刻
zuò zhàn shì qì dà zēng yī qǐ dǎ bài le dí jūn
作战**士气**大增，一起**打败**了敌军。

When he took off his mask, the soldiers **recognized** him and immediately had a great fighting **morale**, **defeating** the enemy together.

zhè gè gù shì bèi biān chéng le yī shǒu jūn rén dài miàn jù de gē wǔ
这个故事被**编成**了一首军人戴面具的歌舞：
lán líng wáng rù zhèn qū qū zi fēi cháng zhù míng hòu lái shèn zhì
《兰陵王入阵曲》，曲子非常**著名**，后来**甚至**
chuán rù le rì běn
传入了日本。

Later, this story was **compiled into** a musical performance of soldiers wearing masks: "The Song of Battle for Prince Lanling", which was so **famous** that **even** introduced to Japan later.

kě shì zhè yàng wán měi de lán líng wáng què zhāo lái le hěn duō rén de jí dù bāo kuò qí guó de guó wáng

可是，这样**完美**的兰陵王却招来了很多人的**嫉妒**，包括齐国的国王。

However, such a **perfect** Prince Lanling attracted the **jealousy** of many people, including the King of Qi.

yī cì guó wáng sòng le yī gè měi nǚ jiàn dié qù lán líng wáng shēn biān mìng lìng zhǎo jī huì cì shā tā

一次，国王送了一个美女**间谍**去兰陵王身边，命令找机会**刺杀**他。

Once, the king sent a beauty **spy** to Prince Lanling's side and ordered to find opportunities to **assassinate** him.

kě shì nà nǚ zi zài hé lán líng wáng xiāng chǔ yī duàn shí jiān hòu bù jǐn chè dǐ fàng qì le cì shā rèn wù hái shēn shēn de ài shàng le tā

可是，那女子在和兰陵王**相处**一段时间后，不仅**彻底**放弃了刺杀**任务**，还深深地**爱上**了他。

Yet, after **getting along** with Prince Lanling for a short period, the woman not only **totally** gave up the assassination **task**, but deeply **fell in love with** him.

lán líng wáng dé zhī zhēn xiāng hòu shēn shòu gǎn dòng yě ài shàng le nà nǚ zi bìng bǎ tā liú zài le shēn biān

兰陵王**得知**真相后，深受**感动**，也爱上了那女子，**并**把她留在了身边。

After Prince Lanling **learned** the truth, he was deeply **moved**, he fell in love with the woman too, **and** kept her by his side.

zhǐ shì jǐ nián hòu guó wáng yòu zhǎo le gè jiè kǒu bī lán líng wáng hē xià dú jiǔ tā sǐ de shí hòu zhǐ yǒu sān shí èr suì

只是，几年后，国王又找了个**借口**逼兰陵王喝下**毒酒**，他死的时候只有三十二岁。

However, a few years later, the king found another **excuse**, and forced Prince Lanling to drink **poisonous wine**, at that time he died, he was only thirty-two years old.

lán líng wáng sǐ hòu chéng qiān shàng wàn de rén wèi tā tòng kū qí guó yě shī qù le tā de zhàn shén jǐ nián hòu bèi dí guó miè wáng le

兰陵王死后，**成千上万**的人为他**痛哭**。齐国也**失去**了它的战神，几年后被敌国**灭亡**了。

After Prince Lanling died, **tens of thousands** of people **wept bitterly** for him. The state of Qi also **lost** its god of war and was **destroyed** by enemy states a few years later.

Culture Corner

Prince Lanling (兰陵王) is still one of the most beloved male figures from ancient China. As a young man with an incredibly handsome face, a mysterious background, and a noble prince with great military achievement, he has been adored by both men and women throughout Chinese history. His stories are also widely presented in various Chinese films and TV dramas, and is also a popular figure in traditional Chinese opera.

你认为兰陵王是个怎样的人。请讨论，如果你是他，明明知道国王故意想杀你，你会怎么做？

What kind of person do you think Prince Lanling was? Please discuss, if you were him and clearly knew that the king intentionally wanted to kill you, what would you do?

A 不反抗，永远对国王忠心。
No resistance, remain loyal to the king forever.

B 反抗，然后逃走。
Resist and escape.

C 反抗，推翻国王，让自己当国王。
Resist and overthrow the king to become the king myself.

D 想办法威胁国王，让他不敢杀自己。
Find a way to threaten the king so that he wouldn't dare to kill me.

Key Vocabulary

Pinyin	Word	Part of speech	Meaning
jiāng jūn	将军	*n.*	general
wáng zǐ	王子	*n.*	prince
cōng míng líng lì	聪明伶俐	*idiom*	super smart
cái huá héng yì	才华横溢	*idiom*	enormously talented
dǎ zhàng	打仗	*v.*	to fight (wars)
yīng jùn	英俊	*adj.*	handsome
wán měi	完美	*adj.*	perfect
chéng qiān shàng wàn	成千上万	*idiom*	tens of thousands
néng wén néng wǔ	能文能武	*idiom*	exceed in literature and martial arts
chóng bài	崇拜	*v.*	to admire/ worship
jí dù	嫉妒	*n.* *adj.*	jealousy jealous
jiàn dié	间谍	*n.*	spy
cì shā	刺杀	*v.*	to assassinate
jiè kǒu	借口	*n.*	excuse
zhēng níng	狰狞	*adj.*	hideous
shī qù	失去	*v.*	to lose
jùn měi	俊美	*adj.*	pretty (man)
wēi hè	威吓	*v.*	to intimidate

Sentence Patterns

... 之一

one of ...

subject + **是** (shì) + noun phrase + **之一** (zhī yī)

lán líng wáng shì zhōng guó sì dà měi nán zhī yī

兰陵王是中国四大美男之一。

Prince Lanling was one of the four most handsome men in ancient China.

既不...也不...

neither ... nor ...

既不 (jì bù) + A + **也不** (yě bù) + B

tā jì bù jiāo ào, yě bù zuò zuò

他既不骄傲，也不做作。

He was neither proud nor pretentious.

CHINESE VERSION

兰陵王是六朝时期著名的将军，也是中国四大美男之一。

兰陵王名叫高长恭，是齐国的王子,从小就聪明伶俐、才华横溢。

他不仅能文能武，而且长相英俊，既不骄傲，也不做作，是个几乎完美的男子。

他也有很出色的军事才华，在很年轻的时候就当上了将军。

可是由于他的脸太俊美，在战场上不能威吓敌人。所以，他就请人为他做了一个狰狞的面具。

后来每次打仗，他都会戴上面具，由于他常常打胜仗，齐国的人民很崇拜他，称他为战神。

有一次，敌国的几万士兵包围了齐国的金墉城，兰陵王却带领五百精锐部队冲进包围，到达城门下。

他当时戴着面具，因此城上的士兵们都不确定是谁，于是叫他摘下面具。

在他摘下面具的时候，士兵们认出了他，立刻作战士气大增，一起打败了敌军。

这个故事被编成了一首军人戴面具的歌舞:《兰陵王入阵曲》，曲子非常著名，后来甚至传入了日本。

可是，这样完美的兰陵王却招来了很多人的嫉妒，包括齐国的国王。

一次，国王送了一个美女间谍去兰陵王身边，命令找机会刺杀他。

可是，那女子在和兰陵王相处一段时间后，不仅彻底放弃了刺杀任务，还深深地爱上了他。

兰陵王得知真相后，深受感动，也爱上了那女子，并把她留在了身边。

只是，几年后，国王又找了个借口逼兰陵王喝下毒酒，他死的时候只有三十二岁。

兰陵王死后，成千上万的人为他痛哭。齐国也失去了它的战神，几年后被敌国灭亡了。

qū yuán

Qu Yuan

(Dragon Boat Festival Origin)

qū yuán shì zhōng guó gǔ dài wěi dà de shī rén hé zhèng zhì jiā, tā yǒu jí gāo de lì shǐ dì wèi, bèi yù wéi "zhōng huá shī zǔ".

屈原是中国古代伟大的**诗人**和**政治家**，他有极高的历史**地位**，被**誉为**"中华诗祖"。

Qu Yuan was a great **poet** and **statesman** in ancient China, who holds an extremely high historical **status**, and was **honored as** the "Chinese Poetry Ancestor."

měi nián nóng lì de wǔ yuè chū wǔ shì duān wǔ jié, zhè shì zhōng guó sì dà chuán tǒng jié rì zhī yī, shì wèi le jì niàn qū yuán.

每年**农历**的五月初五是**端午节**，这是中国四大**传统**节日之一，是为了**纪念**屈原。

Every year on the fifth day of the fifth month of the **lunar calendar** is the **Dragon Boat Festival** - one of the four **traditional** Chinese festivals, which is to **commemorate** Qu Yuan.

chūn qiū zhàn guó shí qī, qū yuán chū shēng zài chǔ guó de yī gè guì zú jiā tíng. tā cóng xiǎo jiù shì gè tiān cái, bù jǐn xìng gé dú lì, ér qiě ài hào xiě shī.

春秋**战国**时期，屈原出生在楚国的一个**贵族家庭**。他从小就是个**天才**，不仅性格**独立**，而且爱好写诗。

During the Spring and Autumn (**Warring States**) Period, Qu Yuan was born in a **noble family** in the State of Chu. He had been a **genius** since he was a child, not only had an **independent** personality, but also loved writing poetry.

qū yuán shì zhèng fǔ de gāo jí guān yuán chǔ wáng yī kāi shǐ hěn xìn rèn tā
屈原是政府的**高级**官员。楚王一开始很**信任**他
kě shì hòu lái què qīn jìn xiǎo rén jiù yuǎn lí tā le
，可是后来却亲近**小人**，就远离他了。

Qu Yuan was a **senior** government official. The King of Chu **trusted** him very much at first, but later, when he became close to the **evildoers**, stayed away from Qu Yuan.

zhī hòu qín guó hé chǔ guó dǎ zhàng chǔ guó bèi dǎ bài le xiàn
之后，秦国和楚国打仗，楚国被**打败**了，陷
rù le yán zhòng de zhèng zhì wēi jī miàn lín zhe yào me gǎi gé yào me
入了严重的**政治危机**，面临着**要么**改革，**要么**
wáng guó de jú miàn
亡国的局面。

After that, war broke out between Qin and Chu, and Chu was **defeated** and sank into a **political crisis**, facing a situation of **either** reforming **or** subjugation.

qū yuán wèi le jiù guó zuò le hěn duō nǔ lì yě tí chū le hěn duō
屈原为了救国，做了很多**努力**，也**提出**了很多
yǒu yòng de jiàn yì kě shì chǔ wáng bù tīng hái liú fàng le qū yuán
有用的**建议**，可是楚王不听，还**流放**了屈原。

In order to save the state, Qu Yuan made a lot of **efforts** and **put forward** many useful **suggestions**, but the king of Chu refused to listen and **exiled** Qu Yuan.

chǔ wáng yuè lái yuè wú néng jǐ nián hòu diào rù qín guó de xiàn jǐng chéng
楚王越来越**无能**，几年后掉入秦国的**陷阱**，成
wéi qiú fàn tā de huǐ hèn dào tā sǐ wéi zhǐ dōu méi yǒu duàn jué
为囚犯。他的悔恨**到**他死**为止**，都没有断绝。

The king became increasingly **incompetent**, and fell into the **trap** of Qin and became a prisoner. His remorse did **not** cease **until** his death.

hòu lái qín guó zài cì qīn fàn chǔ guó chǔ guó de shǒu dū bèi zhàn lǐng
后来，秦国再次**侵犯**楚国，楚国的首都被**占领**
le qū yuán tài shāng xīn jiù tiào hé zì shā le
了。屈原太**伤心**，就跳河**自杀**了。

Later, Qin **invaded** Chu again, and the capital of Chu was **occupied**. Qu Yuan was so **heartbroken** that he jumped into the river to **commit suicide**.

dāng tiān hěn duō rén huá chuán qù zhǎo tā de shī tǐ hái yǒu xiē rén xiàng
当天，很多人**划船**去找他的尸体，还有些人向
hé lǐ rēng zòng zǐ xī wàng yú chī le zòng zi hòu kě yǐ yuǎn lí qū yuán
河里扔**粽子**，希望鱼吃了粽子后可以**远离**屈原
de shī tǐ
的尸体。

On that day, many people **rowed boats** to find his body, with some threw **rice dumplings** into the river, hoping that fish could **stay away from** Qu Yuan's body after eating the zongzi.

wèi le jì niàn qū yuán zhè yī tiān jiù chéng wéi le duān wǔ jié sài lóng
为了**纪念**屈原，这一天就成为了端午节，**赛龙**
zhōu hé chī zòng zi yě chéng wéi le duān wǔ jié de fēng sú
舟和吃粽子也成为了端午节的**风俗**。

To **commemorate** Qu Yuan, this day became the Dragon Boat Festival, and **dragon boat racing** and eating rice dumplings also became the **customs** of the Dragon Boat Festival.

tā de shī kāi chuàng le zhōng guó shī gē shí dài de lǐ chéng bēi bù jǐn
他的诗**开创**了中国诗歌时代的**里程碑**，不仅
zài měi yī dài zhōng guó rén lǐ liú chuán ér qiě yǐng xiǎng le xǔ duō hòu
在每一代中国人里**流传**，而且**影响**了许多后
lái de shī rén bāo kuò lǐ bái
来的诗人，包括**李白**。

His poems **ushered in** a **milestone** of Chinese poetry in the era, not only **passing** in every Chinese generation, but also **influencing** many later poets, including **Li Bai**.

qū yuán bù jǐn shì wěi dà de ài guó shī rén yě shì zhōng guó làng màn
屈原不仅是伟大的**爱国诗人**，也是中国**浪漫**
zhǔ yì wén xué de diàn jī rén tā de zuò pǐn lí sāo jiǔ gē
主义文学的**奠基人**，他的作品《离骚》、《九歌》、
jiǔ zhāng děng dōu shì guó xué jīng diǎn
《九章》等都是**国学经典**。

Qu Yuan was not only a great **patriotic poet**, but also the **founder** of Chinese **romantic literature**. His works "Li Sao", "Nine Songs", "Nine Chapters" and more, are all **classics of Chinese studies**.

nián shì jiè hé píng lǐ shì huì píng xuǎn qū yuán wéi dāng nián jì niàn
1953年，**世界和平理事会**评选屈原为当年纪念
de shì jiè sì dà wén huà míng rén zhī yī
的世界四大**文化名人**之一。

In 1953, the **World Peace Council** selected Qu Yuan as one of four major **cultural celebrities** in the world to be commemorated that year.

CULTURE CORNER

The **Dragon Boat Festival** (端午节) occurs on the fifth day of the fifth month of the Chinese lunar calendar, and is one of the oldest festivals in China. It originates from the highly regarded patriotic poet and literature icon **Qu Yuan** (屈原). In Modern China, people enjoy three days' public holiday to celebrate it, and the most popular activity is the **Dragon Boat Racing** (赛龙舟) - which is where the festival's English name comes from!

你认为屈原是个怎样的人。请讨论楚王死前最后悔的是什么？

What kind of person do you think Qu Yuan was? Please discuss what the King of Chu regretted the most before his death?

A 流放屈原，失去了屈原的辅助。
Exiling Qu Yuan and losing his assistance.

B 自己太笨，被小人影响。
Being too stupid and influenced by evildoers.

C 自己太无能，掉入了秦国的陷进。
Being too incompetent and falling into the trap set by the state of Qin.

D 没有改革，导致自己的国家不够强大。
Failing to enact reforms, resulting in his own state not being strong enough.

Key Vocabulary

zhèng zhì jiā	政治家	*n.*	statesman	tí chū	提出	*v.*	to propose/put forward
dì wèi	地位	*n.*	status	wú néng	无能	*adj.*	incompetent
jì niàn	纪念	*v.*	to commemorate	qiú fàn	囚犯	*n.*	prisoner
tiān cái	天才	*n.*	genius	duàn jué	断绝	*v.*	to end/cease
dú lì	独立	*n.*	independent	qīn lüè	侵略	*v.*	to invade
gāo jí	高级	*adj.*	senior/ high-ranking	zòng zi	粽子	*n.*	rice dumplings
xìn rèn	信任	*v.*	to trust	sài lóng zhōu	赛龙舟	*n.*	dragon boat racing
xiǎo rén	小人	*n.*	evildoer	lǐ chéng bēi	里程碑	*n.*	milestone
wēi jī	危机	*n.*	crisis	jīng diǎn	经典	*n.*	classic

Sentence Patterns

要么…要么…

either … or …

yào me + action 1 + yào me + action 2

要么 + *action 1* + **要么** + *action 2*

chǔ guó miàn lín zhe yào me gǎi gé, yào me wáng guó de jú miàn.

楚国面临着要么改革，要么亡国的局面。

The state of Chu was facing a situation of either reforming or subjugation.

到…为止

up until …

dào + event + wéi zhǐ + clause

到 + *event* + **为止** + *clause*

tā de huǐ hèn dào tā sǐ wéi zhǐ, dōu méi yǒu duàn jué.

他的悔恨到他死为止，都没有断绝。

His remorse did not cease until his death.

Chinese Version

屈原是中国古代伟大的诗人和政治家，他有极高的历史地位，被誉为“中华诗祖”。

每年农历的五月初五是端午节，这是中国四大传统节日之一，是为了纪念屈原。

春秋战国时期，屈原出生在楚国的一个贵族家庭。他从小就是个天才，不仅性格独立，而且爱好写诗。

屈原是政府的高级官员。楚王一开始很信任他，可是后来却亲近小人，就远离他了。

之后，秦国和楚国打仗，楚国被打败了，陷入了严重的政治危机，面临着要么改革，要么亡国的局面。

屈原为了救国，做了很多努力，也提出了很多有用的建议，可是楚王不听，还流放了屈原。

楚王越来越无能，几年后掉入秦国的陷阱，成为囚犯。他的悔恨到他死为止，都没有断绝。

后来，秦国再次侵犯楚国，楚国的首都被占领了。屈原太伤心，就跳河自杀了。

当天，很多人划船去找他的尸体，还有些人向河里扔粽子，希望鱼吃了粽子后可以远离屈原的尸体。

为了纪念屈原，这一天就成为了端午节，赛龙舟和吃粽子也成为了端午节的风俗。

他的诗开创了中国诗歌时代的里程碑，不仅在每一代中国人里流传，而且影响了许多后来的诗人，包括李白。

屈原不仅是伟大的爱国诗人，也是中国浪漫主义文学的奠基人，他的作品《离骚》、《九歌》、《九章》等都是国学经典。

1953年，世界和平理事会评选屈原为当年纪念的世界四大文化名人之一。

mín

jiān

chuán

说

shuō

Chinese Folktales

huā mù lán chuán qí

花木兰传奇

The Legend of Mulan

huā mù lán shì gǔ dài zhù míng de chuán qí nǚ yīng xióng, tā de gù shì zài zhōng guó jiā yù hù xiǎo

花木兰是古代著名的**传奇**女英雄，她的故事在中国**家喻户晓**。

Hua Mulan was a famous **legendary** heroine in ancient times, and her story is **well known** in China.

hěn jiǔ yǐ qián, zài yī gè xiǎo cūn zi lǐ, huā mù lán hé jiā rén guò zhe píng jìng de shēng huó. tā hé pǔ tōng nǚ zǐ yī yàng, měi tiān zhī bù, zuò jiā wù

很久以前，在一个小村子里，花木兰和家人过着**平静**的生活。她和**普通女子**一样，每天织布、做**家务**。

A long time ago, in a small village, Hua Mulan and her family lived a **peaceful** life. Like **ordinary women**, she weaved cloth and did **housework** every day.

kě shì, yǒu yī tiān, zhèng fǔ lái zhāo bīng, guī dìng měi gè jiā tíng dōu děi chū yī gè nán zǐ shàng zhàn chǎng

可是，有一天，**政府**来招兵，**规定**每个家庭都得出一个男子上**战场**。

However, one day, the **government** came to recruit soldiers and **stipulated** that each family should send one man to the **battlefield**.

huā mù lán de fù qīn nián líng hěn dà, shēn tǐ bù hǎo. jiā shàng dì di nián líng tài xiǎo, tā zài sān kǎo lǜ hòu, jué dìng zì jǐ qù zhàn chǎng

花木兰的父亲**年龄很大**，身体不好。加上弟弟**年龄太小**，她**再三考虑**后，**决定**自己去战场。

Hua Mulan's father was **old** (age very big) and in poor health. Plus, her younger brother was **too young**. After **thinking over and over**, she **decided** to go to the battlefield by herself.

zài gǔ dài dǎ zhàng bù shì nǚ rén de shì ér shì nán rén de shì
在古代，打仗**不是**女人的事，**而是**男人的事。
huā mù lán míng bái zì jǐ de cān yǔ shì wéi fǎ de yīn cǐ tā bù
花木兰明白自己的**参与**是**违法**的。因此，她不
dé bù nǚ bàn nán zhuāng
得不**女扮男装**。

In ancient times, fighting wars **was not** a woman's business, **but** a man's. Mulan understood that her **participation** was **illegal**. Therefore, she had to **disguise as a man**.

tā zài jūn duì jiē shòu le jiān kǔ de xùn liàn tiān tiān gào sù zì jǐ
她在军队接受了艰苦的**训练**，天天告诉自己：
yī dìng yào jiān qiáng bù guǎn yǒu duō nán dōu yào jiān chí xià qù
一定要**坚强**！不管有多难，都要**坚持**下去。

In the army, she received tough **training**, everyday she told herself: I must be **strong**! No matter how difficult, I shall **carry on**.

shí duō nián guò qù le huā mù lán cóng yī gè shào nǚ biàn chéng le shēn jīng
十多年过去了，花木兰从一个**少女**变成了**身经**
bǎi zhàn de jiāng jūn
百战的将军。

More than ten years later, Hua Mulan changed from a **teenager** to a very **experienced** general.

zhàn zhēng jié shù hòu huáng dì dǎ suàn jiǎng lì huā mù lán ràng tā zuò
战争**结束**后，皇帝打算**奖励**花木兰，让她做
guān kě shì tā jù jué le yīn wèi duì tā ér yán méi shén me bǐ
官。可是她**拒绝**了，因为**对**她**而言**，没什么比
huí dào jiā xiāng gèng zhòng yào
回到家乡更重要。

After the war **ended**, the emperor planned to **reward** Hua Mulan, and offered her a position as an official. But she **refused**, because **for** her, nothing was more important than returning to her hometown.

huā mù lán zhōng yú qí zhe mǎ huí dào le jiā duō nián bù jiàn tā de
花木兰**终于**骑着马回到了家。多年不见，她的
fù mǔ gèng lǎo le dì di hé mèi mei yě zhǎng dà le
父母更老了，弟弟和妹妹也**长大**了。

Hua Mulan rode her horse to return home **finally**. After all these years, her **parents** looked older, and her brother and sister also **grown up**.

dà jiā kàn jiàn tā dōu fēi cháng jī dòng hái wèi tā zhǔn bèi le shèng dà
大家看见她都非常**激动**，还为她准备了**盛大**
de tuán yuán fàn
的团圆饭。

Everyone was very **excited** to see her and prepared a **grand** reunion dinner for her.

huā mù lán huí dào le fáng jiān huàn shàng le nǚ zǐ de yī fú tā
花木兰回到了房间，**换上**了女子的衣服。她
chū mén hòu huǒ bàn men cái fā xiàn tā shì nǚ zǐ
出门后，**伙伴们**才发现她是女子！

Hua Mulan returned to her room and **changed into** women's clothes. After she went out, her **comrades** (from the battle) finally found out that she was a woman!

dà jiā yòu chī jīng yòu jī dòng měi gè rén dōu wèi tā jiāo ào hòu
大家又**吃惊**、又激动！每个人都为她**骄傲**！后
lái huā mù lán de gù shì jiù kāi shǐ dào chù chuán kāi
来，花木兰的故事就开始**到处**传开。

They were **shocked** and excited! And everyone was **proud** of her! Later, her story started to spread **everywhere**.

yī qiān duō nián guò qù le tā yī rán shì zhōng guó rén xīn zhōng zuì yǒng gǎn
一千多年过去了，她**依然**是中国人心中**最勇敢**
de nǚ yīng xióng
的女英雄。

After more than a thousand years, she is **still** the **bravest** heroine in the hearts of Chinese people.

SUMMARY

Hua Mulan (花木兰 huā mù lán) is one of the most beloved female figures from ancient China. Her bravery, **selflessness** (无私 wú sī), love for her homeland and family are in line with the great traditional values most Chinese people hold – which made her very popular throughout both ancient and modern China. Her stories are also widely presented in various films and TV dramas both in China and abroad.

你认为花木兰是个怎样的人？花木兰为什么被中国人称为伟大的女英雄？

What kind of person do you think Hua Mulan was? Why is she regarded as a great heroine by the Chinese people?

Key Vocabulary

chuán qí 传奇	*n.* *adj.*	legend legendary
jiā yù hù xiǎo 家喻户晓	*idiom*	well-known
píng jìng 平静	*adj.*	peaceful
jiā wù 家务	*n.*	housework
shēn jīng bǎi zhàn 身经百战	*idiom*	very experienced
nián líng 年龄	*n.*	age
cān yǔ 参与	*v.* *n.*	to participate participation
wéi fǎ 违法	*adj.*	illegal
nǚ bàn nán zhuāng 女扮男装	*idiom*	woman disguised as a man
xùn liàn 训练	*n.* *v.*	training to train
jiān qiáng 坚强	*adj.*	strong (mentally)
jiān chí 坚持	*v.*	to carry on
shào nǚ 少女	*n.*	teenager (female)
guī dìng 规定	*v.* *n.*	to stipulate stipulations
jiǎng lì 奖励	*v.*	to reward
jù jué 拒绝	*v.*	to refuse
shèng dà 盛大	*adj.*	grand
jiāo ào 骄傲	*n.* *adj.*	pride proud

Sentence Patterns

不是…而是…

is not … but (rather) …

不是 + *A* + **而是** + *B*

dǎ zhàng bù shì nǚ rén de shì, ér shì nán rén de shì
打仗不是女人的事，而是男人的事。

Fighting wars was not a woman's business, but a man's.

对…而言

for (someone), expressing views

duì ér yán
对 + *subject* + **而言** + *clause*

yīn wèi duì tā ér yán, méi shén me bǐ huí dào jiā xiāng gèng zhòng yào
因为对她而言，没什么比回到家乡更重要。

Because for her, nothing is more important than returning to her hometown.

CHINESE VERSION

花木兰是古代著名的传奇女英雄，她的故事在中国家喻户晓。

很久以前，在一个小村子里，花木兰和家人过着平静的生活。她和普通女子一样，每天织布、做家务。

可是，有一天，政府来招兵，规定每个家庭都得出一个男子上战场。

花木兰的父亲年龄很大，身体不好。加上弟弟年龄太小，她再三考虑后，决定自己去战场。

在古代，打仗不是女人的事，而是男人的事。花木兰明白自己的参与是违法的。因此，她不得不女扮男装。

她在军队接受了艰苦的训练，天天告诉自己：一定要坚强！不管有多难，都要坚持下去。

十多年过去了，花木兰从一个少女变成了身经百战的将军。

战争结束后，皇帝打算奖励花木兰，让她做官。可是她拒绝了，因为对她而言，没什么比回到家乡更重要。

花木兰终于骑着马回到了家。多年不见，她的父母更老了，弟弟和妹妹也长大了。

大家看见她都非常激动，还为她准备了盛大的团圆饭。

花木兰回到了房间，换上了女子的衣服。她出门后，伙伴们才发现她是女子！

大家又吃惊、又激动！每个人都为她骄傲！后来，花木兰的故事就开始到处传开。

一千多年过去了，她依然是中国人心中最勇敢的女英雄。

mèng jiāng nǚ kū cháng chéng

孟姜女哭长城

Lady Meng Jiang Cried the Great Wall

qín cháo shí qī zài yī gè xiǎo cūn zǐ lǐ yǒu gè shàn liáng měi lì de nián qīng nǚ zi jiào mèng jiāng nǚ

秦朝时期，在一个**小村子**里，有个**善良美丽**的年轻女子叫孟姜女。

During the Qin Dynasty, in a **small village**, there was a **kind and beautiful** young woman named Meng Jiangnu.

yī tiān tā zài yuàn zi lǐ xǐ yī fú tū rán fā xiàn dà shù xià cáng le yī gè nán rén xià le tā yī tiào

一天，她在院子里**洗衣服**，突然发现大树下**藏**了一个男人，**吓了她一跳**。

One day, when she was **doing laundry** in her yard, she suddenly found a man **hiding** under the tree, which **startled** her.

nà gè rén mǎ shàng xiàng tā zhāo shǒu shuō qǐng nǐ jiù jiù wǒ ba wǒ jiào fàn xǐ liáng shì lái táo nàn de

那个人马上向她**招手**，说："请你救救我吧！我叫范喜良，是来**逃难**的。"

The man immediately **waved** to her and said, "Please save me! My name is Fan Xiliang, and I'm here to **escape**."

yuán lái qín shǐ huáng wèi le jiàn cháng chéng dào chù zhuā rén yī fāng miàn yào gōng rén gàn zhòng huó lìng yī fāng miàn yòng chāo cháng gōng zuò shí jiān zhé mó tā men

原来秦始皇为了建**长城**到处抓人，**一方面**要工人干重活，**另一方面**用超长工作时间折磨他们。

It turned out that Emperor Qin Shihuang was arresting people everywhere in order to build the **Great Wall**. **On one hand**, workers were required to do heavy labour, **on the other hand** they were tortured with long working hours.

dào mù qián wéi zhǐ yǐ jīng dǎo zhì hěn duō rén bèi è sǐ lèi sǐ le
到目前为止，已经**导致**很多人被饿死、累死了。
mèng jiāng nǚ hěn tóng qíng tā bìng qiě ràng fàn xǐ liáng zàn shí zhù zài tā jiā
孟姜女很同情他，**并且**让范喜良暂时住在她家。

So far, it had **resulted in** many people starving and exhausting to death. Meng Jiangnu sympathized with him **and** let Fan Xiliang live in her house for the time being.

fàn xǐ liáng yòu lǎo shí yòu qín láo lián mèng jiāng nǚ de fù mǔ yě hěn xǐ
范喜良又**老实**又**勤劳**，连孟姜女的父母也很喜
huān tā hěn kuài fàn xǐ liáng hé mèng jiāng nǚ jiù xiāng ài le fù mǔ
欢他。很快，范喜良和孟姜女就**相爱**了，父母
tóng yì hòu tā men jié hūn le
同意后，他们**结婚**了。

Fan Xiliang was **honest** and **hardworking**, even Meng Jiaonu's parents liked him. Soon, Fan Xiliang and Meng Jiangnu **fell in love**. After their parents agreed, they **got married**.

kě shì hūn lǐ hòu de dì sān tiān yǒu yī qún shì bīng tū rán chōng jìn
可是，**婚礼**后的第三天，有一群士兵突然**冲进**
jiā lǐ zhuā le fàn xǐ liáng qù cháng chéng gàn huó
家里，抓了范喜良去长城**干活**。

However, on the third day after the **wedding**, a group of soldiers suddenly **rushed into** the house and arrested Fan Xiliang to take him to **work** on the Great Wall.

mèng jiāng nǚ shāng xīn jí le zhǐ néng zài jiā děng zhàng fū de xiāo xi kě
孟姜女伤心极了，只能在家等丈夫的**消息**，可
shì yī zhí děng bù dào
是**一直**等不到。

Meng Jiangnu was extremely sad and could only wait for **news** of her husband at home, but **always** nothing came.

yú shì tā jué dìng qīn zì qù cháng chéng zhǎo zhàng fū tā cháng tú bá shè
于是，她决定**亲自**去长城找**丈夫**。她**长途跋涉**
jǐ gè yuè hòu zhōng yú zǒu dào le cháng chéng
，几个月后终于走到了长城。

So she decided to go to the Great Wall **in person** to find her **husband**. She **traveled long distances** and finally made it to the Great Wall after a few months.

tā qù le hěn duō gè gōng dì kě shì réng rán zhǎo bù dào zhàng fū
她去了很多个**工地**，可是**仍然**找不到丈夫。
dàn tā bù fàng qì tiān tiān zài cháng chéng dǎ tīng
但她不**放弃**，天天在长城**打听**。

She went to many **construction sites**, but **still** could not find her husband. But she didn't **give up**, and **inquired** at the Great Wall every day.

zhōng yú yǒu yī tiān, yī gè gōng rén gào sù tā: "duì, wǒ rèn shi
终于有一天，一个工人告诉她："对，我认识
fàn xǐ liáng. tā yǐ jīng sǐ le, jiù mái zài cháng chéng jiǎo xià."
范喜良。他已经死了，就**埋在**长城脚下。"

Finally one day, a worker told her: "Yes, I know Fan Xiliang. He is dead and **buried at** the foot of the Great Wall."

mèng jiāng nǚ yòu zhèn jīng, yòu jué wàng, kū zhe qù le cháng chéng jiǎo xià.
孟姜女又**震惊**，又**绝望**，哭着去了长城脚下。
tā guì zài nà lǐ, fǔ mō zhe bīng lěng de shí jiē, bù zhī dào zhàng fū
她**跪**在那里，**抚摸**着冰冷的石阶，不知道丈夫
de shī tǐ zài nǎ kuài shí jiē xià.
的尸体在哪块**石阶**下。

Meng Jiangnu was **shocked** and **desperate**, she walked crying to the foot of the Great Wall. She **knelt** there, **touching** the cold stone steps, not knowing which **stone steps** had her husband's body buried underneath.

tā tòng kǔ jí le, bào zhe shí jiē dà kū qǐ lái, yī zhí kū le sān
她**痛苦**极了，抱着石阶**大哭**起来，一直哭了三
tiān sān yè.
天三夜。

She was in so much **pain** that she hugged the stone steps **crying heavily** for three days and three nights.

zhè shí, tiān tū rán àn le, guā qǐ le hěn dà de fēng, tū rán,
这时，天突然**暗**了，刮起了很大的风，突然，
yī duàn cháng chéng dǎo le, lù chū le fàn xǐ liáng de shī tǐ.
一段长城**倒**了，**露出**了范喜良的尸体。

At this time, the sky suddenly became **dark**, and there was a strong wind, suddenly, a part of the Great Wall **collapsed**, **revealing** Fan Xiliang's body.

mèng jiāng nǚ zǒu guò qù, tā zhōng yú kàn dào le zì jǐ de zhàng fū, zhǐ
孟姜女**走过去**，她终于看到了自己的丈夫，**只**
shì, tā zài yě kàn bù dào tā le.
是，他再也看不到她了。

Meng Jiangnu **walked over**, she finally saw her husband, **however** he couldn't see her anymore.

SUMMARY

Lady Meng Jiang Cried the Great Wall (孟姜女哭长城) is a heartbreaking story that is related to historical facts behind the construction of the Great Wall, which was originally built under the orders of the most hated tyrant emperor Qin Shihuang, to strengthen the country's defense system. Because of his cruelty, countless men were forced to over-work and die for this ambitious project. But Lady Meng's story is one of outstanding loyalty, love and perseverance.

你认为孟姜女是个怎样的人？你觉得她和范喜良的悲剧是可以避免的吗？为什么？

What kind of person do you think Meng Jiangnu was? Do you think the tragedy between her and Fan Xiliang could be avoided? Why?

CULTURE CORNER

Emperor Qin Shihuang (秦始皇) was the founder of the Qin dynasty and the first emperor of a unified China. He is remembered today as one of the most significant figures in Chinese history, having made significant contributions to the development of China as a centralized state and a powerful empire, including many achievements in government, military, and infrastructure. But he is also known for his harsh rule and the brutal methods he used to maintain his power, such as the suppression of dissent and the creation of a vast network of spies. His mausoleum near Xi'an houses the famous **Terracotta Army** (兵马俑), the discovery of which in 1974 was hailed as one of the greatest of the 20th century. It is now a major tourist attraction and one of China's most famous cultural landmarks, attracting millions of visitors each year to the site.

Key Vocabulary

shàn liáng 善良	*adj.*	kind-hearted	qín láo 勤劳	*adj.*	diligent
měi lì 美丽	*adj.*	beautiful	jié hūn 结婚	*v.*	to get married
cáng 藏	*v.*	to hide	hūn lǐ 婚礼	*n.*	wedding
zhāo shǒu 招手	*v.*	to wave	xiāo xi 消息	*n.*	news/ message
táo nàn 逃难	*v.*	to escape (from disasters)	qīn zì 亲自	*adv.*	in-person/ personally
dǎo zhì 导致	*v.*	to result in	cháng tú bá shè 长途跋涉	*idiom*	travel long distances
tóng qíng 同情	*v.*	to sympathize	dǎ tīng 打听	*v.*	to inquire
zàn shí 暂时	*n.*	temporary/ for the time being	jué wàng 绝望	*adj.*	desperate

Sentence Patterns

一方面… 另一方面…

on one hand ... on the other hand ...

yī fāng miàn　lìng yī fāng miàn
一方面 + *A* + 另一方面 + *B*

yī fāng miàn yào gōng rén gàn zhòng huó, lìng yī fāng miàn yòng chāo cháng gōng zuò shí jiān zhé mó tā men
一方面要工人干重活，另一方面用超长工作时间折磨他们。

On one hand, workers are required to do heavy labour, on the other hand they were tortured with long working hours.

… 并且 …

and/plus/moreover

bìng qiě
subject + verb phrase 1 + 并 (且) *+ verb phrase 2*

mèng jiāng nǚ hěn tóng qíng tā, bìng qiě ràng fàn xǐ liáng zàn shí zhù zài tā jiā
孟姜女很同情他，并且让范喜良暂时住在她家。

Meng Jiangnu sympathized with him and let Fan Xiliang live in her house for the time being.

Chinese Version

秦朝时期，在一个小村子里，有个善良美丽的年轻女子叫孟姜女。

一天，她在院子里洗衣服，突然发现大树下藏了一个男人，吓了她一跳。

那个人马上向她招手，说："请你救救我吧！我叫范喜良，是来逃难的。"

原来秦始皇为了建长城到处抓人，一方面要工人干重活，另一方面用超长工作时间折磨他们。

到目前为止，已经导致很多人被饿死、累死了。孟姜女很同情他，并且让范喜良暂时住在她家。

范喜良又老实又勤劳, 连孟姜女的父母也很喜欢他。很快，范喜良和孟姜女就相爱了, 父母同意后，他们结婚了。

可是，婚礼后的第三天，有一群士兵突然冲进家里，抓了范喜良去长城干活。

孟姜女伤心极了，只能在家等丈夫的消息，可是一直等不到。

于是，她决定亲自去长城找丈夫。她长途跋涉，几个月后终于走到了长城。

她去了很多个工地，可是仍然找不到丈夫。但她不放弃，天天在长城打听。

终于有一天，一个工人告诉她："对，我认识范喜良。他已经死了，就埋在长城脚下。"

孟姜女又震惊，又绝望，哭着去了长城脚下。她跪在那里，抚摸着冰冷的石阶，不知道丈夫的尸体在哪块石阶下。

她痛苦极了，抱着石阶大哭起来，一直哭了三天三夜。

这时，天突然暗了，刮起了很大的风，突然，一段长城倒了，露出了 范喜良的尸体。

孟姜女走过去，她终于看到了自己的丈夫，只是，他再也看不到她了。

táng bó hǔ diǎn qiū xiāng

唐伯虎点秋香

The Flirting Scholar

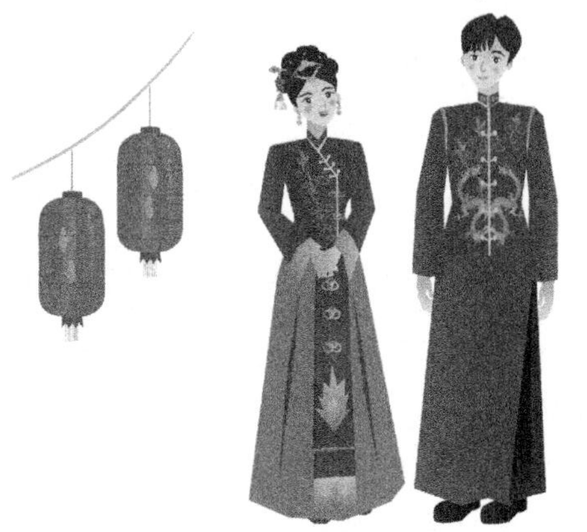

táng bó hǔ shì míng cháo zhù míng de huà jiā shū fǎ jiā hé shī rén tā fēng liú xiāo sǎ shì jiāng nán sì dà cái zǐ zhī yī

唐伯虎是明朝著名的**画家**，**书法**家和诗人。他**风流潇洒**，是江南**四大才子**之一。

Tang Bohu was a famous **painter**, **calligrapher** and poet of the Ming Dynasty. He was **romantic and unrestrained**, and was one of the **four great talents** in south China.

yī cì tā zài lù biān kàn dào yī gè nǚ zǐ zài gěi yī qún qǐ gài sòng shí wù tā hěn gǎn dòng zǒu jìn yī kàn nà nǚ zǐ tái tóu duì tā xiào le xiào

一次，他在路边看到一个女子在给一群**乞丐**送食物。他很**感动**，走近一看，那女子**抬头**对他笑了笑。

Once, on the road he saw a woman delivering food to a group of **beggars**. He was very **moved**, and when he got closer, the woman **looked up** and smiled at him.

táng bó hǔ xīn lǐ yī nuǎn xīn xiǎng yuán lái zhè shì jiè shàng zuì měi de xiào róng shì chōng mǎn ài xīn de xiào róng

唐伯虎心里一**暖**，心想：原来，这世界上最美的**笑容**是充满**爱心**的笑容！

Tang Bohu felt **warm** at heart and thought: It turns out that the most beautiful **smile** in the world is a smile full of **compassion**!

hòu lái táng bó hǔ duì nǚ zi rì sī yè xiǎng dào chù dǎ tīng cái zhī dào nǚ zǐ jiào qiū xiāng shì huà jiā de shì nǚ

后来，唐伯虎对女子**日思夜想**，到处**打听**才知道女子叫秋香，是华家的**侍女**。

Later, Tang Bohu was **thinking** of the woman **day and night**, and when he **inquired** around, he found out that the woman's name was Qiuxiang, and was a **maid** of the Hua family.

zhǐ shì huà jiā shì dà guān rén jiā, fáng zi tài dà, yòu yǒu tài duō shì nǚ hé pú rén. wèi le jiàn dào qiū xiāng, tā bì xū xiǎng bàn fǎ jìn rù huà jiā.

只是华家是**大官人家**，房子太大，又有太多**侍女**和**仆人**。为了见到秋香，他**必须**想办法进入华家。

It's just that the Hua family was a **noble family,** their house is too big, and there are too many **maids** and **servants**. In order to see Qiuxiang, he **must** find a way to enter the Hua family.

yú shì, tā gǎi le míng zì, huà zhuāng chéng yī gè qióng shū shēng, qù huà jiā yìng pìn zhù jiào, fù zé péi huà tài shī de liǎng gè ér zi dú shū.

于是，他改了名字，**化妆**成一个穷书生，去华家**应聘**助教，**负责**陪华太师的两个儿子读书。

So he changed his name, **dressed up** as a poor scholar, and went to the Hua family to **apply** to be a teaching assistant, **responsible for** accompanying the two sons of Lord Hua to study.

kě xī liǎng gè ér zi dú shū bù rèn zhēn, shí ér wán lè, shí ér dǎ dǔn, lǎo shī bù jǐn bù guǎn, hái ràng táng bó hǔ yě bié guǎn.

可惜两个儿子读书不**认真**，**时而**玩乐，**时而**打盹，老师不仅不**管**，还让唐伯虎也别管。

Unfortunately, the two sons didn't study **seriously**, **sometimes** they played aroud, **sometimes** they dozed off. The teacher not only didn't **care**, but also asked Tang Bohu not to care.

yī cì, huà tài shī yào kǎo tā de liǎng gè ér zi duì lián, kàn jiàn yuán zi lǐ de guǒ shù, jiù shuō: pú yè táo yè pú táo yè, cǎo běn mù běn.

一次，华太师要**考**他的两个儿子**对联**，看见园子里的**果树**，就说：蒲叶桃叶葡萄叶，草本木本。

Once, when Lord Hua wanted to **test** his two sons' **couplets matching**, when he saw the **fruit trees** in the garden, he said: Pu leaves, peach leaves, grape leaves, with herbs and woods.

kě shì liǎng gè ér zi dōu huí dá bù chū. yī páng de lǎo shī jiù gēn tài shī shuō: "nín de duì lián tài gāo jí le, jí shǐ shì zhuān jiā yě duì bù chū."

可是两个儿子都**回答不出**。一旁的老师就跟太师说："您的对联太**高级**了，即使是**专家**也对不出。"

However both sons were **unable to answer**. The teacher on the side said to Lord Hua: "Your couplet line is too **advanced**, even **experts** are unable to match it."

zhè shí táng bó hǔ jiù rěn bù zhù xiào le shēng huá tài shī hěn shēng qì
这时唐伯虎就**忍不住**笑了声。华太师很**生气**，
jiù wèn nǐ xiào shén me
就问："你笑什么？"

At this time, Tang Bohu **couldn't help** laughing out. Lord Hua was very **angry** and asked, "What are you laughing at?"

táng bó hǔ shuō nín bié shēng qì wǒ lái shì yī shì zhè shí qiū
唐伯虎说："您别生气，我来试一试。"这时秋
xiāng pèng qiǎo cóng yuán zi jīng guò
香**碰巧**从园子经过。

Tang Bohu said, "Don't be angry, I'll give it a try." At this time, Qiuxiang **happened to** pass by the garden.

táng bó hǔ kàn zhe qiū xiāng hé zhōu wéi de huā jiù huí dá méi huā
唐伯虎看着秋香和**周围**的花，就回答："梅花
guì huā méi guī huā chūn xiāng qiū xiāng
桂花玫瑰花，春香**秋香**！"

Tang Bohu looked at Qiuxiang and flowers **around**, replied, "Plum blossoms, sweet-scented osmanthus, roses, with spring fragrance and **autumn fragrance** (Qiuxiang's name)!"

huà tài shī tīng le hěn gāo xìng fēi cháng xīn shǎng tā mǎ shàng jiě gù le
华太师听了很高兴，非常**欣赏**他，马上**解雇**了
nà wèi lǎo shī ràng táng bó hǔ dài tì
那位老师，让唐伯虎**代替**。

Lord Hua was very happy to hear it, and **admired** him very much, he immediately **dismissed** the teacher and **replaced** him with Tang Bohu.

hòu lái liǎng gè ér zi zài táng bó hǔ de zhǐ dǎo xià xué xí jìn bù de
后来，两个儿子**在**唐伯虎的**指导下**学习进步得
fēi cháng kuài
非常快。

Later, **under the guidance of** Tang Bohu, the two sons made great progress in their studies.

huá tài shī wèi le gǎn xiè tā jiù zhǎo le shí gè piào liàng de shì nǚ ràng
华太师为了**感谢**他，就找了十个漂亮的侍女让
táng bó hǔ xuǎn dāng qī zi táng bó hǔ lì kè xuǎn le qiū xiāng
唐伯虎选当**妻子**，唐伯虎**立刻**选了秋香。

In order to **thank** him, Lord Hua found ten beautiful maids for Tang Bohu to choose as his **wife**, and Tang Bohu **immediately** chose Qiuxiang.

dào le jié hūn dāng tiān táng bó hǔ cái xiàng dà jiā biǎo míng le zhēn zhèng de
到了结婚当天，唐伯虎才向大家**表明**了真正的
shēn fèn jǐn guǎn dà jiā hěn jīng yà dàn shì dōu hěn wèi tā gāo xìng
身份，**尽管**大家很惊讶，**但是**都很为他高兴。

On the wedding day, Tang Bohu finally **revealed** his true **identity** to everyone. **Despite** everyone being surprised, (but) they were very happy for him.

Summary

The **Flirting Scholar** (唐伯虎点秋香) is one of the most famous Chinese folk tales, even in modern China, the story has been frequently retold through shows and films, ranking as one of the best Chinese comedies. Also known as **Tang Yin** (唐寅), he was one of the most notable painters in the history of Chinese art. One of his paintings was sold for $275,000 in an art auction in New York in 2012.

你认为唐伯虎是个怎样的人？你怎么看待他追求秋香的手段？

What kind of person do you think Tang Bohu was? What do you think of his method of chasing Qiuxiang?

Culture Corner

duì lián
对联 or matching couplets originated in the Five Dynasties era (907-979 AD) of China and gained in popularity and relevance in the later Ming and Qing dynasties. You can often see duilian in China today written on red paper and stuck on either side of doors and entryways, particularly around Lantern and Spring Festival. As in the story, a popular competition is that of dueling duilian, whereby one person composes the first part, with a second person having to complete the couplet with something that not only matches in theme and has the same number of characters but also with each character pair being related in meaning, as well as rules regarding the tones. It is certainly a great challenge of intellect, linguistic mastery, and wit.

Key Vocabulary

huà jiā 画家	*n.*	painter	fù zé 负责	*v.*	be responsible for
qǐ gài 乞丐	*n.*	beggar	kǎo 考	*v.*	to test
xiào róng 笑容	*n.*	smile	duì lián 对联	*n.*	couplets matching
ài xīn 爱心	*n.*	compassion	zhuān jiā 专家	*n.*	expert
rì sī yè xiǎng 日思夜想	*idiom*	to think day and night	rěn bù zhù 忍不住	*vp.*	cannot bear/ resist
bì xū 必须	*adv.*	have to	jiě gù 解雇	*v.*	to dismiss
huà zhuāng 化妆	*v.*	to make up/ dress up	biǎo míng 表明	*v.*	to revel/ indicate
yīng pìn 应聘	*v.*	to apply (jobs)	shēn fèn 身份	*n.*	identity
fēng liú xiāo sǎ 风流潇洒	*idiom*	romantic and unrestrained (man)	kě xī 可惜	*adv.*	it's a pity/ unfortunately

Sentence Patterns

时而…时而…

sometimes ... sometimes ...

shí ér　shí ér
时而 + *A* + **时而** + *B*

liǎng gè ér zi shí ér wán lè， shí ér dǎ dǔn
两个儿子时而玩乐，时而打盹。

The two sons sometimes play aroud, sometimes doze off.

尽管…但是…

despite ... (but) ...

jǐn guǎn　dàn shì
尽管 + *clause 1* + **但是** + *clause 2*

jǐn guǎn dà jiā hěn jīng yà， dàn shì dōu hěn wèi tā gāo xìng
尽管大家很惊讶，但是都很为他高兴。

Although everyone was surprised, (but) they were very happy for him.

Chinese Version

唐伯虎是明朝著名的画家，书法家和诗人。他风流潇洒，是江南四大才子之一。

一次，他在路边看到一个女子在给一群乞丐送食物。他很感动，走近一看，那女子抬头对他笑了笑。

唐伯虎心里一暖，心想：原来，这世界上最美的笑容是充满爱心的笑容！

后来，唐伯虎对女子日思夜想，到处打听才知道女子叫秋香，是华家的侍女。

只是华家是大官人家，房子太大，又有太多侍女和仆人。为了见到秋香，他必须想办法进入华家。

于是，他改了名字，化妆成一个穷书生，去华家应聘助教，负责陪华太师的两个儿子读书。

可惜两个儿子读书不认真，时而玩乐，时而打盹，老师不仅不管，还让唐伯虎也别管。

一次，华太师要考他的两个儿子对联，看见园子里的果树，就说：蒲叶桃叶葡萄叶，草本木本。

可是两个儿子都回答不出。一旁的老师就跟太师说："您的对联太高级了，即使是专家也对不出。"

这时唐伯虎就忍不住笑了声。华太师很生气，就问："你笑什么？"

唐伯虎说："您别生气，我来试一试。" 这时秋香碰巧从园子经过。

唐伯虎看着秋香和周围的花，就回答："梅花桂花玫瑰花，春香秋香!"

华太师听了很高兴，非常欣赏他，马上解雇了那位老师，让唐伯虎代替。

后来，两个儿子在唐伯虎的指导下学习进步得非常快。

华太师为了感谢他，就找了十个漂亮的侍女让唐伯虎选当妻子，唐伯虎立刻选了秋香。

到了结婚当天，唐伯虎才向大家表明了真正的身份，尽管大家很惊讶，但是都很为他高兴。

liáng shān bó yǔ zhù yīng tái

梁山伯与祝英台

The Butterfly Lovers

cóng qián yǒu gè cōng míng piāo liàng de nǚ hái jiào zhù yīng tái, yóu yú shì nǚ zi, zhǐ néng zài jiā shàng xué.

从前有个**聪明漂亮**的女孩叫祝英台，**由于**是女子，**只**能在家上学。

Once upon a time, there was a **smart and beautiful** girl named Zhu Yingtai. **Because** she was female, she could **only** attend school at home.

hòu lái, zài tā bù duàn yāo qiú xià, fù mǔ yǔn xǔ tā nǚ bàn nán zhuāng qù le xué xiào shàng xué.

后来，在她**不断**要求下，父母允许她**女扮男装**去了学校上学。

Later, at her **constant** request, her parents allowed her to go to school, but **disguised as a man**.

zài xué xiào lǐ, zhù yīng tái rèn shi le tóng xué liáng shān bó. liáng shān bó bù jǐn shì xué xiào lǐ zuì yōu xiù de xué shēng, ér qiě qiān xū yǒu lǐ.

在学校里，祝英台认识了**同学**梁山伯。梁山伯不仅是学校里**最优秀**的学生，而且**谦虚有礼**。

At school, Zhu Yingtai met her **classmate** Liang Shanbo. Liang Shanbo was not only the **most excellent** student in the school, but also **modest and polite**.

hěn kuài, tā men jiù chéng wéi le zuì hǎo de péng yǒu. màn màn de, zhù yīng tái ài shàng le liáng shān bó, cháng cháng jiàn jiē xiàng tā biǎo bái.

很快，他们就成为了最好的朋友。**慢慢地**，祝英台**爱上**了梁山伯，常常**间接**向他表白。

Soon, they became best friends. **Gradually**, Zhu Yingtai **fell in love with** Liang Shanbo and often confessed to him **indirectly**.

kě shì, liáng shān bó yǐ wéi zhù yīng tái shì nán zǐ, suī rán duì tā yǒu hǎo gǎn, què jiǎ zhuāng bù míng bái.

可是，梁山伯**以为**祝英台是男子，虽然对她有好感，却**假装**不明白。

However, Liang Shanbo **thought** that Zhu Yingtai was a man. Although he felt for her, he **pretended** not to understand.

yī cì, tā men qù jiāo wài sàn bù, zhù yīng tái duì tā shuō: "rú guǒ yǒu yī gè hé wǒ yī mó yī yàng de nǚ zǐ chū xiàn le, nǐ huì ài shàng tā ma?"

一次，他们去**郊外**散步，祝英台对他说：“如果有一个和我**一模一样**的女子**出现**了，你会爱上她吗？”

Once, when they went for a walk in the **suburbs**, Zhu Yingtai said to him, "If a woman **exactly the same** with me **appeared**, would you fall in love with her?"

liáng shān bó liǎn hóng le, tā bù hǎo yì si de xiào le xiào, shuō: "dāng rán! zhè huì shì wǒ de fú qì."

梁山伯**脸红**了，他**不好意思**地笑了笑，说：“当然！这会是我的**福气**。”

Liang Shanbo **blushed**, he smiled **sheepishly** and said, “Of course! This will be my **blessing**.”

hòu lái tā men bì yè le. zài fēn kāi de nà tiān, zhù yīng tái zhōng yú gǔ qǐ yǒng qì gào sù liáng shān bó tā shì nǚ zǐ.

后来他们**毕业**了。在**分开**的那天，祝英台终于**鼓起勇气**告诉梁山伯她是女子。

They later **graduated**. On the day of **parting**, Zhu Yingtai finally **summoned up the courage** to tell Liang Shanbo that she was a woman.

liáng shān bó yòu chī jīng yòu kāi xīn. tā men sī xià jué dìng yào yǒng yuǎn zài yī qǐ, liáng shān bó yě chéng nuò zhù yīng tái huì qù tā jiā tí qīn.

梁山伯又**吃惊**又开心。他们**私下**决定要**永远**在一起，梁山伯也**承诺**祝英台会去她家**提亲**。

Liang Shanbo was **shocked** and happy. They **privately** decided to be together **forever**, Liang Shanbo also **promised** to Zhu Yingtai that he would go to her home to **propose marriage**.

jǐ gè yuè hòu, liáng shān bó dài zhe lǐ wù qù le zhù yīng tái jiā, kě zhù yīng tái de fù mǔ kàn bù qǐ tā zhè gè qióng xué shēng, jù jué le tā.

几个月后，梁山伯带着**礼物**去了祝英台家，可祝英台的父母**看不起**他这个穷学生，**拒绝**了他。

A few months later, Liang Shanbo went to Zhu Yingtai's house with **gifts**, but Zhu Yingtai's parents **looked down on** him as a poor student, so **rejected** him.

gèng zāo gāo de shì tā men yǐ jīng wèi zhù yīng tái zhǎo le yī wèi guān yuán de ér zi hěn kuài jiù huì jié hūn

更糟糕的是，他们已经为祝英台找了一位**官员**的儿子，很快就会结婚。

To make matters worse, they had found an **official**'s son for Zhu Yingtai, and they will be married soon.

liáng shān bó shòu bù liǎo dǎ jī yī huí jiā jiù shēng bìng le tā xiǎng jì rán bù néng hé zhù yīng tái jié hūn zì jǐ jiù zhōng shēn bù qǔ

梁山伯受不了**打击**，一回家就生病了。他想：**既然**不能和祝英台结婚，自己**就**终身不娶。

Liang Shanbo couldn't stand the **blow** and fell ill as soon as he returned home. He thought: **Since** he can't marry Zhu Yingtai, **then** he himself will not marry for the rest of his life.

zhù yīng tái yě bèi fù mǔ guān zài jiā lǐ tā xiě le yī fēng xìn gěi liáng shān bó gào sù tā bù lùn shēng sǐ tā zhǐ huì jià gěi tā

祝英台也被父母**关**在家里，她写了**一封信**给梁山伯，告诉他：**不论**生死，她**只**会嫁给他。

Zhu Yingtai was also **locked** at home by her parents. She wrote **a letter** to Liang Shanbo, telling him that **regardless of** life or death, she would **only** marry him.

liáng shān bó fēi cháng sī niàn zhù yīng tái bìng qíng yě yuè lái yuè yán zhòng yī gè yuè hòu sǐ le zhù yīng tái zhī dào hòu kū le jǐ tiān gǎn jué zì jǐ de xīn chè dǐ suì le

梁山伯非常**思念**祝英台，**病情**也越来越**严重**，一个月后死了。祝英台知道后哭了几天，感觉自己的心彻底**碎**了。

Liang Shanbo **missed** Zhu Yingtai very much, and his **condition** became more and more **severe**, and died a month later. After Zhu Yingtai found out, she cried for several days, feeling that her heart was thoroughly **broken**.

zài tā bèi fù mǔ bī qù hūn lǐ de lù shàng tā gù yì ràng duì wǔ zài liáng shān bó de mù qián tíng xià

在她被父母**逼**去婚礼的路上，她**故意**让队伍在梁山伯的**墓**前停下。

On the way to the wedding **forced** by her parents, she **deliberately** asked her entourage team to stop at Liang Shanbo's **tomb**.

jiē zhe tā tuō xià le hóng sè de xīn niáng zhuāng chuān zhe bái yī zǒu dào le liáng shān bó de mù bēi

接着，她脱下了红色的**新娘装**，穿着白衣走到了梁山伯的**墓碑**。

Then, she took off her red **bridal dress** and walked to Liang Shanbo's **tombstone** in white.

tā yī biān liú lèi, yī biān fǔ mō zhe liáng shān bó de míng zì, rán hòu
她一边流泪，一边**抚摸**着梁山伯的名字，然后
tā ná dāo huá le shǒu zhǐ, yòng xuě zài mù bēi shàng xiě xià zì jǐ de míng
她拿刀**划**了手指，用**血**在墓碑上写下自己的名
zì
字。

While weeping, she **touched** Liang Shanbo's name, then she **scratched** her finger with a knife and wrote her name on the tombstone with **blood**.

zhè shí, tū rán guā qǐ le dà fēng, yī zhèn léi shēng hòu, liáng shān bó
这时，突然刮起了**大风**，一阵**雷声**后，梁山伯
de mù mén dǎ kāi le. zhù yīng tái kàn dào le liáng shān bó, jiù tiào le
的墓门打开了。祝英台看到了梁山伯，就**跳了**
xià qù, mù mén yě mǎ shàng guān le
下去，墓门也马上关了。

At this time, a **strong wind** suddenly blew, and after a burst of **thunder**, the door of Liang Shanbo's tomb opened. When Zhu Yingtai saw Liang Shanbo, she **jumped down**, and the door of the tomb closed immediately.

rán hòu, tiān biàn qíng le, chū xiàn le cǎi hóng, yǒu liǎng zhī hú dié cóng
然后，天变晴了，出现了**彩虹**，有两只**蝴蝶**从
mù mén fēi chū. dà jiā dōu shuō zhè shì tā men, tā men zhōng yú zài yī
墓门飞出。大家都说这是他们，他们终于**在一**
qǐ le
起了。

Then, the sky became clear, a **rainbow** appeared, and two **butterflies** flew out of the tomb door. Everyone say that it's them and they're finally **together**.

SUMMARY

The **Butterfly Lovers** (梁山伯与祝英台) is the top Chinese tragic love story and is often referred to as the Eastern Romeo and Juliet. In ancient China, marriages were arranged by parents and free-willing relationships were rare. Even in modern China, it is common for parents to try to intervene in their children's relationships and marriages. For many Chinese people, the in-law relationships are still one of the hardest to handle, which still contributes to the rising **divorce rate** (离(lí)婚(hūn)率(lǜ)) in modern China.

你认为梁山伯和祝英台分别是怎样的人？对于他们选择以殉情的代价在一起，**你有什么看法？**

What kind of people do you think Liang Shanbo and Zhu Yingtai were respectively? Regarding their choice to be together with the price of death, **what's your view?**

Key Vocabulary

bù duàn 不断	*adv.*	continue/ constant	kàn bù qǐ 看不起	*vp.*	look down on
yōu xiù 优秀	*adj.*	excellent	jù jué 拒绝	*v.*	to reject
qiān xū yǒu lǐ 谦虚有礼	*idiom*	modest and polite	dǎ jī 打击	*n.*	blow
jiàn jiē 间接	*adj.*	indirect	sī niàn 思念	*v.*	to miss/ yearn
yǐ wéi 以为	*v.*	believe/think (wrongly)	yán zhòng 严重	*adj.*	severe
yī mó yī yàng 一模一样	*idiom*	exactly the same	liǎn hóng 脸红	*v.*	to blush
zhōng shēn bù qǔ 终身不娶	*vp.*	to stay unmarried for life (for men)	jiǎ zhuāng 假装	*v.*	to pretend

Sentence Patterns

既然… 就…

since … then …

jì rán 既然 + *condition* + jiù 就 + *result*

tā xiǎng: jì rán bù néng hé zhù yīng tái jié hūn, zì jǐ jiù zhōng shēn bù qǔ.
他想：既然不能和祝英台结婚，自己就终身不娶。

He thought: Since he can't marry Zhu Yingtai, then he himself will not marry for the rest of his life.

不论… 只…

regardless … would only …

bù lùn 不论 + *condition* + zhǐ 只 + *result*

tā gào sù tā: bù lùn shēng sǐ, tā zhǐ huì jià gěi tā.
她告诉他：不论生死，她只会嫁给他。

She told him: regardless of life or death, she would only marry him.

Chinese Version

从前有个聪明漂亮的女孩叫祝英台，由于是女子，只能在家上学。

后来，在她不断要求下，父母允许她女扮男装去了学校上学。

在学校里，祝英台认识了同学梁山伯。梁山伯不仅是学校里最优秀的学生，而且谦虚有礼。

很快，他们就成为了最好的朋友。慢慢地，祝英台爱上了梁山伯，常常间接向他表白。

可是，梁山伯以为祝英台是男子，虽然对她有好感，却假装不明白。

一次，他们去郊外散步，祝英台对他说："如果有一个和我一模一样的女子出现了，你会爱上她吗？"

梁山伯脸红了，他不好意思地笑了笑，说："当然！这会是我的福气。"

后来他们毕业了。在分开的那天，祝英台终于鼓起勇气告诉梁山伯她是女子。

梁山伯又吃惊又开心。他们私下决定要永远在一起，梁山伯也承诺祝英台会去她家提亲。

几个月后，梁山伯带着礼物去了祝英台家，可祝英台的父母看不起他这个穷学生，拒绝了他。

更糟糕的是，他们已经为祝英台找了一位官员的儿子，很快就会结婚。

梁山伯受不了打击，一回家就生病了。他想：既然不能和祝英台结婚，自己就终身不娶。

祝英台也被父母关在家里，她写了一封信给梁山伯，告诉他：不论生死，她只会嫁给他。

梁山伯非常思念祝英台，病情也越来越严重，一个月后死了。祝英台知道后哭了几天，感觉自己的心彻底碎了。

在她被父母逼去婚礼的路上，她故意让队伍在梁山伯的墓前停下。

接着，她脱下了红色的新娘装，穿着白衣走到了梁山伯的墓碑。

她一边流泪，一边抚摸着梁山伯的名字，然后她拿刀划了手指，用血在墓碑上写下自己的名字。

这时，突然刮起了大风，一阵雷声后，梁山伯的墓门打开了。祝英台看到了梁山伯，就跳了下去，墓门也马上关了。

然后，天变晴了，出现了彩虹，有两只蝴蝶从墓门飞出。大家都说这是他们，他们终于在一起了。

The Four Beauties of China

sì

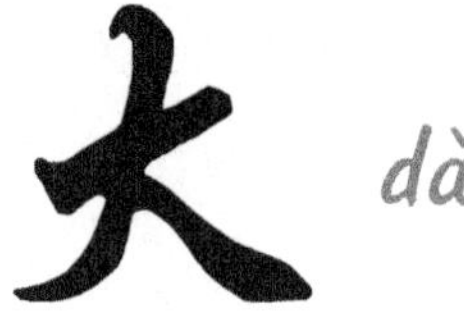
dà

měi

女
nǚ

jiàn dié měi nǚ xī shī

间谍美女：西施

Xi Shi : The Spy Beauty

西施

chūn qiū shí qī zhōng guó bèi fēn wéi qī gè bù tóng de xiǎo guó jiā yǒu
春秋时期，中国被**分为**七个不同的小国家。有
yī nián yuè guó hé wú guó dǎ zhàng yuè guó bèi dǎ bài le
一年，越国**和**吴国**打仗**，越国被**打败**了。

During the Spring and Autumn Period, China was **divided into** seven different small states. One year, the state of Yue was **at war with** the state of Wu. And Yue was **defeated**.

yuè wáng bèi wú wáng zhuā qù dāng nú lì tiān tiān yǎng mǎ tā hèn jí le
越王被吴王抓去当**奴隶**，天天养马。他**恨**极了
wú wáng biǎo miàn shùn cóng xīn lǐ què xiǎng zhe bào chóu
吴王，表面**顺从**，心里却想着**报仇**。

The King of Yue was captured by the King of Wu as a **slave**, and had to tend to horses every day. He **hated** the King of Wu so much, appearing **obedient** outside, but thinking of **revenge** in his heart.

yuè wáng wò xīn cháng dǎn jìn le zuì dà nǔ lì tǎo hǎo wú wáng jǐ nián
越王**卧薪尝胆**，**尽**了**最大努力**讨好吴王。几年
hòu wú wáng zhōng yú fàng sōng le jǐng tì biàn shì fàng le tā
后，吴王终于放松了警**惕**，便**释放**了他。

The King of Yue **maintained his resolve for revenge**, **trying his best** to please the King of Wu. After a few years, the King of Wu finally let down his **guard** and **released** him.

yuè wáng huí dào yuè guó hòu dào chù xún zhǎo měi nǚ yīn wèi tā zhī dào
越王回到越国后，**到处**寻找美女，因为他知道
wú wáng zuì dà de ruò diǎn shì hào sè kě yǐ yòng měi rén jì bào chóu
吴王最大的**弱点**是**好色**，可以用“美人计”报仇。

After the King of Yue returned to his state, he looked for beautiful women **everywhere**, because he knew that the King of Wu's greatest **weakness** was **lust for women**, and he could use the “Beauty Strategy” for his revenge.

hěn kuài tā zài yī gè xiǎo cūn zi lǐ zhǎo dào le yī wèi guó sè tiān xiāng
很快，他在一个小村子里找到了一位**国色天香**
de měi nǚ xī shī tā zài gè fāng miàn péi xùn le xī shī bǎ tā
的美女：西施。他在各方面**培训**了西施，把她
biàn chéng le yī gè jiàn dié
变成了一个**间谍**。

Soon, He found a **heavenly beautiful** woman in a small village: Xi Shi. He **trained** Xi Shi in all aspects and turned her into a **spy**.

péi xùn wán chéng hòu yuè wáng jiù pài nián qīng guān yuán fàn lí bǎ xī shī sòng
培训**完成**后，越王就**派**年轻官员范蠡把西施送
qù wú guó xiàn gěi wú wáng
去吴国**献**给吴王。

After the training was **completed**, the King of Yue **sent** a young official Fan Li to escort Xishi to the state of Wu to **present** her to the King of Wu.

zài qù wú guó de lù shàng fàn lí hé xī shī zhāo xī xiāng chǔ hěn kuài
在去吴国的路上，范蠡和西施**朝夕相处**，很快
jiù xiāng ài le kě shì wèi le wán chéng yuè wáng de bào chóu rèn wù
就**相爱**了。可是，**为了**完成越王的报仇任务，
tā men xuǎn zé le fàng shǒu
他们选择了放手。

On the way to Wu, Fan Li and Xi Shi **spent a long time getting on with one another**, and soon **fell in love**. However, **in order to** complete the revenge mission of their king, they chose to let go of the relationship.

xī shī dào dá wú guó hòu wú wáng jiù lì kè mí shàng le tā hái zhuān
西施到达吴国后，吴王就立刻**迷上**了她，还**专**
mén wèi tā xiū jiàn le gōng diàn
门为她修建了宫殿。

After Xi Shi arrived in Wu, the King of Wu became **fascinated by** her immediately. He even built a palace **specifically** for her.

wú wáng tiān tiān hé tā zài yī qǐ yuè lái yuè bù guǎn zhèng zhì xī shī
吴王天天和她在一起，越来越不管**政治**。西施
yě chéng wéi le shì wú wáng zuì ài de fēi pín
也成为了是吴王最爱的**妃嫔**。

He stayed with her every day, becoming more and more ignorant of **politics**. Xi Shi became the king's favourite **concubine**.

shí nián hòu wú guó biàn ruò yuè wáng dài bīng lái hé wú guó dǎ zhàng
十年后，吴国变**弱**，越王带兵来和吴国打仗。
zhè yī cì yuè guó yíng le wú guó bèi miè wáng le
这一次，越国**赢**了，吴国被**灭亡**了。

Ten years later, the state of Wu became **weak**, and the King of Yue brought troops to fight Wu. This time, Yue **won** the war and Wu was **destroyed**.

wú wáng yě zhōng yú míng bái le hé xī shī de yī qiè zhǐ shì yīn móu tā
吴王也终于明白了和西施的**一切**只是**阴谋**，他
shāng xīn yù jué jiù zì shā le
伤心欲绝，就**自杀**了。

The King of Wu also finally realized that **everything** between him and Xi Shi was just a **conspiracy**. He was **so heartbroken** that he **committed suicide**.

xī shī suī rán wán chéng le tā de rèn wù kě shì tā hěn nèi jiù méi
西施虽然完成了她的**任务**，可是她很**内疚**，没
yǒu huí dào yuè guó ér shì shén mì de shī zōng le
有回到越国，而是神秘地**失踪**了。

Although Xi Shi completed her **mission**, she felt very **guilty** and did not return to Yue, instead she mysteriously **disappeared**.

yǒu rén shuō tā zì shā le yě yǒu rén shuō fàn lí zhǎo dào le
有人说，她**自杀**了。也有人说，范蠡找到了
tā dài tā lí kāi le
她，**带**她**离开**了。

Some people said that she **committed suicide**, others said that Fan Li found her and **took** her **away**.

?

十年的相处，**你觉得西施有没有爱过吴王？你认为西施的最终的结局是什么？**

After ten years of getting along, **do you think Xi Shi had ever loved the King of Wu? What do you think was the final ending of Xi Shi?**

Culture Corner

Xi Shi (西施) comes is the earliest amongst the Four Beauties of China in history. Despite her humble beginning as a village girl, she was trained as the most successful spy leading to the downfall of the State of Wu. For her homeland, she was regarded as a heroine, however for the state of Wu, she was certainly the most hated, leaving her a controversial figure. Today, Xi Shi is remembered as a symbol of female beauty and grace in Chinese culture. Her story has been passed down through the generations in various forms of literature, poetry, and art. She is still revered and celebrated in Chinese society, and her name is synonymous with beauty and elegance. The famous West Lake (西湖) in Hangzhou is said to be the incarnation of Xi Shi.

Key Vocabulary

shùn cóng 顺从	*adj.*	obedient	wán chéng 完成	*v.*	to complete
zhāo xī xiāng chǔ 朝夕相处	*idiom*	spend a long time getting on	bào chóu 报仇	*n.* *v.*	revenge to revenge
wò xīn cháng dǎn 卧薪尝胆	*idiom*	maintain one's resolve	fàng shǒu 放手	*v.*	to let go
jǐng tì 警惕	*n.*	guard/alert	zhuān mén 专门	*adv.*	specially
shì fàng 释放	*v.*	to release	ruò diǎn 弱点	*n.*	weakness
guó sè tiān xiāng 国色天香	*idiom*	heavenly beautiful (woman)	yīn móu 阴谋	*n.*	conspiracy
péi xùn 培训	*v.*	to train	rèn wù 任务	*n.*	task/mission
jiàn dié 间谍	*n.*	spy	nèi jiù 内疚	*adj.*	guilty
shāng xīn yù jué 伤心欲绝	*idiom*	extremely heartbroken (want to end)	shī zōng 失踪	*v.*	to disappear

Sentence Patterns

尽最大努力…

try ones' best to …

subject + **尽最大努力** (jìn zuì dà nǔ lì) + *action*

tā jìn le zuì dà nǔ lì tǎo hǎo wú wáng
他尽了最大努力讨好吴王。

He tried his best to please the King of Wu.

为了…

in order to …

为了 + *objective* + *clause*

wèi le wán chéng yuè wáng de bào chóu rèn wù, tā men xuǎn zé le fàng shǒu
为了完成越王的报仇任务，他们选择了放手。

In order to complete the revenge mission of their king, they chose to let go of the relationship.

CHINESE VERSION

春秋时期，中国被分为七个不同的小国家。有一年，越国和吴国打仗，越国被打败了。

越王被吴王抓去当奴隶，天天养马。他恨极了吴王，表面顺从，心里却想着报仇。

越王卧薪尝胆，尽了最大努力讨好吴王。几年后，吴王终于放松了警惕，便释放了他。

越王回到越国后，到处寻找美女，因为他知道吴王最大的弱点是好色，可以用"美人计"报仇。

很快，他在一个小村子里找到了一位国色天香的美女：西施。他在各方面培训了西施，把她变成了一个间谍。

培训完成后，越王就派年轻官员范蠡把西施送去吴国献给吴王。

在去吴国的路上，范蠡和西施朝夕相处，很快就相爱了。可是，为了完成越王的报仇任务，他们选择了放手。

西施到达吴国后，吴王就立刻迷上了她，还专门为她修建了宫殿。

吴王天天和她在一起，越来越不管政治。西施也成为了是吴王最爱的妃嫔。

十年后，吴国变弱，越王带兵来和吴国打仗。这一次，越国赢了，吴国被灭亡了。

吴王也终于明白了和西施的一切只是阴谋，他伤心欲绝，就自杀了。

西施虽然完成了她的任务，可是她很内疚，没有回到越国，而是神秘地失踪了。

有人说，她自杀了。也有人说，范蠡找到了她，带她离开了。

22 wú dí měi nǚ : wáng zhāo jūn
无敌美女：王昭君

Wang Zhaojun : The Invincible Beauty

gōng yuán qián 54 nián, wáng zhāo jūn chū shēng zài yī gè pǔ tōng jiā tíng。
公元前54年，王昭君出生在一个**普通家庭**。
yǒu yī nián, huáng dì xiàng quán guó xuǎn měi rén zuò pín fēi, wáng zhāo jūn bèi xuǎn shàng le。
有一年，皇帝向**全国**选美人做嫔妃，王昭君被**选上**了。

In 54 **BC**, Wang Zhaojun was born in an **ordinary family**. One year, the emperor was selecting beautiful woman from **all over the country** to be his concubines, and Wang Zhaojun was **selected**.

wáng zhāo jūn dào huáng gōng hòu, què méi néng jiàn dào huáng dì。 yuán lái, zhè děi kào yī gè huà jiā bǎ tā men de huà xiàng sòng gěi huáng dì lái xuǎn zé。
王昭君到**皇宫**后，却没能见到皇帝。**原来**，这得**靠**一个画家把她们的**画像**送给皇帝来选择。

After Wang Zhaojun arrived at the **palace**, she was unable to see the emperor. **It turned out** this **depended on** a painter giving **portraits** to the emperor to select.

měi rén men dōu huì lù huà jiā, zhǐ yǒu wáng zhāo méi yǒu zhè yàng zuò, yīn wèi tā jué de zhè zhǒng xíng wéi hěn kě chǐ。
美人们都**贿赂**画家，**只有**王昭没有这样做，因为她觉得这种行为很**可耻**。

Beauties all **bribed** the painter, **only** Wang Zhaojun did not, because she thought this kind of behavior was **shameful**.

huà jiā hěn shēng qì, jué de wáng zhāo jūn xīn gāo qì ào。 jiù gù yì bǎ tā huà chéng chǒu nǚ。 yú shì, wáng zhāo jūn luò xuǎn, zhǐ néng dāng gōng nǚ。
画家很生气，觉得王昭君**心高气傲**。就故意把她画成**丑女**。于是，王昭君**落选**，只能当宫女。

The painter was very angry and felt that Wang Zhaojun was **proud and arrogant**, so he deliberately painted her as an **ugly woman**. Therefore, Wang Zhaojun **failed the selection**, and had to be a court lady.

jǐ nián hòu xiōng nú de guó wáng cháng tú bá shè lái bài jiàn huáng dì
几年后，匈奴的国王**长途跋涉**来拜见皇帝，
qǐng qiú lián yīn
请求**联姻**。

A few years later, the King of the Huns **traveled long distances** to meet the emperor and ask for a **marriage alliance**.

dāng shí de xiōng nú yòu xiǎo yòu qióng gōng zhǔ men dōu jué de bù zhí dé
当时的**匈奴**又小又穷，公主们都觉得**不值得**
jià guò qù suǒ yǐ dōu jù jué le
嫁过去，所以都拒绝了。

At that time, **the Huns** were small and poor, so princesses all felt that it was **not worth** marrying over, so they all refused.

yú shì huáng dì jiù dǎ suàn zhǎo yī gè gōng nǚ fēng wéi gōng zhǔ pài qù
于是，皇帝就打算找一个宫女**封为**公主，派去
lián yīn wáng zhāo jūn bù xiǎng lǎo sǐ zài gōng lǐ jiù zhǔ dòng bào míng
联姻。王昭君不想老死在宫里，就主动**报名**。

Therefore, the emperor planned to find a court lady to be **named as** a princess to send for the **marriage alliance**. Wang Zhaojun didn't want to die old in the palace, so she took the initiative to **sign up**.

xiōng nú de guó wáng yī jiàn dào tā jiù bèi tā mí zhù le guó wáng gāo
匈奴的国王**一**见到她，**就**被她迷住了。国王高
xìng jí le dài zhe tā qù gǎn xiè huáng dì
兴极了，带着她去**感谢**皇帝。

As soon as the King of the Huns saw her, he was fascinated by her. The King was very happy and took her to **thank** the emperor.

jiù zhè yàng huáng dì dì yī cì jiàn dào le wáng zhāo jūn shēn shēn de bèi
就这样，皇帝第一次见到了王昭君，深深地被
tā de měi zhèn jīng le huáng dì fēi cháng shě bù dé ràng wáng zhāo jūn lí
她的美**震惊**了。皇帝非常**舍不得**让王昭君离
kāi hěn shāng xīn bù néng gǎi biàn zhè yī qiè
开，很伤心不能**改变**这一切.

Through this, the emperor saw Wang Zhaojun for the first time and was deeply **astonished** by her beauty. The emperor was very **reluctant** to let Wang Zhaojun leave, and was very sad that he couldn't **change** anything.

wáng zhāo jūn zǒu hòu huáng dì diào chá le huà xiàng de shì fā xiàn zhēn xiàng
王昭君走后，皇帝**调查**了画像的事，发现**真相**
hòu fēi cháng nǎo huǒ jiù bǎ nà gè huà jiā shā le
后，非常**恼火**，就把那个画家杀了。

After Wang Zhaojun left, the emperor **investigated** the portrait matter and when he found out the **truth**, he was very **furious** and killed the painter.

wáng zhāo jūn dào xiōng nú hòu, chéng wéi le hé píng dà shǐ, hái dài qù le guó nèi xiān jìn de wén huà hé jì shù.

王昭君到匈奴后，成为了**和平大使**，还带去了国内**先进**的文化和**技术**。

After Wang Zhaojun arrived in the Huns, she became an **ambassador of peace** and brought **advanced** culture and **technology** from her country.

tā fēi cháng shòu huān yíng, yī zhí dào tā qù shì wéi zhǐ, dōu hěn shòu xiōng nú rén de ài dài.

她非常**受欢迎**，一直到她去世为止，都很**受**匈奴人的**爱戴**。

She was very **popular** and was very **loved by** the Huns until her death.

如果你是王昭君，你会选择慢慢地老死宫中，还是像她一样，选择冒险去陌生的国家联姻？请给出理由。

If you were Wang Zhaojun, would you choose to slowly die in the palace, or, like her, choose to venture to a foreign country for the marriage alliance? Please give reasons.

CULTURE CORNER

Wang Zhaojun (王昭君) was not afraid to be different. Her story continues to be celebrated in Chinese culture, serving as an example of strength and resilience in the face of adversity! Hence being known as the invincible beauty. Due to her courage and sacrifice, China enjoyed decades of peace with the Huns. She is generally considered to be the most loved among of the Four Beauties. The Zhaojun Museum near Hohhot, the capital city of Inner Mongolia, was built to commemorate her and also contains the Museum of Hun Culture.

Key Vocabulary

huì lù 贿 赂	*v.*	to bribe	gǎn xiè 感 谢	*v.*	to thank (formal)
kě chǐ 可 耻	*adj.*	shameful	zhèn jīng 震 惊	*v.*	to astonish
xīn gāo qì ào 心 高 气 傲	*idiom*	proud and arrogant	diào chá 调 查	*v.*	to investigate
chǒu nǚ 丑 女	*n.*	ugly woman	zhēn xiàng 真 相	*n.*	truth
luò xuǎn 落 选	*v.*	to fail selection	nǎo huǒ 恼 火	*adj.*	furious/ annoyed
cháng tú bá shè 长 途 跋 涉	*idiom*	travel long distance	hé píng 和 平	*n.*	peace
zhí dé 值 得	*v.*	worth	dà shǐ 大 使	*n.*	ambassador
bào míng 报 名	*v.*	to sign up	xiān jìn 先 进	*adj.*	advanced
shòu huān yíng 受 欢 迎	*adj.*	popular	jì shù 技 术	*n.*	technology

Sentence Patterns

(不)值得...

(not) worth doing

bù zhí dé
(不) 值得 + *action*

gōng zhǔ men dōu jué de bù zhí dé jià guò qù
公主们都觉得不值得嫁过去。

Princesses all felt that it was not worth marrying over.

受...爱戴

loved by ... (used more for seniors, leaders)

shòu ài dài
A + 受 + *B* + 爱戴

tā hěn shòu xiōng nú rén de ài dài
她很受匈奴人的爱戴。

She was very loved by the Huns.

CHINESE VERSION

公元前54年，王昭君出生在一个普通家庭。有一年，皇帝向全国选美人做嫔妃，王昭君被选上了。

王昭君到皇宫后，却没能见到皇帝。原来，这得靠一个画家把她们的画像送给皇帝来选择。

美人们都贿赂画家，只有王昭没有这样做，因为她觉得这种行为很可耻。

画家很生气，觉得王昭君心高气傲。就故意把她画成丑女。于是，王昭君落选，只能当宫女.

几年后，匈奴的国王长途跋涉来拜见皇帝，请求联姻。

当时的匈奴又小又穷，公主们都觉得不值得嫁过去，所以都拒绝了。

于是，皇帝就打算找一个宫女封为公主，派去联姻。王昭君不想老死在宫里，就主动报名。

匈奴的国王一见到她，就被她迷住了。国王高兴极了，带着她去感谢皇帝。

就这样，皇帝第一次见到了王昭君，深深地被她的美震惊了。皇帝非常舍不得让王昭君离开，很伤心不能改变这一切.

王昭君走后，皇帝调查了画像的事，发现真相后，非常恼火，就把那个画家杀了。

王昭君到匈奴后，成为了和平大使，还带去了国内先进的文化和技术。

她非常受欢迎，一直到她去世为止，都很受匈奴人的爱戴。

xīn jī měi nǚ diāo chán

心机美女：貂蝉 23

Diao Chan : The Scheming Beauty

貂
蝉

diāo chán shì zhōng guó sì dà měi nǚ zhōng zuì shén mì de nǚ rén ， ér qiě méi yǒu rén qīng chǔ tā de chū shēn bèi jǐng 。

貂蝉是中国四大美女中最**神秘**的女人，而且没有人清楚她的**出身背景**。

Diao Chan was the most **mysterious** woman amongst the four beauties of China, and no one knew her **background by birth**.

dà jiā zhǐ zhī dào tā shì gè gē nǚ ， yīn wèi cóng xiǎo bèi dà guān yuán wáng yǔn shōu yǎng ， suǒ yǐ duì tā hěn zhōng chéng 。

大家只知道她是个歌女，因为**从小**被大官员王允**收养**，所以对他很**忠诚**。

People just knew that she was a singer. Since being **adopted** by the great official Wang Yun **from a young age**, she remained very **loyal** to him.

dāng shí ， wáng yǔn zuì dà de dí rén jiào dǒng zhuō ， shì yī gè è dú de dà guān 。 dǒng zhuō kòng zhì zhe huáng dì hé zhèng fǔ ， bù jǐn luàn shā rén ， hái chī rén ròu 。

当时，王允最大的**敌人**叫董卓，是一个**恶毒**的大官。董卓**控制**着皇帝和政府，不仅**乱杀**人，还吃人肉。

At that time, Wang Yun's greatest **enemy** was Dong Zhuo, who was a **vicious** official, Dong Zhuo **controlled** the emperor and the government, not only **randomly killing** people, but also eating human flesh.

wáng yǔn yī zhí hěn xiǎng shā sǐ dǒng zhuō ， kě shì dǒng zhuō yǒu gè wǔ gōng gāo qiáng de gān ér zi lǚ bù 。

王允一直很想**杀死**董卓，可是董卓有个**武功高强**的**干儿子**吕布。

Wang Yun had always wanted to **kill** Dong Zhuo, but Dong Zhuo had a **godson** with **great martial kills**, named Lu Bu.

dǒng zhuō yǒu lǚ bù de bǎo hù dà jiā dōu shā bù liǎo tā zhí dào
董卓有吕布的**保护**，大家都杀不了他。**直到**，
wáng yǔn xiǎng dào le měi rén jì jiù pài diāo chán qù yǐn yòu lǚ bù
王允想到了“美人计”，就派貂蝉去**引诱**吕布。

With the **protection** of Lu Bu, no one was able to kill Dong Zhuo. **Until** Wang Yun thought of the "Beauty Strategy," he sent Diao Chan to **seduce** Lu Bu.

lǚ bù yī jiàn dào diāo chán jiù fēng kuáng de ài shàng le tā rán hòu
吕布**一见**到貂蝉，**就**疯狂地爱上了她。然后，
wáng yǔn yòu bǎ diāo chán jià gěi dǒng zhuō
王允又把貂蝉**嫁给**董卓。

As soon as Lu Bu saw Diao Chan, he fell in love with her madly. Then, Wang Yun **married** Diao Chan to Dong Zhuo.

lǚ bù měi tiān kàn zhe zuì ài de nǚ rén hé bié rén zài yī qǐ fēi cháng
吕布每天看着最爱的女人和别人在一起，非常
shāng xīn jué wàng gēn tā xiāng bǐ dǒng zhuō jiǎn zhí shì shì shàng zuì xìng fú
伤心绝望。**跟**他**相比**，董卓简直是世上最幸福
de nán rén
的男人。

Everyday Lu Bu watched his most belove woman being with another, feeling extremely **heartbroken and desperate**. **Compared to** him, Dong Zhuo was simply the happiest man in the world.

diāo chán cōng míng de wán nòng zhè liǎng gè nán rén yī biān tǎo hǎo dǒng zhuō
貂蝉聪明地**玩弄**这两个男人，一边**讨好**董卓，
yī biān qiāo qiāo de hé lǚ bù yuē huì
一边悄悄地和吕布**约会**。

Diao Chan **played** smartly between these two men. While **pleasing** Dong Zhuo, she would secretly **date** Lu Bu.

tā hái jīng cháng xiàng lǚ bù bào yuàn dǒng zhuō shuō zì jǐ zhǐ ài lǚ bù yī
她还经常向吕布**抱怨**董卓，说自己只爱吕布一
gè rén lǚ bù shòu diāo chán de yǐng xiǎng yuè lái yuè hèn dǒng zhuō
个人。吕布**受**貂蝉的**影响**，越来越恨董卓。

She also often **complained** to Lu Bu about Dong Zhuo, claiming that she loved Lu Bu alone. **Under the influence of** Diao Chan, Lu Bu hated Dong Zhuo more and more.

zuì zhōng lǚ bù wèi le hé diāo chán zài yī qǐ jiù hé wáng yǔn jié méng
最终，吕布为了和貂蝉在一起，就和王允**结盟**
bǎ dǒng zhuō shā sǐ le
，把董卓杀死了。

Finally, in order to be with Diao Chan, Lu Bu formed an **alliance** with Wang Yun and killed Dong Zhuo.

zhī hòu lǚ bù bèi huáng dì fēng wéi dà jiāng jūn yě zhōng yú hé diāo chán zài yī qǐ le
之后，吕布被皇帝封为**大将军**，也终于和貂蝉在一起了。

Afterwards, Lu Bu was named a **Great General** by the emperor, and was finally with Diao Chan.

kě shì tā men xìng fú de shēng huó le jǐ nián hòu lǚ bù jiù bèi tā de dí rén cáo cāo shā le
可是，他们**幸福**地生活了几年后，吕布就被他的**敌人**曹操杀了。

However, after they lived **happily** for a few years, Lu Bu was killed by his **enemy** Cao Cao.

lǚ bù sǐ hòu diāo chán jiù shén mì de shī zōng le méi yǒu rén zhī dào tā qù le nǎ lǐ
吕布死后，貂蝉就神秘地**失踪**了，没有人知道她去了哪里。

After Lu Bu died, Diao Chan mysteriously **disappeared**, and no one knew where she went.

?

你觉得貂蝉是什么样的人？你觉得貂蝉有没有爱过吕布？请给出理由。

What kind of person do you think Diao Chan was? Do you think Diao Chan had ever loved Lu Bu? Please give reasons.

Diao Chan (貂蝉) came third amongst the Four Beauties of China. She had a mysterious background as well as a mysterious ending, and no one knew how she really felt within the plot. However if not because of her help, Dongzhuo - one of the the most hated official in Chinese history, would not be easily killed.

This story is from the **Romance of the Three Kingdoms** (三国演义), you can read more stories from this classic novel in the next chapter!

Key Vocabulary

bèi jǐng 背景	*n.*	background	jué wàng 绝望	*adj.*	desperate
shōu yǎng 收养	*v.*	to adopt	xìng fú 幸福	*adj.*	happy (deeply)
zhōng chéng 忠诚	*adj.*	loyal	wán nòng 玩弄	*v.*	to play/trick
dí rén 敌人	*n.*	enemy	tǎo hǎo 讨好	*v.*	to please
è dú 恶毒	*adj.*	vicious	yuē huì 约会	*v.*	to date
kòng zhì 控制	*v.*	to control	bào yuàn 抱怨	*v.*	to complain
wǔ gōng gāo qiáng 武功高强		great in martial kills	jié méng 结盟	*v.*	to form an alliance
yǐn yòu 引诱	*v.*	to seduce	jiāng jūn 将军	*n.*	general

Sentence Patterns

跟… 相比

compared with …

A + gēn 跟 + B + xiāng bǐ 相比

gēn tā xiāng bǐ, dǒng zhuō jiǎn zhí shì shì shàng zuì xìng fú de nán rén.
跟他相比，董卓简直是世上最幸福的男人。

Compared with him, Dong Zhuo is simply the happiest man in the world.

受…影响

under the influence of

A + shòu 受 + B + yǐngxiǎng 影响

lǚ bù shòu diāo chán de yǐng xiǎng, yuè lái yuè hèn dǒng zhuō.
吕布受貂蝉的影响，越来越恨董卓。

Under the influence of Diaochan, Lu Bu hated Dong Zhuo more and more.

Chinese Version

貂蝉是中国四大美女中最神秘的女人，而且没有人清楚她的出身背景。

大家只知道她是个歌女，因为从小被大官员王允收养，所以对他很忠诚。

当时，王允最大的敌人叫董卓，是一个恶毒的大官。董卓控制着皇帝和政府，不仅乱杀人，还吃人肉。

王允一直很想杀死董卓，可是董卓有个武功高强的干儿子吕布。

董卓有吕布的保护，大家都杀不了他。直到，王允想到了“美人计”，就派貂蝉去引诱吕布。

吕布一见到貂蝉，就疯狂地爱上了她。然后，王允又把貂蝉嫁给董卓。

吕布每天看着最爱的女人和别人在一起，非常伤心绝望。跟他相比，董卓简直是世上最幸福的男人。

貂蝉聪明地玩弄这两个男人，一边讨好董卓，一边悄悄地和吕布约会。

她还经常向吕布抱怨董卓，说自己只爱吕布一个人。吕布受貂蝉的影响，越来越恨董卓。

最终，吕布为了和貂蝉在一起，就和王允结盟，把董卓杀死了。

之后，吕布被皇帝封为大将军，也终于和貂蝉在一起了。

可是，他们幸福地生活了几年后，吕布就被他的敌人曹操杀了。

吕布死后，貂蝉就神秘地失踪了，没有人知道她去了哪里。

24 王朝美女：杨贵妃

wáng cháo měi nǚ yáng guì fēi

Consort Yang : Beauty of the Dynasty

yáng guì fēi shì zhōng guó táng cháo zuì měi de nǚ rén. tā shì yīn yuè jiā hé wǔ dǎo jiā, yě shì huáng dì táng xuán zōng de guì fēi.

杨贵妃是中国唐朝最美的女人。她是**音乐家**和**舞蹈家**，也是皇帝唐玄宗的**贵妃**。

Consort Yang was the most beautiful woman in Tang dynasty. She was a **musician** and **dancer** and the **noble concubine** of Emperor Xuan Zong.

yáng guì fēi běn míng yáng yù huán, gōng yuán nián, tā chū shēng zài yī gè guì zú jiā tíng, cóng xiǎo jiù shì yǒu míng de měi rén hé cái nǚ.

杨贵妃**本名**杨玉环，**公元**719年，她出生在一个**贵族家庭**，从小就是有名的**美人**和**才女**。

Consort Yang's **original name** is Yang Yuhuan. In 719 **AD**, she was born in a **noble family**. She was a famous **beauty** and **talented girl** since she was a child.

zài gǔ dài, guì zú nǚ rén de shǐ mìng dōu shì: yòng hǎo de hūn yīn wèi zì jǐ de jiā tíng dài lái róng yào hé lì yì.

在古代，贵族女人的**使命**都是：用好的婚姻为自己的家庭带来**荣耀**和**利益**。

In ancient China, the **mission** of aristocratic women was to use good marriages to bring **glory** and **benefits** to their families.

yú shì, yáng yù huán de jiā rén jiù bǎ tā jià gěi le huáng dì de ér zi lǐ mào. tā men jié hūn hòu, xìng fú de shēng huó le jǐ nián.

于是，杨玉环的家人就把她**嫁给**了皇帝的儿子李瑁。他们**结婚**后，幸福地生活了几年。

Therefore, Yang Yuhuan's family **married** her **to** the emperor's son Li Mao. After they **got married**, they lived happily for several years.

kě shì , yǒu yī tiān , huáng dì jiàn dào le tā , shēn shēn de bèi tā xī yǐn le 。 huáng dì wèi le dé dào tā , bù zé shǒu duàn , shén zhì bù guǎn zì jǐ ér zi de gǎn shòu 。

可是，有一天，皇帝见到了她，深深的被她**吸引**了。皇帝为了得到她，**不择手段**，甚至不管自己儿子的**感受**。

However, one day, the emperor saw her and was deeply **attracted** by her. In order to get her, the emperor **used all means possible**, even neglected his own son's **feelings**.

yáng yù huán miàn duì huáng dì fēng kuáng de zhuī qiú , zhǐ néng shùn cóng 。 ér tā de zhàng fū , suī rán hèn fèn nù , yě bù gǎn wéi bèi tā de huáng dì fù qīn 。

杨玉环面对皇帝疯狂的**追求**，只能顺从。**而她**的丈夫，虽然恨**愤怒**，也不敢**违背**他的皇帝父亲。

Facing with the emperor's crazy **pursuit**, Yang Yuhuan could only obey. **As for** her husband, though **furious**, did not dare to **disobey** his emperor father.

huáng dì zì cóng yǒu le yáng yù huán , jiù zhǐ xiǎng shí shí kè kè hé tā zài yī qǐ , měi tiān tán qín wán lè , bù guǎn zhèng zhì 。

皇帝**自从**有了杨玉环，**就**只想时时刻刻和她在一起，每天弹琴玩乐，不管政治。

Ever since the emperor had Yang Yuhuan with him, he **just** wanted to be with her all the time, playing music and having fun every day, totally ignored his political duties.

huáng dì tài ài yáng yù huán le , chéng nuò huì yǒng yuǎn ài tā , hái bù duàn de jiǎng shǎng tā de jiā rén , zhè ràng suǒ yǒu rén dōu fēi cháng jí dù 。

皇帝太爱杨玉环了，**承诺**会永远爱她，还**不断**地**奖赏**她的家人，这让所有人都非常**嫉妒**。

The emperor loved Yang Yuhuan so much, he **promised** to love her forever, and **rewarded** her family **constantly**, which made everyone else very **jealous**.

shí duō nián hòu , "ān shǐ zhī luàn" bào fā , huáng gōng bèi dí jūn zhàn lǐng le 。 huáng dì dài zhe yáng yù huán táo pǎo 。

十多年后，"安史之乱"**爆发**，皇宫被**敌军**占领了。皇帝带着杨玉环**逃跑**。

More than ten years later, the "An Lushan Rebellion" **broke out** and the Emperor's palace was occupied by **enemy forces**. The emperor took Yang Yuhuan to **escape**.

zài táo pǎo de lù shàng , huáng dì shēn biān de jiāng jūn men kāi shǐ wēi xié huáng dì , yāo qiú shā sǐ yáng yù huán 。

在逃跑的路上，皇帝身边的将军们开始**威胁**皇帝，**要求**杀死杨玉环。

On their way of escaping, the generals around the emperor began to **threaten** the emperor and **demanded** that Yang Yuhuan be killed.

yīn wèi cóng tā men de jiǎo dù lái kàn shì huáng dì duì zhè gè nǚ rén fēng

因为**从**他们**的角度来看**，是皇帝对这个女人疯

kuáng de ài zào chéng le zhè chǎng zhèng zhì zāi nàn

狂的爱，造成了这场**政治灾难**。

Because **from** their **perspective**, it was the emperor's crazy love for this woman that caused this **political disaster**.

huáng dì suī rán shè bù dé dàn wèi le zì bǎo zuì zhōng hái shì shā

皇帝虽然**舍不得**，但为了自保，**最终**还是杀

sǐ le yáng yù huán tā dāng shí zhǐ yǒu suì

死了杨玉环，她**当时**只有38岁。

Although the emperor was **reluctant**, in order to protect himself, he **eventually** killed Yang Yuhuan, who was only 38 years old **by then**.

你同情杨玉环吗？皇帝是真的爱她吗？在他杀死杨玉环后，他后悔吗？请给出理由。

Do you sympathize with Yang Yuhuan? Did the emperor really love her? After he killed Yang Yuhuan, did he regret it? Please give reasons.

Culture Corner

Yang Yuhuan (杨玉环) was the most recent of the Four Beauties of China, and is the most famous of them. The Tang dynasty was the most prominent dynasty of ancient China and emperor Xuan Zong was diligent and hugely successful during the first half of his reign, however the "An Lushan Rebellion," one of the biggest disasters in Chinese history, ruined everything and became the turning point of a prosperous dynasty and resulted in the death of nearly a third of China's population. Regardless of the cause of the disaster, it is unfair to blame one single woman for it!

Key Vocabulary

yīn yuè jiā	音乐家	*n.*	musician	fèn nù	愤怒	*adj.*	furious
wǔ dǎo jiā	舞蹈家	*n.*	dancer	wéi bèi	违背	*v.*	to disobey
jiā tíng	家庭	*n.*	family	chéng nuò	承诺	*v.* *n.*	to promise promise
shǐ mìng	使命	*n.*	mission	jiǎng shǎng	奖赏	*v.*	to reward
róng yào	荣耀	*n.*	glory	bào fā	爆发	*v.*	break out
lì yì	利益	*n.*	benefit	táo pǎo	逃跑	*v.*	run away
bù zé shǒu duàn	不择手段	*idiom*	by all means (negative)	wēi xié	威胁	*v.*	to threaten
gǎn shòu	感受	*n.*	feeling	zāi nàn	灾难	*n.*	disaster

Sentence Patterns

自从…就…

ever since …

自从 + *event/time* + **就** + *result*

huáng dì zì cóng yǒu le yáng yù huán, jiù zhǐ xiǎng shí shí kè kè hé tā zài yī qǐ
皇帝自从有了杨玉环，就只想时时刻刻和她在一起。

Ever since the emperor had Yang Yuhuan with him, he just wanted to be with her all the time.

从…的角度来看

from the perspective of …

cóng **从** + *noun* + de jiǎo dù lái kàn **的角度来看** + *clause*

yīn wèi cóng tā men de jiǎo dù lái kàn, shì huáng dì duì zhè gè nǚ rén fēng kuáng de ài, zào chéng le zhè chǎng zhèng zhì zāi nán
因为从他们的角度来看，是皇帝对这个女人疯狂的爱，造成了这场政治灾难。

Because from their perspective it was the emperor's crazy love for this woman that caused this political disaster.

CHINESE VERSION

杨贵妃是中国唐朝最美的女人。她是音乐家和舞蹈家，也是皇帝唐玄宗的贵妃。

杨贵妃本名杨玉环，公元719年，她出生在一个贵族家庭，从小就是有名的美人和才女。

在古代，贵族女人的使命都是：用好的婚姻为自己的家庭带来荣耀和利益。

于是，杨玉环的家人就把她嫁给了皇帝的儿子李瑁。他们结婚后，幸福地生活了几年。

可是，有一天，皇帝见到了她，深深的被她吸引了。皇帝为了得到她，不择手段，甚至不管自己儿子的感受。

杨玉环面对皇帝疯狂的追求，只能顺从。而她的丈夫，虽然恨愤怒，也不敢违背他的皇帝父亲。

皇帝自从有了杨玉环，就只想时时刻刻和她在一起，每天弹琴玩乐，不管政治。

皇帝太爱杨玉环了，承诺会永远爱她，还不断地奖赏她的家人，这让所有人都非常嫉妒。

十多年后，“安史之乱”爆发，皇宫被敌军占领了。皇帝带着杨玉环逃跑。

在逃跑的路上，皇帝身边的将军们开始威胁皇帝，要求杀死杨玉环。

因为从他们的角度来看，是皇帝对这个女人疯狂的爱，造成了这场政治灾难。

皇帝虽然舍不得，但为了自保，最终还是杀死了杨玉环，她当时只有38岁。

sān

guó

gù

事 shì

Romance of the Three Kingdoms

táo yuán jié yì

桃园结义

Oath of the Peach Garden

hàn cháo hòu qī, huáng dì wú néng, zhèng fǔ fǔ bài。 quán guó bào fā le
汉朝后期，皇帝**无能**，政府**腐败**。全国**爆发**了
nóng mín qǐ yì, zhèng fǔ bù dé bù dào chù zhāo bīng。
农民起义，政府**不得不**到处招兵。

In the late Han Dynasty, the emperor was **incompetent** and the government was **corrupt**. Peasant uprising **broke out** across the country, and the government **had to** recruit troops everywhere.

yǒu yī jù zhōng guó míng yán jiào：“luàn shì chū yīng xióng。” ér zhè yě shì
有一句**中国名言**叫：“乱世出英雄。”而这也是
hěn duō rén de mèng xiǎng, bāo kuò liú bèi。
很多人的**梦想**，包括刘备。

There is a **famous Chinese saying**: “Heroes come out of troubled times.”And this was also the **dream** of many people, including Liu Bei.

liú bèi rén dào zhōng nián, suī rán shì huáng shì chéng yuán, dàn shì hěn
刘备人到**中年**，虽然是皇室**成员**，但是很
qióng, méi yǒu quán lì。
穷，没有**权力**。

Liu Bei reached **middle age**, although he was a **member** of the royal family, he was poor and had no **power**.

tā měi tiān zài jiē shàng mài cǎo xié zhèng qián, biǎo miàn shàng shì gè pǔ tōng rén
他每天在街上卖草鞋**挣钱**，表面上是个**普通人**
，xīn lǐ què mèng xiǎng zhe zuò guó jiā de tǒng zhì zhě。
，心里却梦想着做国家的**统治者**。

He was selling straw shoes on the street every day to **earn money**. On the surface, he looked like an **ordinary person**, but in his heart he dreamt of being the **ruler** of the country.

yī tiān liú bèi kàn dào le zhèng fǔ zhāo bīng de gào shì tā yī biān yáo
一天，刘备看到了政府招兵的**告示**，他一边摇
tóu yī biān tàn qì jué de zì jǐ hěn méi yòng
头，一边**叹气**，觉得自己很**没用**！

One day, when Liu Bei saw the government recruitment **notice**, he shook his head and **sighed**, feeling **useless**!

tū rán tā tīng dào yǒu rén shuō le yī jù nǐ zhè gè dà nán rén
突然，他听到有人说了一句："你这个大男人，
gàn ma tàn qì
干嘛叹气？"

Suddenly, he heard someone said to him: "Hey, man-up! (You big man, why sigh?)"

liú bèi hěn chī jīng yī tái tóu kàn dào le yī gè gāo dà de hēi liǎn
刘备很**吃惊**，一抬头，看到了一个高大的黑脸
zhuàng hàn liú bèi jué de tā hěn yǒu yì si jiù kāi shǐ hé tā liáo tiān
壮汉。刘备觉得他很有意思，就开始和他**聊天**。

Liu Bei was very **shocked**, he raised head and saw a tall, big black-faced **strong man**, whom he thought was very interesting, so he started to **chat** with him.

yuán lái zhè gè rén jiào zhāng fēi shì gè shā zhū de lì qì hěn dà
原来，这个人叫张飞，是个**杀猪的**，力气很大。
suī rán yǒu diǎn cū lǔ dàn shì xìng gé háo shuǎng lè yú zhù rén
虽然有点**粗鲁**，但是**性格**豪爽，**乐于助人**。

It turned out that this man was called Zhang Fei, he was a **butcher** and had great strength. Although a bit **rude**, he had a bold **personality** and **enjoyed helping others**.

liú bèi gào sù zhāng fēi zì jǐ yǒu yuǎn dà de mù biāo dàn shì méi qián yě
刘备告诉张飞自己有远大的**目标**，但是没钱也
méi quán pà wú fǎ shí xiàn
没权，怕无法**实现**。

Liu Bei told Zhang Fei that he had big **goals**, but had no money or power, hence worried that he would not be able to **achieve** them.

zhāng fēi jué de liú bèi hěn yǒu chéng xīn jiù gào sù tā wǒ jiā lǐ
张飞觉得刘备很**有诚心**，就告诉他："我家里
yǒu yī diǎn ér jī xù yě xǔ kě yǐ bāng dào nǐ
有一点儿**积蓄**，也许可以帮到你。"

Zhang Fei felt that Liu Bei was very **sincere**, so he told him: I have a bit of **savings** at home, perhaps it could help you.

liú bèi tīng hòu xìng gāo cǎi liè dǎ suàn hé zhāng fēi jiāo péng yǒu jiù qǐng
刘备听后**兴高采烈**，打算**和**张飞**交朋友**，就请
tā qù cān guǎn hē jiǔ le
他去餐馆喝酒了。

Liu Bei was **extremely happy**, and planned **to make friends with** Zhang Fei, so he invited Zhang Fei to the restaurant to have a drink.

tā men zài hē jiǔ de shí hòu tū rán tīng dào páng biān de yī gè hóng liǎn
他们在喝酒的时候，**突然**听到旁边的一个红脸
zhuàng hàn dà hǎn kuài ná jiǔ lái wǒ gǎn zhe qù bào míng dāng bīng ne
壮汉大喊：“快拿酒来，我赶着去**报名**当兵呢。”

While they were drinking, they **suddenly** heard a red-faced **strong man** nearby shouting: "Quickly get me the wine, I'm rushing to **sign up** as a soldier."

zhè gè rén jiào guān yǔ yóu yú shā le qī fù ruò xiǎo de huài dàn bù
这个人叫关羽，**由于**杀了欺负弱小的坏蛋，不
néng huí jiā dào chù liú làng
能回家，**到处流浪**。

This man was called Guan Yu. **Due to** killing a jerk who bullied the weak, he was not able to go home, but **wandered around**.

liú bèi jué de guān yǔ bù shì yī bān rén jiù qǐng tā guò lái jiā rù tā
刘备觉得关羽不是**一般人**，就请他过来**加入**他
men tā men sān gè rén yī biān hē jiǔ yī biān liáo tiān fēi cháng tòng
们。他们三个人一边喝酒，一边聊天，非常**痛**
kuài hěn kuài jiù chéng wéi le zhì qù xiāng tóu de péng yǒu
快，很快就成为了**志趣相投**的朋友。

Liu Bei felt that Guan Yu was not an **ordinary person**, so invited him to **join** them. Three of them were chatting while drinking, feeling very **happy**. They soon became **like-minded** friends.

hòu lái tā men de guān xi yuè lái yuè hǎo yī tiān tā men qù le zhāng
后来他们的**关系**越来越好。一天，他们去了张
fēi de táo huā yuán zài táo huā shù xià jié bài chéng xiōng dì
飞的**桃花园**，在桃花树下**结拜成兄弟**。

Later their **relationship** became better and better. One day, they went to Zhang Fei's **peach blossom garden**, and the three of them **swore to be brothers**, under the peach blossom tree.

tā men fā shì bù qiú tóng nián tóng yuè tóng rì shēng dàn qiú tóng nián
他们**发誓**：“不求同年同月同日**生**，但求同年
tóng yuè tóng rì sǐ liú bèi dāng dà gē guān yǔ shì èr gē zhāng fēi
同月同日**死**。”刘备当大哥，关羽是二哥，张飞
shì sān dì
是三弟。

They **vowed** that: “We might not have **born** on the same day and same year, but we are willing to **die** on the same day and same year.” Liu Bei became the big brother, Guan Yu the second brother, and Zhang Fei the third brother.

zhāng fēi hái qǐng rén wèi tā men dǎ zào le sān bǎ dāo jiàn liú bèi de shuāng
张飞还请人为他们打造了三把**刀剑**：刘备的**双**

gǔ jiàn guān yǔ de qīng lóng yǎn yuè dāo zhāng fēi de zhàng bā shé máo
股剑，关羽的**青龙偃月刀**，张飞的**丈八蛇矛**。

Zhang Fei also had three **swords** made for them: Liu Bei's **Double-stranded Sword**, Guan Yu's **Green Dragon Moon Sword** and Zhang Fei's **Zhang Eight Snake Spear**.

tā men zhǔn bèi cóng cǐ tà shàng yīng xióng zhī lù zǔ jiàn zì jǐ de jūn duì
他们准备**从此**踏上英雄之路，**组建**自己的军队！

They were ready to embark on the heroic road **from that moment** and **to form** their own army!

你觉得刘备是个怎样的人？他跟张飞和关羽结拜成兄弟是真心的吗？请给出理由。

What kind of person do you think Liu Bei was? Was he truly sincere to swear brothers with Zhang Fei and Guan Yu? Please give reasons.

Culture Corner

The Oath of the Peach Garden (桃园结义) is the opening chapter of renowned historic novel **Romance of the Three Kingdoms** (三国演义). The oath bound the three men, who later played important roles in the establishment of the state of Shu Han during the Three Kingdoms period in Chinese history. The swords made for them are also amongst the most legendary Chinese weapons. And the legend of their brotherhood became so influential that for thousands of years many people follow the same path when swearing as close mates.

Key Vocabulary

wú néng 无能	*adj.*	incompetent	tàn qì 叹气	*v.*	to sign
fǔ bài 腐败	*adj.*	corrupt	chéng xīn 诚心	*adj.*	sincere
mèng xiǎng 梦想	*n.*	dream/aim	lè yú zhù rén 乐于助人	*idiom*	happy to help others
zhōng nián 中年	*n.*	mid-age	mù biāo 目标	*n.*	goal
chéng yuán 成员	*n.*	member	shí xiàn 实现	*v.*	to achieve
zhèng qián 挣钱	*v.*	to earn money	jī xù 积蓄	*n.*	savings
pǔ tōng rén 普通人	*n.*	normal people	xìng gāo cǎi liè 兴高采烈	*idiom*	extremely happy
tǒng zhì zhě 统治者	*n.*	ruler	zhì qù xiāng tóu 志趣相投	*idiom*	like-minded
gào shì 告示	*n.*	signpost/ notice	fā shì 发誓	*v.*	to vow

Sentence Patterns

和…交朋友

make friends with …

hé jiāo péng yǒu
A + **和** + *B* + **交朋友**

liú bèi dǎ suàn hé zhāng fēi jiāo péng yǒu
刘备打算和张飞交朋友。

Liu Bei planned to make friends with Zhang Fei.

由于…

due to …

yóu yú
由于 + *cause* + *effect*

yóu yú shā le qī fù ruò xiǎo de huài dàn, tā bù néng huí jiā, dào chù liú làng
由于杀了欺负弱小的坏蛋，他不能回家，到处流浪。

Due to killing a jerk who bullied the weak, he was not able to go home, but wandering around.

Chinese Version

汉朝后期，皇帝无能，政府腐败。全国爆发了农民起义，政府不得不到处招兵。

有一句中国名言叫："乱世出英雄。" 而这也是很多人的梦想，包括刘备。

刘备人到中年，虽然是皇室成员，但是很穷，没有权力。

他每天在街上卖草鞋挣钱，表面上是个普通人，心里却梦想着做国家的统治者。

一天，刘备看到了政府招兵的告示，他一边摇头，一边叹气，觉得自己很没用！

突然，他听到有人说了一句："你这个大男人，干嘛叹气？"

刘备很吃惊，一抬头，看到了一个高大的黑脸壮汉。刘备觉得他很有意思，就开始和他聊天。

原来，这个人叫张飞，是个杀猪的，力气很大。虽然有点粗鲁，但是性格豪爽，乐于助人。

刘备告诉张飞自己有远大的目标，但是没钱也没权，怕无法实现。

张飞觉得刘备很有诚心，就告诉他："我家里有一点儿积蓄，也许可以帮到你。"

刘备听后兴高采烈，打算和张飞交朋友，就请他去餐馆喝酒了。

他们在喝酒的时候，突然听到旁边的一个红脸壮汉大喊："快拿酒来，我赶着去报名当兵呢。"

这个人叫关羽，由于杀了欺负弱小的坏蛋，不能回家，到处流浪。

刘备觉得关羽不是一般人，就请他过来加入他们。他们三个人一边喝酒，一边聊天，非常痛快，很快就成为了志趣相投的朋友。

后来他们的关系越来越好。一天，他们去了张飞的桃花园，在桃花树下结拜成兄弟。

他们发誓："不求同年同月同日生，但求同年同月同日死。"刘备当大哥，关羽是二哥，张飞是三弟。

张飞还请人为他们打造了三把刀剑：刘备的双股剑，关羽的青龙偃月刀，张飞的丈八蛇矛。

他们准备从此踏上英雄之路，组建自己的军队！

chì bì zhī zhàn

赤壁之战

The Battle of Red Cliffs

jǐ nián hòu liú bèi zài zhāng fēi guān yǔ de bāng zhù xià jiā rù le
huáng shì qīn qi liú biǎo de zhèn yíng

几年后，刘备**在张飞、关羽的帮助下**，加入了皇室**亲戚**刘表的阵营。

A few years later, **with the help of** Zhang Fei and Guan Yu, Liu Bei joined the camp of Liu Biao, a **relative** from the royal family.

nà shí hòu quán guó yǒu jūn shì shí lì de dà guān dōu tuō lí le zhōng yāng zhèng
fǔ jiàn lì le zì jǐ de guó jiā huò zhèng quán

那时候全国有**军事实力**的大官都**脱离**了中央政府，**建立**了自己的国家或**政权**。

At that time, high-ranking officials with **military strength** all over the country **broke away** from the central government and **established** their own state or **regime**.

shí lì zuì qiáng de cáo cāo zài chéng gōng tǒng yī zhōng guó běi fāng hòu zhǔn
bèi xiāo miè wú guó hé liú biǎo zhèng quán

实力最强的**曹操**，在成功**统一**中国北方后，准备**消灭**吴国和刘表**政权**。

The most powerful was **Cao Cao**, after successfully **unifying** the northern China, he was ready to **destroy** the state of Wu and Liu Biao's **regime**.

dāng shí liú biǎo gāng sǐ ér liú biǎo de ér zi miàn duì cáo cāo de jūn duì
yě bù zhàn ér xiáng yú shì liú bèi jiù dài zhe liú biǎo de bù fēn jūn duì
táo zǒu le

当时刘表刚死，而刘表的儿子面对曹操的军队也**不战而降**，于是刘备就带着刘表的部分军队**逃走**了。

At that time, Liu Biao had just died, and Liu Biao's son **surrendered without fighting** against Cao Cao's army, so Liu Bei **fled** with part of Liu Biao's army.

jiē zhe liú bèi zài dà chén zhū gé liàng de bāng zhù xià chéng gōng yǔ sūn
接着，刘备**在**大臣诸葛亮的**帮助下**成功与孙
quán lǐng dǎo de wú guó lián méng zhǔn bèi yī qǐ duì kàng cáo cāo
权领导的吴国**联盟**，准备一起**对抗**曹操。

Then, **with the help of** minister Zhuge Liang, Liu Bei successfully **formed an alliance** with the state of Wu led by Sun Quan, ready to **fight against** Cao Cao together.

hěn kuài sūn quán jiù pài jiāng jūn zhōu yú hé liú bèi yī qǐ dài zhe bā wàn
很快，孙权就**派**将军周瑜和刘备一起带着八万
lián méng jūn dào le chì bì hé cáo cāo de èr shí duō wàn jūn duì zài jiāng
联盟军到了**赤壁**，和曹操的二十多万军队在江
shàng duì zhì
上**对峙**。

Soon, Sun Quan **sent** general Zhou Yu, along with Liu Bei to the **Red Cliffs**, together with 80,000 alliance forces, and **confront** Cao Cao's over 200,000 troops on the river.

zhōu yú hé liú bèi shāng liang jì cè liú bèi shuō wǒ fāng shí lì yǒu xiàn
周瑜和刘备商量**计策**，刘备说："我方实力有限
bù néng xiǎng zuò shén me jiù zuò shén me zhōu yú biǎo shì tóng yì
，不能**想做什么就做什么**。"周瑜表示同意，
yuàn yì děng dài shí jī
愿意等待**时机**。

Zhou Yu and Liu Bei discussed **strategies**, and Liu Bei said: "Our side's strength is limited, we can't **do whatever we want**." Zhou Yu agreed and was willing to wait for the **opportunity**.

hòu lái cáo cāo wèi le fáng zhǐ tū xí bǎ suǒ yǒu de zhàn chuán lián zài
后来，曹操为了**防止**突袭，把所有的战船**连**在
yī qǐ ér zhè què ràng zhōu yú xiǎng dào le huǒ gōng de jì cè
一起。而这却让周瑜想到了**火攻**的计策。

Later, in order to **prevent** sudden attacks, Cao Cao **connected** all the warships together. But this made Zhou Yu think of the **fire attack** strategy.

dàn shì lián méng jūn bù gǎn zhí jiē jìn gōng yú shì zhōu yú jiù xiě
但是**联盟军**不敢直接**进攻**。于是，周瑜就**写**
xìn gěi cáo cāo biǎo shì yuàn yì tóu xiáng
信给曹操，表示愿意**投降**。

But the **alliance forces** did not dare to **attack** directly. So Zhou Yu **wrote** to Cao Cao, expressing his willingness to **surrender**.

cáo cāo shōu dào xìn hòu xuǎn zé le xiāng xìn jiā shàng tā de jūn duì shí
曹操收到信后，选择了**相信**，加上他的军队**实**
lì gèng qiáng yú shì hěn kuài jiù duì lián méng jūn diào yǐ qīng xīn
力更强，于是很快就对联盟军**掉以轻心**。

After Cao Cao received the letter, he chose to **believe** it, plus his army **strength** was stronger, he quickly **lowered his guard** towards the alliance army.

jié guǒ zài yī gè wǎn shàng zhū gé liàng hé zhōu yú lì yòng fēng xiàng pài rén qiāo qiāo qù cáo cāo de zhàn chuán shàng fàng huǒ

结果，在一个晚上，诸葛亮和周瑜**利用**风向派人**悄悄**去曹操的战船上**放火**。

As a result, one night, Zhuge Liang and Zhou Yu **took advantage** of the wind direction, and sent soldiers to **set fire** to Cao Cao's warship **in secret**.

cáo cāo cuò bù jí fáng mìng lìng jiù huǒ kě shì fēng tài dà le mǎ shàng suǒ yǒu de zhàn chuán dōu zháo huǒ le

曹操**措不及防**，命令**救火**，可是风太大了，马上所有的战船都**着火**了。

Cao Cao was **caught off guard** and ordered to **put out the fire**, but the wind was so strong that immediately all the warships **caught fire**.

jiē zhe lián méng jūn chèng jī jìn gōng hěn kuài jiù xiāo miè le cáo cāo jī hū yī bàn de jūn duì

接着，联盟军**乘机**进攻，很快就**消灭**了曹操几乎一半的军队。

Then, the alliance forces **took the opportunity** to attack and quickly **wiped out** almost half of Cao Cao's army.

cáo cāo sǔn shī tài dà zhī néng dài lǐng shèng yú de jūn duì táo pǎo tā nù huǒ chōng tiān fēi cháng hòu huǐ duì dí rén diào yǐ qīng xīn

曹操**损失**太大，只能**带领**剩余的军队逃跑，他**怒火冲天**，非常后悔对敌人**掉以轻心**。

Cao Cao **lost** too much and could only **lead** the remaining army to escape. He was **extremely furious** and regretted so much **lowering the guard** to the enemy.

ér liú bèi què zài zhè chǎng dà zhàn hòu shí lì dà zēng bù jiǔ jiù qù le sì chuān jiàn lì shǔ guó

而刘备却在这场大战后实力**大增**，不久就去了四川**建立**蜀国。

Yet, Liu Bei's strength **increased greatly** after this battle, and soon he went to Sichuan to **establish** the state of Shu.

chì bì zhī zhàn de jié guǒ yě ràng zhōng guó màn màn jìn rù le sān guó shí dài tā men fēn bié shì cáo cāo de wèi guó liú bèi de shǔ guó hé sūn quán de wú guó

赤壁之战的结果也让中国慢慢进入了**三国时代**。它们**分别**是曹操的魏国，刘备的蜀国，和孙权的吴国。

The result of the **Battle of Red Cliffs** also made China gradually enter the **era of the Three Kingdoms**. They were Cao Cao's state of Wei, Liu Bei's state of Shu, and Sun Quan's state of Wu **respectively**.

SUMMARY

The Battle of Red Cliffs (赤壁之战) was a decisive battle fought in China during the Three Kingdoms period, in the year 208 AD. The battle was fought between the forces of the warlord Cao Cao and the allied forces of the warlords Liu Bei and Sun Quan, and was a critical moment in the formation of the Three Kingdoms, which would later become the foundation of the kingdom of Shu, the kingdom of Wu, and the kingdom of Wei.

The battle took place along the Yangtze River and was notable for its use of naval warfare and innovative tactics. The forces of Liu Bei and Sun Quan were able to use their naval prowess and clever stratagems to defeat the much larger army of Cao Cao and secure their control over the southeastern regions of China.

你觉得曹操是个怎样的人？如果他没有对敌人掉以轻心，你觉得他会被打败吗？请给出理由。

What kind of person do you think Cao Cao was? Do you think he would be defeated if he didn't lower his guard to his enemies? Please give reasons.

CULTURE CORNER

The Three Kingdoms period is widely considered one of the most dramatic periods in Chinese history, and it is often depicted in Chinese literature, film, TV, and video games. It produced many of China's most famous individuals.

Today, Liu Bei's tomb can be found inside of Wuhou Temple in Chengdu. As for Cao Cao, he was revered and feared for his ruthlessness and cunning so much that there is a famous saying: "**Speak Cao Cao and he shall appear**" (说曹操，曹操到 shuō cáo cāo, cáo cāo dào), which is much like the English phrase "Speak of the Devil." Cao Cao's son, Cao Pi (曹丕 cáo pī), became the first emperor of Cao Wei (曹魏 cáo wèi) after forcing the last ruler of the Eastern Han to abdicate.

Key Vocabulary

亲戚	qīn qi	*n.*	relative	防止	fáng zhǐ	*v.*	to prevent
军事	jūn shì	*n.*	military	投降	tóu xiáng	*v.*	to surrender
实力	shí lì	*n.*	strength	进攻	jìn gōng	*v.*	to attack
脱离	tuō lí	*v.*	to break away	利用	lì yòng	*v.*	take advantage of
掉以轻心	diào yǐ qīng xīn	*idiom*	lower one's guard	统一	tǒng yī	*v.*	to unify
政权	zhèng quán	*n.*	regime	着火	zháo huǒ	*v.*	be on fire
措不及防	cuò bù jí fáng	*idiom*	be caught off guard	联盟	lián méng	*n.* *v.*	alliance to form alliance
不战而降	bù zhàn ér xiáng	*idiom*	to surrender without fighting	时代	shí dài	*n.*	era
怒火冲天	nù huǒ chōng tiān	*idiom*	extremely angry	计策	jì cè	*n.*	strategy

Sentence Patterns

在…的帮助下

with the help of ...

在 (zài) + *noun* + **的帮助下** (de bāng zhù xià) + *result*

刘备在张飞、关羽的帮助下，加入了皇室亲戚刘表的阵营。

liú bèi zài zhāng fēi、guān yǔ de bāng zhù xià, jiā rù le huáng shì qīn qi liú biǎo de zhèn yíng.

With the help of Zhang Fei and Guan Yu, Liu Bei joined the camp of Liu Biao, a relative from the royal family.

想…什么就…什么

indicate just do whatever someone wants

想 (xiǎng) + *verb* + **什么** (shén me) + **就** (jiù) + *verb* + **什么** (shén me)

刘备说："我方实力有限，不能想做什么就做什么。"

liú bèi shuō: "wǒ fāng shí lì yǒu xiàn, bù néng xiǎng zuò shén me jiù zuò shén me."

Liu Bei said: "Our side's strength is limited, we can't do whatever we want."

Chinese Version

几年后，刘备在张飞、关羽的帮助下，加入了皇室亲戚刘表的阵营。

那时候全国有军事实力的大官都脱离了中央政府，建立了自己的国家或政权。

实力最强的曹操，在成功统一中国北方后，准备消灭吴国和刘表政权。

当时刘表刚死，而刘表的儿子面对曹操的军队也不战而降，于是刘备就带着刘表的部分军队逃走了。

接着，刘备在大臣诸葛亮的帮助下成功与孙权领导的吴国联盟，准备一起对抗曹操。

很快，孙权就派将军周瑜和刘备一起带着八万联盟军到了赤壁，和曹操的二十多万军队在江上对峙。

周瑜和刘备商量计策，刘备说："我方实力有限，不能想做什么就做什么。"周瑜表示同意，愿意等待时机。

后来，曹操为了防止突袭，把所有的战船连在一起。而这却让周瑜想到了火攻的计策。

但是联盟军不敢直接进攻。于是，周瑜就写信给曹操，表示愿意投降。

曹操收到信后，选择了相信，加上他的军队实力更强，于是很快就对联盟军掉以轻心。

结果，在一个晚上，诸葛亮和周瑜利用风向派人悄悄去曹操的战船上放火。

曹操措不及防，命令救火，可是风太大了，马上所有的战船都着火了。

接着，联盟军乘机进攻，很快就消灭了曹操几乎一半的军队。

曹操损失太大，只能带领剩余的军队逃跑，他怒火冲天，非常后悔对敌人掉以轻心。

而刘备却在这场大战后实力大增，不久就去了四川建立蜀国。

赤壁之战的结果也让中国慢慢进入了三国时代。它们分别是曹操的魏国，刘备的蜀国，和孙权的吴国。

kōng chéng jì

空城计

Empty Fort Strategy

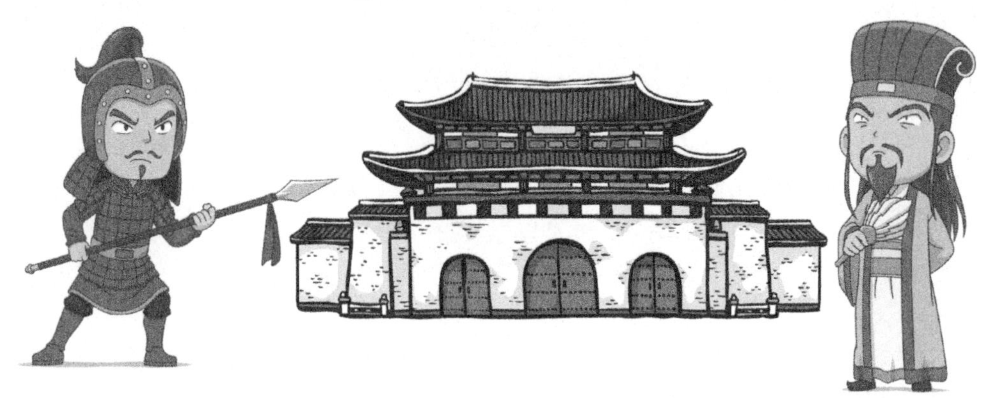

duō nián hòu liú bèi bìng sǐ bǎ shǔ guó chuán gěi zì jǐ de ér zi liú
多年后，刘备**病死**，把蜀国**传给**自己的儿子刘
shàn zhè shí sān guó zhī jiān wèi le tǒng yī quán zhōng guó zào chéng
禅。这时，三国之间为了统一全中国，**造成**
le bù duàn de zhàn zhēng
了不断的战争。

Years later, Liu Bei **died of illness** and **passed on** the state of Shu to his son Liu Shan. At this time, in order to unify the whole of China, the three states **caused** constant wars within one another.

kě shì liú shàn tiān shēng zhì zhàng yīn wèi tā de xiǎo míng jiào ā dòu suǒ
可是刘禅**天生智障**，因为他的**小名**叫阿斗，所
yǐ bèi dà jiā xiào chēng wéi fú bù qǐ de ā dòu
以被大家**笑称**为："扶不起的阿斗。"

However, Liu Shan was **born with mental retardation**, because his **nickname** was A Dou, everyone **jokingly referred** to him as: "A Dou, the dummy who can't be helped".

yīn cǐ hěn duō guó jiā dà shì dōu děi kào shǒu xiàng zhū gé liàng yǒu yī
因此，很多**国家大事**都得靠**首相**诸葛亮。有一
nián zhū gé liàng dài lǐng jūn duì hé wèi guó dǎ zhàng
年，诸葛亮**带领**军队和魏国打仗。

Hence, many important **state affairs** depended on the **Prime Minister** Zhuge Liang. One year, Zhuge Liang **led** the army to fight with the state of Wei.

dāng shí zhū gé liàng de jūn duì gāng gāng jīng lì le yī chǎng dà bài sǔn
当时，诸葛亮的军队刚刚**经历**了一场大败，**损**
shī hěn dà zhǐ néng zài xī chéng xiū xī
失很大，**只能**在西城休息。

At that time, Zhuge Liang's side had just **experienced** a big defeat, the **loss** was huge that he and his army **could only** rest in the West City.

kě shì zhè shí hòu wèi guó de dà jiāng jūn sī mǎ yì dài lǐng jūn duì dào
可是，这时候魏国的**大将军**司马懿带领军队**到**
dá le chéng wài zhǔn bèi jìn gōng
达了城外，准备**进攻**。

However, at this time, Wei's **great general** Sima Yi led his army **arriving** outside of the city, ready to **attack**.

dà jiā tīng dào zhè gè xiāo xi dōu hěn hài pà yīn wèi zhū gé liàng de
大家听到这个消息，都很**害怕**，因为诸葛亮的
jūn duì zhǐ yǒu jǐ qiān rén ér sī mǎ yì de jūn duì yǒu shí wǔ wàn rén
军队只有几千人，而司马懿的**军队**有十五万人。

Everyone in the city was very **scared** when they heard the news, because Zhuge Liang's **army** has only a few thousand men, while Sima Yi's **army** had 150,000 men.

hěn duō rén dōu quàn zhū gé liàng táo pǎo kě shì tā méi yǒu tā sī kǎo
很多人都**劝**诸葛亮逃跑，可是他没有。他**思考**
le yī huì ér rán hòu dàn dìng de gào sù dà jiā wǒ yǒu yī gè
了一会儿，然后**淡定**地告诉大家："我有一个
bàn fǎ néng ràng sī mǎ yì tuì bīng
办法，能让司马懿**退兵**。"

Many people **persuaded** Zhuge Liang to escape, but he did not. He **thought** a while, then told everyone **calmly**: "I have a way to get Sima Yi to **retreat**."

shǒu xiān zhū gé liàng ràng shì bīng men dǎ kāi chéng mén rán hòu ràng yī xiē
首先，诸葛亮让士兵们打开城门，**然后**让一些
shì bīng dǎ bàn chéng bǎi xìng de yàng zi zài chéng mén sǎo dì zuì hòu
士兵打扮成**百姓**的样子，在城门扫地。**最后**，
tā yī gè rén pá shàng le chéng qiáng
他一个人爬上了城墙。

Firstly, Zhuge Liang asked the soldiers to open the city gate, **then** he asked some of them disguised as **ordinary citizens** sweeping the ground at the city gates. **Finally**, he climbed to the city gate alone.

tā zài chéng qiáng yī biān kàn fēng jǐng yī biān tán qín kàn shàng qù fēi cháng
他在城墙**一边**看风景，**一边**弹琴，看上去非常
yōu rán zì dé
悠然自得。

He was watching the scenery **while** playing Guqin (Chinese musical instrument) at the city wall, looking **very relaxed**.

sī mǎ yì de qián fāng bù duì kàn dào zhè yàng de qíng kuàng gǎn jué fēi cháng
司马懿的**前方部队**看到这样的情况，感觉非常
mí huò jiù jí máng bǎ zhè jiàn shì gào sù le sī mǎ yì
迷惑，就**急忙**把这件事告诉了司马懿。

Sima Yi's **frontline troops** felt very **confused** when they seeing this and **hurriedly** reported it to Sima Yi.

sī mǎ yì bù xiāng xìn xiào zhe shuō zhè zěn me kě néng yú
司马懿不**相信**，笑着说："这怎么可能？"于
shì tā jiù yī gè rén qí zhe mǎ qù le chéng mén
是，他就一个人骑着马去了**城门**。

Sima Yi didn't **believe** it, he smiled and said, "How is this possible? So he himself rode a horse to the **city gate**.

tā zhēn de kàn jiàn le chéng mén dà kāi zhe ér zhū gé liàng zuò zài chéng qiáng
他真的看见了城门**大开**着，而诸葛亮坐在城墙
shàng yōu rán zì dé de tán qín
上**悠然自得**地弹琴。

He really saw that the city gate was **wide open**, and Zhuge Liang was indeed sitting on the city wall playing the music **relaxingly**.

sī mǎ yì jué de yòu mí huò yòu hài pà tā bù zhī dào chéng lǐ de
司马懿觉得**又**迷惑，**又**害怕，他不知道城里的
zhēn shí qíng kuàng hěn dān xīn zhè shì yī gè xiàn jǐng
真实**情况**，很担心这是一个**陷阱**。

Sima Yi felt felt confused **and** scared. He didn't know the real **situation** in the city, and was worried that this was a **trap**.

sī kǎo piàn kè hòu tā jué dìng fàng qì jìn gōng mìng lìng tā de jūn duì
思考**片刻**后，他决定**放弃**进攻，命令他的军队
mǎ shàng tuì bīng
马上**退兵**。

After thinking for **a moment**, he decided to **give up** the attack and ordered his army to **retreat** immediately.

zhū gé liàng de wēi jī jiù zhè yàng jiě jué le tā bù dàn méi yǒu táo pǎo
诸葛亮的**危机**就这样解决了。他不但没有逃跑
ér qiě hái yòng tā de zhì huì hé yǒng qì xià pǎo le qiáng dà de dí rén
，而且还用他的**智慧**和**勇气**吓跑了强大的敌人。

Zhuge Liang's **crisis** was resolved in this way. Not only did he not escape, but he used his **wisdom** and **courage** to scare away powerful enemies.

zhōng guó de zhù míng jūn shì zhù zuò sūn zi bīng fǎ zhōng shuō zhī jǐ
中国的**著名**军事著作《孙子兵法》中说：**知己**
zhī bǐ bǎi zhàn bǎi shèng
知彼，百战百胜。

In the **renowned** Chinese military masterpiece "Sun Tzu The Art of War", it is said: **if you know yourself and know the enemy, you need not fear the result of one hundred battles**.

zhū gé liàng jiù shì yīn wèi liǎo jiě sī mǎ yì zhī dào tā duō yí bù
诸葛亮就是因为**了解**司马懿，知道他**多疑**，不
gǎn mào xiǎn cái chéng gōng yòng le kōng chéng jì
敢冒险，才**成功**用了"空城计"。

It was because Zhuge Liang **knew** Sima Yi **well**, and knew that he was **suspicious** and dared not to risk, so he **successfully** used the "empty fort strategy."

Summary

The **Empty City/Fort Strategy** (空 城 计) is the thirty-second strategy among the **Thirty-six Strategems** (三 十 六 计), a collection of Chinese military tactics and strategies used to gain advantage in war and politics, inspired by **Sun Tzu The Art of War** (孙子兵法). The strategy embodies the idea of using wit and intelligence to win battles rather than brute force, just as Sun Tzu said:

yòng bīng zhě shèng ér bù zhàn ér zhì zhě wéi shàng
用兵者，胜而不战，而治者为上

The supreme art of war is to subdue the enemy without fighting

你觉得诸葛亮是个怎样的人？如果你是他，但是不了解司马懿，**你会选择逃跑还是照样会使用空城计？**请给出理由。

What kind of person do you think Zhuge Liang was? If you were him, but didn't know Sima Yi well, would you choose to run away or still use the empty fort strategy? Please give reasons.

Culture Corner

Zhuge Liang (诸葛亮), also known as Kong Ming (孔明), was a highly regarded military strategist during the Three Kingdoms period in ancient China. He served as the Prime Minister of Shu, a state located in present-day Sichuan province. As a testament to his impact, the Wuhou Temple in Chengdu was built to commemorate him, this is also where Liu Bei's tomb lies.

Sima Yi was a prominent figure in the State of Cao Wei, serving as a general and eventually as a regent. He staged a successful coup d'état, becoming the most powerful person in Wei and laying the foundation for his grandson, Sima Yan, to establish the Jin dynasty as its first emperor.

Learning Tip

扶不起的阿斗 (fú bù qǐ de ā dòu) (A Dou, the dummy who cannot be helped) is a common colloquialism used to describe "hopeless idiots." Sometimes, no matter how much you try and help someone, they just can't be helped! The origin of this phrase comes from Liu Bei's son, as explained in the story.

Key Vocabulary

造成 (zào chéng)	*v.*	to cause	淡定 (dàn dìng)	*adj.*	calm
天生 (tiān shēng)	*adj.*	inherent	智障 (zhì zhàng)	*n.*	retardation/ extreme low IQ
退兵 (tuì bīng)	*v.*	to retreat	悠然自得 (yōu rán zì dé)	*idiom*	very relaxed and feeling free
小名 (xiǎo míng)	*n.*	nickname	部队 (bù duì)	*n.*	troops
首相 (shǒu xiàng)	*n.*	prime minister	迷惑 (mí huò)	*adj.*	confused
带领 (dài lǐng)	*v.*	to lead	急忙 (jí máng)	*adv.*	hurriedly/ hastily
损失 (sǔn shī)	*n.*	loss	情况 (qíng kuàng)	*n.*	situation
进攻 (jìn gōng)	*v.*	to attack	陷阱 (xiàn jǐng)	*n.*	trap
害怕 (hài pà)	*adj.*	afraid	片刻 (piàn kè)	*n.*	a moment
军队 (jūn duì)	*n.*	army	危机 (wēi jī)	*n.*	crisis
思考 (sī kǎo)	*v.*	to think (deeply)	智慧 (zhì huì)	*n.*	wisdom

Sentence Patterns

造成...

to cause ...

zào chéng
subject + **造成** + *negative result*

sān guó zhī jiān wèi le tǒng yī quán zhōng guó, zào chéng le bù duàn de zhàn zhēng
三国之间为了统一全中国，造成了不断的战争。

In order to unify the whole of China, the three states caused constant wars within one another.

首先...然后...最后

firstly ... then ... finally ...

shǒuxiān rán hòu zuì hòu
首先 + *action 1* + **然后** + *action 2* + **最后** + *action 3*

shǒu xiān, zhū gé liàng ràng shì bīng men dǎ kāi chéng mén, rán hòu ràng yī xiē shì bīng dǎ bàn chéng bǎi xìng de yàng zi, zài chéng mén sǎo dì. zuì hòu, tā yī gè rén pá shàng le chéngqiáng
首先，诸葛亮让士兵们打开城门，然后让一些士兵打扮成百姓的样子，在城门扫地。最后，他一个人爬上了城墙。

Firstly, Zhuge Liang asked the soldiers to open the city gate, then he asked some of them disguised as ordinary citizens sweeping the ground at the city gates. Finally, he climbed to the city gate alone.

CHINESE VERSION

多年后，刘备病死，把蜀国传给自己的儿子刘禅。这时，三国之间为了统一全中国，造成了不断的战争。

可是刘禅天生智障，因为他的小名叫阿斗，所以被大家笑称为“扶不起的阿斗”。

因此，很多国家大事都得靠首相诸葛亮。有一年，诸葛亮带领军队和魏国打仗。

当时，诸葛亮的军队刚刚经历了一场大败，损失很大，只能在西城休息。

可是，这时候魏国的大将军司马懿带领军队到达了城外，准备进攻。

大家听到这个消息，都很害怕，因为诸葛亮的军队只有几千人，而司马懿的军队有十五万人。

很多人都劝诸葛亮逃跑，可是他没有。他思考了一会儿，然后淡定地告诉大家：“我有一个办法，能让司马懿退兵。”

首先，诸葛亮让士兵们打开城门，然后让一些士兵打扮成百姓的样子，在城门扫地。最后，他一个人爬上了城墙。

他在城墙一边看风景，一边弹琴，看上去非常悠然自得。

司马懿的前方部队看到这样的情况，感觉非常迷惑，就急忙把这件事告诉了司马懿。

司马懿不相信，笑着说：“这怎么可能？”于是，他就一个人骑着马去了城门。

他真的看见了城门大开着，而诸葛亮坐在城墙上悠然自得地弹琴。

司马懿觉得又迷惑，又害怕，他不知道城里的真实情况，很担心这是一个陷阱。

思考片刻后，他决定放弃进攻，命令他的军队马上退兵。

诸葛亮的危机就这样解决了。他不但没有逃跑，而且还用他的智慧和勇气吓跑了强大的敌人。

中国的著名军事著作《孙子兵法》中说:知己知彼,百战百胜。

诸葛亮就是因为了解司马懿，知道他多疑，不敢冒险，才成功用了“空城计”。

Chinese Proverbs

谚 yàn
语 yǔ
故 gù
事 shì

guì rén duō wàng shì

贵人多忘事 28

táng cháo shí qī yǒu gè xué zhě jiào wáng líng rán, tā cóng xiǎo jiù mèng xiǎng zhe dāng guān. kě shì, zhī yǒu tōng guò kē jǔ kǎo shì cái huì yǒu jī huì bèi pìn yòng wéi guān yuán.

唐朝时期有个**学者**叫王泠然，他从小就**梦想着**当官。可是，只有通过**科举考试**才会有机会**被聘用为**官员。

During the Tang Dynasty, there was a **scholar** named Wang Lingran, who **dreamed of** becoming an official since he was young. At that time, only those who passed the **imperial examination** would have the opportunity to **be employed as** an official.

duì yú pǔ tōng xué zhě, bù jǐn yào tōng guò dì fāng de kǎo shì, hái yào tōng guò zhōng yāng zhèng fǔ de kǎo shì.

对于普通学者，**不仅**要通过地方的考试，**还**要通过中央政府的考试。

For ordinary scholars, it is necessary to pass **not only** the local examinations, **but also** the examinations of the central government.

yīn cǐ, wáng líng rán fēi cháng nǔ lì, zài yī cì kǎo shì zhōng huò dé le hěn gāo de chéng jì, bèi fēng wéi jìn shì.

因此，王泠然非常努力，在一次考试中获得了很高的**成绩**，被封为**进士**。

Therefore, Wang Lingran worked very hard and got a high **score** in an exam, and received the title of **Imperial Scholar**.

tā fēi cháng gāo xìng, xiǎng zhe hěn kuài jiù kě yǐ dāng guān le. kě shì tā děng le hěn jiǔ, yě méi yǒu bèi zhèng fǔ pìn yòng.

他非常高兴，想着很快就可以**当官**了。可是他等了很久，也没有被政府**聘用**。

He was very happy, thinking that he could **become an official** soon. But he was not **hired** by the government after waiting for a long time.

hòu lái tā cái fā xiàn yào dāng guān guāng tōng guò kǎo shì bù gòu hái
后来，他才发现要当官，**光**通过考试**不**够，还
děi kào guān xì bì xū yǒu gāo guān de tuī jiàn cái néng chéng gōng
得靠“关系”，**必须**有高官的**推荐**才能成功。

Later, he discovered that **only** passing the exam is **not** enough to be selected as an official, but it also depends on “connections,” he **must** have a **recommendation** from a senior official to succeed.

zhè shí tā tū rán xiǎng qǐ le yī gè lǎo péng yǒu gāo chāng yǔ hěn duō
这时，他突然想起了一个**老朋友**高昌宇。很多
nián qián tā men shì fēi cháng hǎo de péng yǒu cháng cháng yī qǐ yán jiū wén
年前，他们是非常好的朋友，常常一起**研究**文
xué
学。

At this time, he suddenly thought of his **old friend** Gao Changyu. Many years ago, they were very good friends and often **studied** literature together.

zài gāo chāng yǔ yù dào jīng jì kùn nán de shí hòu yě shì wáng líng rán wèi
在高昌宇遇到**经济困难**的时候，也是王泠然**为**
tā tí gòng le jīng jì zhī yuán
他**提供**了经济支援。

When Gao Changyu encountered **financial difficulties**, it was also Wang Lingran who **provided** financial support **for** him.

dāng shí tā men chéng nuò duì fāng huì yǒng yuǎn xiāng hù bāng zhù zuò yī
当时，他们**承诺**对方会永远相互帮助，做**一**
bèi zi de péng yǒu kě shì jǐ nián hòu gāo chāng yǔ dāng shàng le gāo
辈子的朋友。可是，几年后高昌宇当上了**高**
guān jiù zài yě bù hé tā lián xì le
官，就再也不和他**联系**了。

At the time, they **promised** each other that they would always help each other and be friends for **a whole life**. However, a few years later, Gao Changyu became a **high-ranking official** and never **contacted** him again.

suī rán wáng líng rán yǒu diǎn shī wàng dàn hái shì zhǔ dòng lián xì le gāo chāng
虽然王泠然有点**失望**，但还是**主动**联系了高昌
yǔ tā gěi gāo chāng yǔ xiě le xìn qǐng qiú gāo chāng yǔ zài zhèng fǔ tuī
宇。他给高昌宇写了信，**请求**高昌宇在政府**推**
jiàn tā wéi guān yuán
荐他为官员。

Although Wang Lingran was a little **disappointed**, he still **took the initiative** to contact Gao Changyu. He wrote a letter to Gao Changyu, **asking** Gao Changyu to **recommend** him as an official in the government.

kě shì guò le hěn jiǔ wáng líng rán yě méi yǒu shōu dào huí xìn tā bù
可是，过了很久王泠然也没有收到**回信**。他不
fàng qì zài hòu lái de liǎng nián jì xù gěi gāo chāng yǔ xiě xìn
放弃，在后来的两年**继续**给高昌宇写信。

However, after a long time, Wang Lingran did not receive a **reply**. He did not **give up** and **continued** to write letters to Gao Changyu for the next two years.

zhōng yú yǒu yī tiān tā shōu dào huí xìn le kě shì gāo chāng yǔ zài xìn
终于有一天，他**收到**回信了。可是高昌宇在信
zhōng biǎo shì bù jì dé dāng nián de chéng nuò hái gào sù tā bié zài xiě xìn
中表示不**记得**当年的承诺，还告诉他别再写信
le
了。

Finally one day, he **received** a reply. However, Gao Changyu said in the letter that he did not **remember** the promise he made back then, and told him not to write any more letters.

wáng líng rán fēi cháng shēng qì tā ná qǐ bǐ xiě le huí fù nǐ
王泠然非常**生气**，他拿起笔，写了回复："你
zhēn shì guì rén duō wàng shì xiàn zài nǐ shì gāo guān jiù chè dǐ wàng le
真是**贵人多忘事**！现在你是高官，就**彻底**忘了
lǎo péng yǒu
老朋友！"

Wang Lingran was very **angry**, he picked up the pen and wrote a reply: "You **noble men just forget things**! Now that you are a high-ranking official, you have **completely** forgotten your old friend!"

tā yuè xiě yuè shēng qì yú shì yòu jiā le yī jù
他越写越生气，于是又**加**了一句：

The more he wrote, the angrier he became, so he also **added**:

nǐ bié wàng le shì shì nán liào jiāng lái yě xǔ wǒ de guān zhí huì
"你别忘了，**世事难料**，将来也许我的**官职**会
bǐ nǐ gèng gāo nǐ xiàn zài bù bāng wǒ yǐ hòu wǒ yě bù huì bāng
比你更高，你现在不帮我，以后我也不会帮
nǐ zán men yī dāo liǎng duàn
你，咱们**一刀两断**！"

"Don't forget, **things are unpredictable**. Maybe my **position** will be higher than yours in the future. If you don't help me now, I won't help you in the future. Let's **end our ties** (cut into two halves with a knife)!

Summary

In this original story behind the proverb we see a proud official who ignored his friends after becoming successful. Do you think that success and power can lead people to become self-centered or does it simply exaggerate existing characteristics?

Culture Corner

Wang Lingran struggles to succeed because of his lack of good **"connections"** (关 系), something that remains relevant even in modern Chinese society. Building and maintaining good relationships is still considered important for personal and professional success.

Learning Tip

贵人多忘事 is a Chinese proverb, translated as "noble men have short memories." The saying is often used to refer to the tendency of people in positions of power or influence to become forgetful or neglectful of those around them, especially of promises they have made or obligations they have incurred.

1 你真是**贵人多忘事**，上周答应今天请我吃饭，现在却说不记得了。

You are such **a noble man with a short memory**. Last week, you promised to treat me a meal today, but now you are saying not remembering.

2 他总是**贵人多忘事**，我受不了了。

He always **forgets his commitments**, I can't stand it anymore.

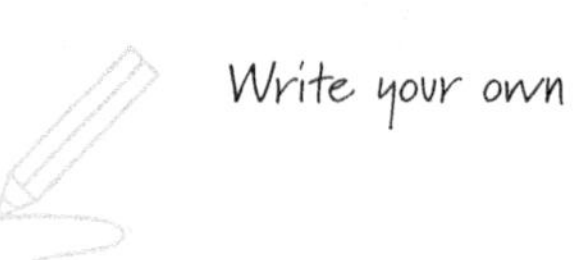

Key Vocabulary

pìn yòng 聘用	*v.*	to hire/employ	lián xì 联系	*v.*	to contact
zhōng yāng 中央	*n.*	central	shī wàng 失望	*adj.*	disappointed
chéng jì 成绩	*n.*	score	zhǔ dòng 主动	*v.*	take the initiative
tuī jiàn 推荐	*v.* *n.*	to recommend recommendation	jì xù 继续	*v.*	to carry on
bì xū 必须	*adv.*	must	huí xìn 回信	*n.* *v.*	reply to reply
yán jiū 研究	*v.*	to study/research	chè dǐ 彻底	*adv.*	completely
jīng jì 经济	*n.* *adj.*	economy financial	yī bèi zi 一辈子	*n.*	a whole life
kùn nán 困难	*n.*	difficulty	yī dāo liǎng duàn 一刀两断	*idiom*	end ties/ relationships
zhī yuán 支援	*n.*	support (material)	shì shì nán liào 世事难料	*idiom*	things in the world are unpredictable

Sentence Patterns

光…不

only … not enough (to reach desired result)

guāng 光 + *condition* + bù 不 + *result*

guāng tōng guò kǎo shì bù gòu
光通过考试不够。

Only by passing the exam is not enough.

为…提供…

provide … for

A + wèi 为 + *B* + tí gòng 提供 + *noun*

wáng líng rán wèi tā tí gōng le jīng jì zhī yuán
王泠然为他提供了经济支援。

Wang Lingran provided financial support for him.

Chinese Version

唐朝时期有个学者叫王泠然，他从小就梦想着当官。可是，只有通过科举考试才会有机会被聘用为官员。

对于普通学者，不仅要通过地方的考试，还要通过中央政府的考试。

因此，王泠然非常努力，在一次考试中获得了很高的成绩，被封为进士。

他非常高兴，想着很快就可以当官了。可是他等了很久，也没有被政府聘用。

后来，他才发现要当官，光通过考试不够，还得靠“关系”，必须有高官的推荐才能成功。

这时，他突然想起了一个老朋友高昌宇。很多年前，他们是非常好的朋友，常常一起研究文学。

在高昌宇遇到经济困难的时候，也是王泠然为他提供了经济支援。

当时，他们承诺对方会永远相互帮助，做一辈子的朋友。可是，几年后高昌宇当上了高官，就再也不和他联系了。

虽然王泠然有点失望，但还是主动联系了高昌宇。他给高昌宇写了信，请求高昌宇在政府推荐他为官员。

可是，过了很久王泠然也没有收到回信。他不放弃，在后来的两年继续给高昌宇写信。

终于有一天，他收到回信了。可是高昌宇在信中表示不记得当年的承诺，还告诉他别再写信了。

王泠然非常生气，他拿起笔，写了回复：“你真是贵人多忘事！现在你是高官，就彻底忘了老朋友！”

他越写越生气，于是又加了一句：

“你别忘了，世事难料，将来也许我的官职会比你更高，你现在不帮我，以后我也不会帮你，咱们一刀两断!”

jūn zǐ bào chóu shí nián bù wǎn

君子报仇，十年不晚

Never Too Late to Take Revenge

cóng qián yǒu yī gè nóng mín jiào lǐ jūn tā yǒu gè mào měi rú huā de qī zi jiào xiù zhī

从前，有一个**农民**叫李君，他有个**貌美如花**的妻子叫秀芝。

Once upon a time, there was a **farmer** named Li Jun, and he had a **very beautiful** wife named Xiuzhi.

tā men hěn xiāng ài lǐ jūn zhòng tián xiù zhī zhī bù rì zi guò de suī rán hěn jiǎn dān dàn hěn xìng fú

他们很**相爱**，李君种田，秀芝织布，日子过得虽然很**简单**，但很**幸福**。

They were very **in love**. Li Jun was farming and Xiuzhi was weaving. Although their life was **simple**, they were very **happy**.

yǒu yī tiān xiù zhī qù chéng lǐ mài bù yù dào le yī gè huā huā gōng zǐ lǐ hé

有一天，秀芝去城里**卖布**，遇到了一个**花花公子**李和。

One day, Xiuzhi went to the city to **sell cloth** and encountered a **playboy** Li He.

lǐ hé kàn shàng le xiù zhī de měi mào jiù tiáo xì tā xiù zhī yòu shēng qì yòu hài pà zhǔn bèi lí kāi

李和看上了秀芝的**美貌**，就**调戏**她。秀芝又生气又害怕，准备**离开**。

Li He took a fancy to Xiuzhi's **beauty** and **teased** her. Xiuzhi was angry and scared, and was about to **leave**.

kě shì lǐ hé què ràng pū rén bǎ xiù zhī bǎng jià dào tā jiā lǐ xiǎng qiáng jiān tā xiù zhī bù duàn fǎn kàng yī tóu zhuàng sǐ zài le zhù zi shàng

可是，李和却让仆人把秀芝**绑架**到他家里，想**强奸**她。秀芝不断**反抗**，一头撞死在了**柱子**上。

However, Li He asked servants to **kidnap** Xiuzhi to his house and wanted to **rape** her. Xiuzhi kept **resisting** and slammed her head into the **pillar** and died.

lǐ jūn tīng dào hòu, mǎ shàng gǎn qù, què zhǐ kàn dào le xiù zhī bīng lěng de shī tǐ.
李君听到后，马上**赶去**，却只看到了秀芝冰冷的**尸体**。

After Li Jun heard it, he **rushed over** immediately, but only saw Xiuzhi's cold **body**.

tā yòu tòng xīn yòu jué wàng, xiǎng zhuā lǐ hé qù jǐng chá jú. kě shì lǐ hé yǒu qián yǒu shì, lián jǐng chá dōu bù gǎn dòng tā.
他又**痛心**又绝望，想抓李和去**警察局**。可是李和**有钱有势**，**连**警察都不敢动他。

He was so **distressed** and desperate, and wanted to seize Li He to the **police station**. But Li He was **rich and powerful**, **even** the police dared not to touch him.

lǐ hé shèn zhì ràng pū rén bǎ lǐ jūn dǎ de biàn tǐ lín shāng, rán hòu bǎ tā rēng dào le yuǎn chù de shān lín lǐ.
李和**甚至**让仆人把李君打得**遍体鳞伤**，然后把他**扔**到了远处的山林里。

Li He **even** had his servants give Li Jun **bruises all over the body**, then **threw** him into the distant forest.

lǐ jūn shāng de tài yán zhòng, hūn mí le liǎng tiān liǎng yè, xìng kuī bèi yī gè hé shàng kàn jiàn, bǎ tā bēi huí le sì miào.
李君伤得太**严重**，**昏迷**了两天两夜，幸亏被一个**和尚**看见，把他背回了**寺庙**。

Li Jun was so **seriously** injured that he **was in a coma** for two days and two nights. Fortunately, a **monk** saw him and carried him back to the **temple**.

lǐ jūn xǐng lái hòu, zhī dào shì hé shàng jiù le tā, fēi cháng gǎn jī. tā fā xiàn zhè gè hé shàng tiān tiān zài yuàn zi lǐ liàn wǔ, shì gè wǔ shù gāo shǒu.
李君醒来后，知道是和尚**救**了他，非常**感激**。他发现这个和尚天天在院子里**练武**，是个武术**高手**。

When Li Jun woke up, he knew that it was the monk who **saved** him, and he was very **grateful**. He found that this monk **practiced martial arts** in the courtyard every day and was a **master** of martial arts.

yú shì, lǐ jūn guì xià qiú hé shàng jiāo tā wǔ gōng. hé shàng běn lái hěn yóu yù, kě tīng dào lǐ jūn bēi cǎn de gù shì hòu jiù tóng yì le.
于是，李君**跪下**求和尚教他武功。和尚本来很**犹豫**，可听到李君**悲惨**的故事后就同意了。

So Li Jun **knelt down** and begged the monk to teach him martial arts. The monk was **hesitant** at first, but he agreed after hearing Li Jun's **tragic** story.

hòu lái lǐ jūn tiān tiān gēn hé shàng nǔ lì xué wǔ lì zhì chéng wéi wǔ shù gāo shǒu
后来，李君天天跟和尚努力学武，**立志**成为武术高手。

Later, Li Jun studied hard with the monk to learn martial arts every day, **determined** to become a martial arts master.

lǐ jūn gào sù zì jǐ jiù suàn huā shí nián de shí jiān wǒ yě yào liàn hǎo wǔ shù rán hòu wèi qī zi bào chóu
李君告诉自己："**就算**花十年的时间，我**也要**练好武术，然后为妻子报仇。"

Li Jun told himself: "**Even if** it takes ten years, I **have to** practice martial arts well, then avenge my wife."

shí nián hòu lǐ jūn de mù biāo shí xiàn le zhēn de chéng wéi le wǔ shù gāo shǒu yú shì tā dài zhe jiàn xià shān qù le lǐ hé jiā
十年后，李君的**目标**实现了，真的成为了**武术高手**。于是，他带着**剑**下山去了李和家。

Ten years later, Li Jun's **goal** was achieved, he really became a **martial arts master**. So, he took the **sword** down the mountain to Li He's house.

tā yī jiǎo tī kāi mén pú rén men kàn jiàn hòu mǎ shàng qù dǎ tā què hěn kuài quán bù bèi tā dǎ dǎo le
他一脚**踢**开门，**仆人们**看见后，马上去打他，却很快全部被他**打倒**了。

He **kicked** the door open, and when the **servants** saw him, they immediately went to beat him, but he quickly **knocked** them all **down**.

tā zhōng yú zhuā zhù le lǐ hé dà shēng wèn nǐ hái jì dé wǒ de qī zi xiù zhī ma
他终于**抓住**了李和，大声问："你还**记得**我的妻子秀芝吗？"

He finally **seized** Li He and asked loudly, "Do you **remember** my wife Xiuzhi?"

lǐ hé yòu jīng yòu pà lián máng qiú lǐ jūn ráo mìng lǐ jūn yī jiàn cì jìn le tā de xīn zàng shā sǐ le tā
李和又惊又怕，**连忙**求李君**饶命**。李君一剑**刺进**了他的心脏，杀死了他。

Li He was shocked and scared, **rashly** begging Li Jun to **spare** his **life**. Li Jun **stabbed into** his heart with his sword and killed him.

rán hòu tā yòng jiàn zài qiáng shàng xiě xià le jūn zǐ bào chóu shí nián bù wǎn
然后，他用剑在墙上写下了：**君子报仇，十年不晚**！

Then, he wrote on the wall with the sword: **Never too Late to Take Revenge**!

SUMMARY

The story behind this proverb shows us a tragic story of revenge, but the story itself is to show the importance of **strong determination** (决心 jué xīn) when it comes to achieve goals in life. Ten years is a long time for any goal, but as long as you are determined for success, the time doesn't matter, but the result.

Learning Tip

君子报仇，十年不晚 is a Chinese proverb, translated as: Never too Late to Take Revenge, used to show strong determination to achieve goals, not necessarily always relating to revenge.

1 别忘了：**君子报仇，十年不晚**。你好好加油，以后当上总监，他就不敢欺负你了。

Don't forget: **never too late to take revenge**. Just work hard, and when you become a director in the future, he will not dare to bully you.

2 **君子报仇，十年不晚**！我要继续加油，成立公司，让所有人都不敢看低我。

Never too late to take revenge! I will continue to work hard and set up my company so that no one dares to look down on me.

KEY VOCABULARY

mào měi rú huā 貌美如花	*idiom*	as beautiful as a flower (woman)	měi mào 美貌	*n.*	beauty (appearance)
huā huā gōng zǐ 花花公子	*idiom*	playboy	jǐng chá jú 警察局	*n.*	police station
biàn tǐ lín shāng 遍体鳞伤	*idiom*	bruises all over the body	yán zhòng 严重	*adj.*	serious/ severe
tiáo xì 调戏	*v.*	to tease/ harass	gǎn jī 感激	*adj.*	grateful
bǎng jià 绑架	*v.*	to kidnap	yóu yù 犹豫	*adj.*	hesitant
qiáng jiān 强奸	*v.*	to rape	bēi cǎn 悲惨	*adj.*	tragic
fǎn kàng 反抗	*v.*	to resist	lì zhì 立志	*v.*	determine to
wǔ shù gāo shǒu 武术高手	*n.*	martial arts master	tòng xīn 痛心	*adj.*	distressed/ heart-broken
yǒu qián yǒu shì 有钱有势	*idiom*	rich and powerful	shī tǐ 尸体	*n.*	dead body

SENTENCE PATTERNS

连…

even (stress a higher degree)

clause 1 + lián **连** + *clause 2*

kě shì lǐ hé yǒu qián yǒu shì, lián jǐng chá dōu bù gǎn dòng tā.
可是李和有钱有势，连警察都不敢动他。

But Li He was rich and powerful, even the police dared not to touch him.

就算…也…

even if ... (emphasize result/determination)

jiù suàn **就算** + *action 1* + yě **也** + *action 2*

jiù suàn huā shí nián de shí jiān, wǒ yě yào liàn hǎo wǔ shù.
就算花十年的时间，我也要练好武术。

Even if it takes ten years, I have to practice martial arts well

CHINESE VERSION

从前，有一个农民叫李君，他有个貌美如花的妻子叫秀芝。

他们很相爱，李君种田，秀芝织布，日子过得虽然很简单，但很幸福。

有一天，秀芝去城里卖布，遇到了一个花花公子李和。

李和看上了秀芝的美貌，就调戏她。秀芝又生气又害怕，准备离开。

可是，李和却让仆人把秀芝绑架到他家里，想强奸她。秀芝不断反抗，一头撞死在了柱子上。

李君听到后，马上赶去，却只看到了秀芝冰冷的尸体。

他又痛心又绝望，想抓李和去警察局。可是李和有钱有势，连警察都不敢动他。

李和甚至让仆人把李君打得遍体鳞伤，然后把他扔到了远处的山林里。

李君伤得太严重，昏迷了两天两夜，幸亏被一个和尚看见，把他背回了寺庙。

李君醒来后，知道是和尚救了他，非常感激。他发现这个和尚天天在院子里练武，是个武术高手。

于是，李君跪下求和尚教他武功。和尚本来很犹豫，可听到李君悲惨的故事后就同意了。

后来，李君天天跟和尚努力学武，立志成为武术高手。

李君告诉自己："就算花十年的时间，我也要练好武术，然后为妻子报仇。"

十年后，李君的目标实现了，真的成为了武术高手。于是，他带着剑下山去了李和家。

他一脚踢开门，仆人们看见后，马上去打他，却很快全部被他打倒了。

他终于抓住了李和，大声问：“你还记得我的妻子秀芝吗？”

李和又惊又怕，连忙求李君饶命。李君一剑刺进了他的心脏，杀死了他。

然后，他用剑在墙上写下了：君子报仇，十年不晚！

jiàng zài jūn jūn mìng yǒu suǒ bù shòu

30 将在军，君命有所不受

A General in the Field Is Not Bound by Orders from His Sovereign

孙子兵法

sūn wǔ shì chūn qiū shí qī de qí guó rén zhù míng de jūn shì jiā zhèng
孙武是**春秋时期**的齐国人，**著名**的军事家、政
zhì jiā tā bèi zūn wéi sūn zǐ hé dōng fāng bīng xué de bí zǔ
治家。他**被尊为**“孙子”和“东方兵学的鼻祖”。

Sun Wu was a citizen of the state of Qi in the **Spring and Autumn Period**, a **renowned** military strategist and statesman. He was **regarded as** "Master Sun" and "the originator of eastern military science".

tā de zhù zuò sūn zi bīng fǎ bèi zūn wéi bīng xué shèng diǎn
他的**著作**《孙子兵法》，**被尊为**“兵学圣典”，
zài zhōng guó nǎi zhì shì jiè jūn shì jiè xué shù jiè hé zhé xué jiè dōu
在中国**乃至**世界军事界、学术界、和哲学界都
yǒu jí gāo de dì wèi
有极高的**地位**。

His **masterpiece** "Sun Tzu The Art of War" is **regarded as** the "Sacred Book of Military Studies" and has a very high **status** in military, academic, and philosophical disciplines in China and **even** the world.

sūn wǔ běn lái shì gè mò luò guì zú dàn yǒu hěn gāo de jūn shì cái
孙武**本来**是个没落**贵族**，但有很高的军事**才**
huá zài sān shí duō suì de shí hòu tā jiù xiě xià le sūn zi bīng
华。在三十多岁的时候，他就写下了《孙子兵
fǎ
法》。

Sun Wu was **originally** a declining **nobleman**, but he had great military **talent**. In his thirties, he wrote "The Art of War".

tā de zhì yǒu jiān zhèng fǔ dà guān wǔ zi xū kàn dào hòu fēi cháng xīn shǎng
他的**挚友**兼政府大官伍子胥看到后，非常**欣赏**
jiù xiàng wú wáng tuī jiàn le sūn wǔ
，就**向**吴王**推荐**了孙武。

His **soul mate** and government official Wu Zixu saw it and **admired** it very much, so he **recommended** Sun Wu **to** the King of Wu.

sūn wǔ jiàn dào wú wáng zhī hòu chéng shàng le zì jǐ de shū wú wáng
孙武见到吴王之后，**呈上**了自己的书。吴王
kàn hòu zàn bù jué kǒu wèi le kǎo chá sūn zǐ de lǐng dǎo néng lì
看后，**赞不绝口**。为了考察孙子的**领导能力**，
tā tiāo xuǎn le yī bǎi duō míng gōng nǚ ràng sūn wǔ cāo liàn
他**挑选**了一百多名宫女让孙武**操练**。

After Sun Wu met the King, he **presented** his book to him. The king was **full of praise** after seeing it. In order to test his **leadership ability**, he **selected** more than 100 palace maids for Sun Wu for the **drill**.

sūn wǔ bǎ gōng nǚ men fēn wéi liǎng duì zhǐ dìng wú wáng zuì xǐ ài de liǎng
孙武把宫女们**分为**两队，**指定**吴王最喜爱的两
wèi pín fēi wéi duì zhǎng tóng shí zhǐ dìng yī gè shì wèi zhí xíng jūn fǎ
位嫔妃为**队长**，同时指定一个侍卫**执行**军法。

Sun Wu **divided** the palace maids **into** two teams, and **appointed** two of the King's favorite concubines as **captains**, and at the same time appointed a bodyguard to **carry out** the military law.

dàn cāo liàn kāi shǐ hòu gōng nǚ men què dāng chéng yóu xì bù tīng hào lìng
但**操练**开始后，宫女们却当成**游戏**，不听号令
pěng fù dà xiào dǎo zhì duì wǔ dà luàn
，**捧腹大笑**，导致队伍大乱。

But after the **drill** started, the palace maids regarded it as a **game**, ignoring orders and **laughing heavily**, causing chaos in the contingent.

sūn wǔ biàn gēn jù jūn fǎ yào shā liǎng wèi duì zhǎng wú wáng kàn dào le
孙武便**根据**军法要杀两位队长。吴王看到了，
jiù zhāo jí de shuō wǒ yǐ jīng zhī dào nǐ de néng lì le qǐng bié
就**着急**地说："我已经知道你的**能力**了。请别
shā tā men wǒ yào shì méi yǒu tā men chī fàn shuì jué dōu bù huì
杀她们，我要是没有她们，吃饭睡觉都不会
hǎo
好！"

Sun Wu wanted to kill the two captains **according to** military law. When the king saw it, he said **anxiously**: "I already know your **ability**. Please don't kill them. If I don't have them, I won't be able to eat or sleep well!"

sūn wǔ què jiān jué de shuō jiàng zài jūn jūn mìng yǒu suǒ bù shòu
孙武却**坚决**地说：“**将在军，君命有所不受。**”
jiē zhe mìng lìng shā le liǎng wèi duì zhǎng jì xù cāo liàn
接着**命令**杀了两位队长，继续操练。

Sun Wu, however, said **firmly**: “**A general in the field is not bound by the orders from his sovereign.**” Then he **ordered** the two captains to be killed and continued the drill.

dāng sūn wǔ zài cì fā hào shī lìng de shí hòu gōng nǚ men mǎ shàng yán sù
当孙武再次**发号施令**的时候，宫女们马上**严肃**
qǐ lái jìn tuì yǒu xù zhèn xíng shí fēn zhěng qí
起来，**进退有序**，阵形十分**整齐**。

When Sun Wu **gave the order** again, the maids immediately became **serious**, **advancing and retreating in an orderly manner**, and the formation was very **neat**.

ér wú wáng shī qù le liǎng wèi pín fēi xīn lǐ hěn bù shuǎng sūn wǔ jiù
而吴王失去了两位嫔妃，心里很**不爽**。孙武就
gào sù tā jūn fǎ de mù dì zài yú shǎng fá fēn míng zhǐ yǒu duì
告诉他：“军法的**目的**在于**赏罚分明**，只有对
shì bīng wēi yán tā men cái huì tīng hào lìng dǎ zhàng cái néng shèng lì
士兵威严，他们才会听号令，打仗才能胜利。”

As for the king, he lost two concubines and was very **upset**. So Sun Wu told him: “The **purpose** of military law is to **distinguish between rewards and punishments**. Only by being majestic to the soldiers will they obey orders and win wars.”

tīng le sūn wǔ de jiě shì wú wáng bù zài shēng qì lì kè fēng sūn wǔ
听了孙武的**解释**，吴王不再生气，立刻封孙武
wéi jiāng jūn zài sūn wǔ de xùn liàn xià wú guó de jūn shì sù zhì tí
为**将军**。在孙武的训练下，吴国的**军事素质**提
gāo de hěn kuài zuì zhōng chéng wéi zhàn guó wǔ bà zhī yī
高得很快，最终成为**战国五霸**之一。

After hearing Sun Wu’s **explanation**, King Wu was no longer angry, and immediately named Sun Wu as **general**. Under Sun Wu’s training, Wu’s **military quality** improved rapidly and eventually became one of the **Five Hegemons of the Warring States**.

hòu lái wú guó hé chǔ guó dǎ zhàng sūn wǔ zhǐ huī wú guó jūn duì yǐ sān
后来吴国和楚国打仗，孙武**指挥**吴国军队以三
wàn jūn duì duì kàng chǔ guó de èr shí wàn jūn duì lián xù wǔ zhàn wǔ
万军队，对抗楚国的二十万军队，连续**五战五**
jié chuàng zào le zhōng guó jūn shì shǐ shàng yǐ shǎo shèng duō de qí jì
捷，创造了中国军事史上**以少胜多**的**奇迹**。

Later, when the state of Wu fought the state of Chu, Sun Wu **commanded** Wu’s army of 30,000 troops against Shu's 200,000 in **five consecutive battles and five victories**, creating a **miracle** of **winning the war with less army** in China’s military history.

sūn wǔ wǔ shí duō suì de shí hòu zhì yǒu wǔ zi xū bèi shā sūn wǔ
孙武五十多岁的时候，**挚友**伍子胥被杀，孙武
gǎn dào fēi cháng shāng xīn hé shī wàng zhī hòu cí zhí qù le xiāng xià yǐn
感到非常伤心和**失望**。之后**辞职**，去了乡下**隐**
jū
居。

When Sun Wu was in his fifties, his **soul mate** Wu Zixu was killed, and Sun Wu felt very sad and **disappointed**. Then he **resigned** and went to the countryside to **live in seclusion**.

tā de zhù zuò sūn zi bīng fǎ jǐ qiān nián lái bù duàn liú chuán zài
他的**著作**《孙子兵法》几千年来不断**流传**，在
zhèng zhì jīng jì jūn shì wén huà zhé xué děng lǐng yù dōu bèi tuī
政治、经济、军事、文化、哲学等领域都被**推**
guǎng yùn yòng
广运用。

His **masterpiece** "Sun Tzu The Art of War" has **passed on** for thousands of years and has been **widely used** in politics, economy, military, culture, philosophy and other fields.

mù qián wéi zhǐ zhè běn shū yǐ jīng bèi fān yì chéng èr shí duō zhǒng yǔ yán
目前为止，这本书已经被**翻译成**二十多种语言
yǐng xiǎng le wú shù guó nèi wài de jūn shì jiā zhèng zhì jiā zhé xué
，**影响**了无数**国内外**的军事家、政治家、哲学
jiā hé qǐ yè jiā
家和企业家。

So far, the book has been **translated into** more than twenty languages and has **influenced** countless military strategists, politicians, philosophers and entrepreneurs **at home and abroad**.

SUMMARY

The story behind this proverb illustrates Sun Tzu's character and the successful application of his iconic work The Art of War. Today, the book is widely used in politics and business and is a required study in MBA programs at renowned universities such as **Harvard** (hā fú dà xué 哈弗大学). Many Chinese idioms and proverbs have their roots in this classic work.

I have even written a modern bilingual version of **The Art of War for Language Learners**, catering to higher intermediate and advanced students. If you enjoyed this story then you should definitely check it out!

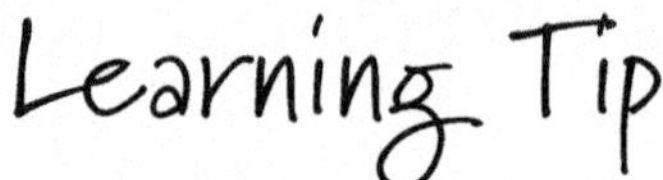

将在军，君命有所不受 is a Chinese proverb, translated as: a general in the field is not bound by the orders from his sovereign, used to indicate that under certain circumstances, one can make his/her own decisions without the consent of their superiors.

1 **将在军，君命有所不受！**这是紧急情况，我们现在就行动，不用请示总统。

A general in the field is not bound by the orders from his sovereign! This is an emergency that we must act on now, no need to consult the President.

2 **将在军，君命有所不受！**既然联系不上总经理，我们就先签合同，之后再向他汇报。

A general in the field is not bound by the orders from his sovereign! Since we can't contact the CEO, we will sign the contract first and report to him later.

Write your own sentence

Key Vocabulary

zhù míng 著名	*adj.*	renowned	zhǐ dìng 指定	*v.*	to appoint
zhù zuò 著作	*n.*	masterpiece	duì zhǎng 队长	*n.*	captain/ team leader
pěng fù dà xiào 捧腹大笑	*idiom*	hold stomach and laugh heavily	dì wèi 地位	*v.*	status
mò luò 没落	*v.*	to decline	jūn shì 军事	*n.*	military
fā hào shī lìng 发号施令	*idiom*	to give order	yán sù 严肃	*adj.*	serious (attitude)
zàn bù jué kǒu 赞不绝口	*idiom*	full of praise	cái huá 才华	*n.*	talent
lǐng dǎo néng lì 领导能力	*n.*	leadership ability	zhì yǒu 挚友	*n.*	close friend/ soul mate
shǎng fá fēn míng 赏罚分明	*idom*	to distinguish between rewards and punishments	qí jì 奇迹	*n.*	miracle
yǐ shǎo shèng duō 以少胜多	*idiom*	to win with disadvantage or less strength (win more with less)	tiāo xuǎn 挑选	*v.*	to select

Sentence Patterns

…被尊为

… is (highly) regarded as …

bèi zūn wéi
A + **被尊为** + *B*

sūn zi bīng fǎ bèi zūn wéi bīng xué shèng diǎn
《孙子兵法》被尊为“兵学圣典”。

"Sun Tzu The Art of War" is regarded as the "Sacred Book of Military Studies."

向…推荐…

recommend … to …

A + **向** + *B* + **推荐** + *noun*

tā jiù xiàng wú wáng tuī jiàn le sūn wǔ
他就向吴王推荐了孙武。

He recommended Sun Wu to the King of Wu.

Chinese Version

孙武是春秋时期的齐国人，著名的军事家、政治家。他被尊为“孙子”和“东方兵学的鼻祖”。

他的著作《孙子兵法》，被尊为“兵学圣典”，在中国乃至世界军事界、学术界、和哲学界都有极高的地位。

孙武本来是个没落贵族，但有很高的军事才华。在三十多岁的时候，他就写下了《孙子兵法》。

他的挚友兼政府大官伍子胥看到后，非常欣赏，就向吴王推荐了孙武。

孙武见到吴王之后，呈上了自己的书。吴王看后，赞不绝口。为了考察孙子的领导能力，他挑选了一百多名宫女让孙武操练。

孙武把宫女们分为两队，指定吴王最喜爱的两位嫔妃为队长，同时指定一个侍卫执行军法。

但操练开始后，宫女们却当成游戏，不听号令，捧腹大笑，导致队伍大乱。

孙武便根据军法要杀两位队长。吴王看到了，就着急地说：“我已经知道你的能力了。请别杀她们，我要是没有她们，吃饭睡觉都不会好！”

孙武却坚决地说："将在军，君命有所不受。"接着命令杀了两位队长，继续操练。

当孙武再次发号施令的时候，宫女们马上严肃起来，进退有序，阵形十分整齐。

而吴王失去了两位嫔妃，心里很不爽。孙武就告诉他：“军法的目的在于赏罚分明，只有对士兵威严，他们才会听号令，打仗才能胜利。”

听了孙武的解释，吴王不再生气，立刻封孙武为将军。在孙武的训练下，吴国的军事素质提高得很快，最终成为战国五霸之一。

后来吴国和楚国打仗，孙武指挥吴国军队以三万军队，对抗楚国的二十万军队，连续五战五捷，创造了中国军事史上以少胜多的奇迹。

孙武五十多岁的时候，挚友伍子胥被杀，孙武感到非常伤心和失望。之后辞职，去了乡下隐居。

他的著作《孙子兵法》几千年来不断流传，在政治、经济、军事、文化、哲学等领域都被推广运用。

目前为止，这本书已经被翻译成二十多种语言，影响了无数国内外的军事家、政治家、哲学家和企业家。

31

liú dé qīng shān zài bù pà méi chái shāo

留得青山在，不怕没柴烧

Where There Is Life, There Is Hope

hěn jiǔ yǐ qián, yǒu gè lǎo rén kào zhe tā jiā de yī zuò shān zuò le yī bèi zi de mù tàn shēng yì

很久以前，有个老人**靠着**他家的一座山做了一辈子的**木炭生意**。

A long time ago, there was an old man who was running a **charcoal business** all his life, **relying on** a mountain of his own.

lǎo rén yǒu liǎng gè ér zi, dà ér zi jiào qīng shān, xiǎo ér zi jiào hóng shān. dàn tā piān ài hóng shān, fán shì dōu guān zhào tā duō yī diǎn

老人有两个儿子，大儿子叫**青山**，小儿子叫**红山**。但他**偏爱**红山，凡事都**关照**他多一点。

The old man had two sons, the older son was called **Qingshan** (green mountian) and the younger son **Hongshan** (red mountian). But he **favored** Hongshan and **took care** of him more in everything.

zài tā kuài qù shì de shí hòu, tā bǎ dōng shān fēn gěi le dà ér zi, bǎ xī shān fēn gěi le xiǎo ér zi

在他快**去世**的时候，他把**东山**分给了大儿子，把**西山**分给了小儿子。

When he was about to **pass away**, he gave the **eastern part of the mountain** to his older son and **western part** to his younger son.

xiǎo ér zi hóng shān fēn dào de zhè piàn shān shù mù mào shèng, néng shēng chǎn gèng duō、zhì liàng gèng hǎo de mù tàn

小儿子红山分到的这片山**树木茂盛**，能**生产**更多、**质量更好**的木炭。

The youngest son, Hongshan, was assigned to the part of the mountain with **lush trees**, which was able to **produce** more and **better-quality** charcoal.

hóng shān hěn qín fèn, tiān tiān kǎn shù, hěn kuài tā de mù tàn shēng yì
红山很**勤奋**，天天砍树，很快他的木炭**生意**
yuè zuò yuè dà, ràng tā chéng wéi le bǎi wàn fù wēng
越做越大，让他成为了**百万富翁**。

Hongshan was very **diligent**, cutting down trees every day, and soon his charcoal **business** grew bigger and bigger, making him a **millionaire**.

kě shì jǐ nián hòu, shān shàng de shù quán bèi tā kǎn wán le. tā shī qù
可是几年后，山上的树全被他砍完了。他失去
le mù tàn lái yuán, mǎ shàng tā de shēng yì jiù pò chǎn le
了木炭**来源**，马上他的生意就**破产**了。

But a few years later, all the trees on the mountain were cut down by him, leaving him without **sources** of charcoal, so immediately his business went **bankrupt**.

yú shì, tā zài kōng shān shàng zhòng shàng le zhuāng jià. bù liào, yǒu yī
于是，他在空山上种上了**庄稼**。**不料**，有一
tiān xià le yī chǎng dà bào yǔ, chōng zǒu le suǒ yǒu de zhuāng jià
天下了一场大暴雨，**冲走**了所有的庄稼。

So, he planted **crops** on the empty mountain. **Unexpectedly**, a heavy rain fell one day and **washed away** all the crops.

hóng shān zǒu tóu wú lù, zhǐ néng qù tóu bēn tā de gē ge qīng shān. yuán
红山**走投无路**，只能去**投奔**他的哥哥青山。原
lái, qīng shān fēn dào de nà piàn shān shù mù xī shǎo, hěn nán shēng chǎn
来，青山分到的那片山树木**稀少**，很难**生产**
tài duō zhì liàng hǎo de mù tàn
太多**质量好**的木炭。

Hong Shan was **left with no choice**, he could only **go to** his older brother Qing Shan for help. It turned out that there were very **few** trees in the part of the mountain that Qingshan was assigned to, and it was difficult to **produce** more **good-quality** charcoal.

dàn shì tā hěn huì guī huà, kǎn le bù chéng cái de shù mù, zuò chéng mù
但是他很会**规划**，砍了**不成材**的树木，做成木
tàn hòu dī jià mài chū. rán hòu zhòng shàng le xīn de shù miáo
炭后**低价**卖出。然后种上了新的**树苗**。

But he was very good at **planning**, he cut down the **unproductive** trees, making them into charcoal and selling at a **low price**. Then he planted new **saplings** to replace them.

yóu yú mù tàn shēng yì tài xiǎo, tā zhǐ néng miǎn qiáng wéi chí shēng jì. yú
由于木炭生意太小，他只能勉强**维持生计**。于
shì, tā zài shān xià jiàn le nóng chǎng, yòu zhòng zhuāng jià, yòu sì yǎng
是，他在山下建了**农场**，又种**庄稼**，又**饲养**
niú yáng
牛羊。

As the charcoal business was so small, he could barely **make ends meet**. So he built a **farm** at the foot of the mountain, planted **crops**, and **raised** cattle and sheep.

jǐ nián hòu shān shàng de shù miáo zhǎng dà le mù tàn shēng yì yě gèng

几年后，山上的**树苗**长大了，木炭**生意**也更

hǎo le ér qiě nóng chǎng de shēng yì yě yuè lái yuè hóng huǒ ràng

好了。而且，农场的生意也越来越**红火**，让

tā chéng wéi le bǎi wàn fù wēng

他成为了**百万富翁**。

After a few years, the **saplings** on the mountain grew up and the charcoal **business** got better. Moreover, the farm business was getting more and more **prosperous**, making him a **millionaire**.

hóng shān kàn dào gē ge rú cǐ chéng gōng qián tú yī piàn guāng míng zhēn

红山看到哥哥**如此**成功，前途一片**光明**，真

shì yòu jí dù yòu xiàn mù

是又**嫉妒**又**羡慕**。

After Hongshan saw his brother being **so** successful, and with such a **bright** prospect, he was **jealous** and **envious**.

tā bù míng bái wèi shén me zì jǐ yōng yǒu yōu shì què lún wèi shī bài

他不明白为什么自己拥有**优势**，却沦为**失败**

zhě ér gē ge zhǐ zhàn liè shì què biàn wéi chéng gōng zhě

者。而哥哥，只占**劣势**，却变为**成功者**。

He didn't understand why he had an **advantage**, yet degraded to a **loser**. However his older brother with the **disadvantage**, yet became a **winner**.

gē ge qīng shān jiě shì shuō nǐ chī shān què bù yǎng shān dāng rán huì

哥哥青山**解释**说："你吃山却不养山，当然会

shān qióng shuǐ jìn nǐ yào yǎng shān zhǐ yǒu bǎo zhèng le shù mù cái néng bǎo

山穷水尽！你要养山，**只有**保证了树木**才**能保

zhèng mù tàn

证木炭。"

The older brother Qing Shan **explained**: "If you live upon mountains but don't keep them, of course you will **run out all resources**! You have to keep the mountains, and **only** when you guarantee the trees, you **can** guarantee charcoal."

hóng shān zhōng yú míng bái le tā diǎn tóu huí dá dào zhēn de shì liú

红山终于明白了，他**点头**回答到："真的是**留**

dé qīng shān zài bù pà méi chái shāo

得青山在，不怕没柴烧！"

Hongshan finally understood, he **nodded** and replied, "It truly is that only by keeping the green mountains (older brother's name), we will not be afraid of running out of firewood (**Where There is Life, There is Hope**)!"

Summary

The tale embodied in this proverb highlights the contrast between two brothers who employ differing methods in managing their business and attain contrasting results. It emphasizes the importance of having a **long-term perspective and vision** (目光长远 mù guāng cháng yuǎn) rather than being narrow-minded and **short-sighted** (目光短浅 mù guāng duǎn qiǎn). It stresses that with astute planning and hard work, one can overcome challenges and ultimately attain success.

Learning Tip

留得青山在，不怕没柴烧 is a Chinese proverb that can be interpreted as "where there is life, there is hope." The idea is that no matter how desperate the situation, as long as we keep our remaining resources and carry on with our energy/hard-work, we will definitely turn it back around to success.

liú dé	qīng shān	zài	bù pà	méi	chái	shāo
留得	青山	在	不怕	没	柴	烧
keep	green mountain	at	not afraid	no	fire-wood	burn

1 **留得青山在，不怕没柴烧**！现在虽然破产了，但我会继续努力，将来一定会重建公司。

Where there is life, there is hope! Although I am now bankrupt, I will continue my hard-work and will definitely rebuild my company in the future.

2 别怕被炒，只要继续提高自己，就不怕找不到新工作！要记住：**留得青山在，不怕没柴烧**!

Don't be afraid of being fired, as long as you keep improving yourself, you won't be afraid of not finding a new job! You must remember: **Where there is life, there is hope**.

Write your own sentence

Key Vocabulary

shēng yì 生意	*n.*	business	xī shǎo 稀少	*adj.*	few/rare
zǒu tóu wú lù 走投无路	*idiom*	be left with no choices	guī huà 规划	*v.* *n.*	to plan plan (formal)
shēng chǎn 生产	*v.*	to produce	nóng chǎng 农场	*n.*	farm
zhì liàng 质量	*n.*	quality	sì yǎng 饲养	*v.*	to raise/keep (livestock)
qín fèn 勤奋	*v.*	diligent	hóng huǒ 红火	*adj.*	prosperous
bǎi wàn fù wēng 百万富翁	*n.*	millionaire	xiàn mù 羡慕	*v.*	to envy
pò chǎn 破产	*v.* *n.*	to bankrupt bankruptcy	shī bài zhě 失败者	*n.*	loser
wéi chí shēng jì 维持生计	*vp.*	to make ends meet	chéng gōng zhě 成功者	*n.*	winner
shān qióng shuǐ jǐn 山穷水尽	*idiom*	run out of all resources (mountains and water all end)	bù liào 不料	*conj.*	unexpectedly

Sentence Patterns

由于…

due to/as...

yóu yú
由于 + *cause* + *effect*

yóu yú mù tàn shēng yì tài xiǎo, tā zhǐ néng miǎn qiáng wéi chí shēng jì
由于木炭生意太小，他只能勉强维持生计。

As the charcoal business was so small, he could barely make ends meet.

只有…才…

only ... can ...

zhǐ yǒu cái
只有 + *condition* + **才** +*result*

zhǐ yǒu bǎo zhèng le shù mù cái néng bǎo zhèng mù tàn
只有保证了树木才能保证木炭。

Only when you guarantee the trees, you can guarantee charcoal.

Chinese Version

很久以前，有个老人靠着他家的一座山做了一辈子的木炭生意。

老人有两个儿子，大儿子叫青山，小儿子叫红山。但他偏爱红山，凡事都关照他多一点。

在他快去世的时候，他把东山分给了大儿子，把西山分给了小儿子。

小儿子红山分到的这片山树木茂盛，能生产更多、质量更好的木炭。

红山很勤奋，天天砍树，很快他的木炭生意越做越大，成为了百万富翁。

可是几年后，山上的树全被他砍完了。他失去了木炭来源，马上他的生意就破产了。

于是，他在空山上种上了庄稼。不料，有一天下了一场大暴雨，冲走了所有的庄稼。

红山走投无路，只能去投奔他的哥哥青山。原来，青山分到的那片山树木稀少，很难生产太多质量好的木炭。

但是他很会规划，砍了不成材的树木，做成木炭后低价卖出。然后种上了新的树苗。

由于木炭生意太小，他只能勉强维持生计。于是，他在山下建了农场，又种庄稼，又饲养牛羊。

几年后，山上的树苗长大了，木炭生意也更好了。而且，农场的生意也越来越红火，让他成为了百万富翁。

红山看到哥哥如此成功，前途一片光明，真是又嫉妒又羡慕。

他不明白为什么自己拥有优势，却沦为失败者。而哥哥，只占劣势，却变为成功者。

哥哥青山解释说：“你吃山却不养山，当然会山穷水尽！你要养山，只有保证了树木才能保证木炭。”

红山终于明白了，他点头回答到：“真的是留得青山在，不怕没柴烧！”

ACCESS AUDIO

I highly encourage you to use the accompanying audio recordings for all of the examples in this book, not only will it help to improve your listening skills but if you are unfamiliar or unsure about the pronunciations of any words in this book, then you can listen to them spoken by native speakers.

INSTRUCTIONS TO ACCESS AUDIO

1. **Scan this QR code** →
   or go to: **www.linglingmandarin.com/books**

2. Locate this book in the list of LingLing Mandarin Books

3. Click the "Access Audio" button   Access Audio

4. Enter the password:

GCSF965

THE NEXT STAGE

Discover the richness of Chinese language and culture with **The Art of War for Language Learners**. This comprehensive book merges the wisdom of China's most renowned classic with modern Chinese language learning, making it perfect for higher-intermediate or advanced learners.

Be the first to get a copy:
https://amzn.to/3LdBJmA

Chinese Conversations for Intermediate is a must-have for anyone who enjoys learning through entertaining stories set in modern China. Experience daily life conversations through relatable, fun stories and master various types of conversations, idioms, and phrases to deepen your understanding of Chinese culture and society.

Available now:
https://amzn.to/3Z3xwHU

Chinese Conversations for Beginners

Chinese Conversations for Intermediate

Manadarin Writing Practice Book

Chinese Stories for Language Learners: Elementary

Chinese Stories for Language Learners: Intermediate

The Art of War for Language Learners

Learn Chinese Vocabulary for Beginners: New HSK 1

Learn Chinese Vocabulary for Beginners: New HSK 2

Learn Chinese Vocabulary for Beginners: New HSK 3

Get notified about **new releases**
https://linglingmandarin.com/notify

ABOUT THE AUTHOR

LingLing is a native Chinese Mandarin educator with an MA in Communication and Language. Originally from China, now living in the UK, she is the founder of the learning brand LingLing Mandarin, which aims to create the best resources for learners to master the Chinese language and achieve deep insight into Chinese culture in a fun and illuminating way. Discover more about LingLing and access more great resources by following the links below or scanning the QR codes.

WEBSITE

linglingmandarin.com

YOUTUBE CHANNEL

youtube.com/c/linglingmandarin

PATREON

patreon.com/linglingmandarin

INSTAGRAM

instagram.com/linglingmandarin

Printed in Great Britain
by Amazon

35264691R00123